WASTED EDUCATION

WASTED EDUCATION

How We Fail Our Graduates in Science, Technology, Engineering, and Math

JOHN D. SKRENTNY

The University of Chicago Press CHICAGO AND LONDON

The University of Chicago Press, Chicago 60637
The University of Chicago Press, Ltd., London
© 2023 by The University of Chicago
Published 2023
Printed in the United States of America

32 31 30 29 28 27 26 25 24 23   1 2 3 4 5

ISBN-13: 978-0-226-82579-3 (cloth)
ISBN-13: 978-0-226-82970-8 (e-book)
DOI: https://doi.org/10.7208/chicago/9780226829708.001.0001

Library of Congress Cataloging-in-Publication Data

Names: Skrentny, John David, author.
Title: Wasted education : how we fail our graduates in science,
    technology, engineering, and math / John D. Skrentny.
Other titles: How we fail our graduates in science, technology,
    engineering, and math
Description: Chicago ; London : The University of Chicago Press,
    2023. | Includes bibliographical references and index.
Identifiers: LCCN 2023009366 | ISBN 9780226825793 (cloth) |
    ISBN 9780226829708 (ebook)
Subjects: LCSH: Skilled labor—United States. | Science and
    industry—United States. | Science students—Employment—
    United States. | Engineering students—Employment—United
    States. | Work environment—United States. | Corporate
    culture—United States.
Classification: LCC HD5724 .S58 2023 | DDC 331.110973—dc23/
    eng/20230417
LC record available at https://lccn.loc.gov/2023009366

♾ This paper meets the requirements of ANSI/NISO Z39.48-1992
(Permanence of Paper).

For Ava and Zoe

CONTENTS

CHAPTER 1

INTRODUCTION
The Great Investment in STEM Education

If education is thought of as an investment, then corporate hiring
practices help define the payoff for that investment.[1]
GERALD DAVIS

In an America riven by political conflict, there is at least one point of
policy consensus: we highly value education in science, technology, engineering, and math (STEM). Both Democratic and Republican members of the US Congress support bills to boost STEM education, and
recent presidents—Biden, Trump, and Obama—all have made funding of STEM education a priority. States as different as California and
Mississippi have targeted public investments in STEM education, and
cities have their own programs as well. Major philanthropies are investing in STEM education, and individual students and families are putting in their own dollars, time, energy, and effort. The number of STEM
majors has surged.

While schools and universities have always taught math and science
skills as part of a well-rounded education, and many advocates push
STEM education especially in the kindergarten through high school
phase for general mathematical and scientific literacy, there are several
prominent rationales for massive investments in STEM education that
extend to the college level and beyond. All share a goal of producing
more workers for STEM occupations.

First, there is the shortage rationale. Employers and their advocates
regularly complain, and have done so for decades, that American universities are not graduating enough STEM majors for them to hire.
They say that their job openings for STEM positions remain open for
months. Some throw up their hands and say they cannot wait any longer for universities to graduate more STEM majors, and they press for
more STEM-educated foreign workers to be admitted to the US to meet
their voracious demand. So urgent are their pleas that they may come

with threats—that they will leave the US to set up operations in foreign countries because of the lack of STEM workers in the US.

Second is the competitiveness rationale. A favorite of policymakers as well as some employers, this line of reasoning emphasizes that STEM grads are crucial because STEM workers innovate, and innovation is the source of economic growth and strength as well as national security. The more we invest in STEM education, the more STEM workers we can have, and thus the more innovation we can have, and thus the more economic growth and strength we can have, allowing the US to compete better with other countries, and thus—at the end of this long chain, though this is rarely stated explicitly—the happier we all will be. The competitiveness rationale basically says that the more STEM workers we have, the better off we are.

The third rationale for investment in STEM education emphasizes diversity. A problem with STEM workers is that they are mostly male and mostly White and Asian. In the diversity rationale, the White or Asian maleness of STEM is a problem for two main reasons: (1) it is bad for the US because it means the US STEM workforce is missing out on talented women, African Americans, and Latinos; and (2) because STEM jobs are typically well paid, the underrepresentation of women, African Americans, and Latinos in STEM majors means they are missing out on middle-class, or even upper-class, lifestyles for which STEM jobs provide a gateway. Greater investment in STEM education, then, is an investment in American equality and a more fair and vibrant society.

A fourth rationale, which I confess is the basis for my own interest in STEM education but is not as prominent in public debates as the other three, relates to what STEM workers do with their skills. In a world facing calamitous climate change, experiencing global pandemics, and drowning in plastic pollution, we need more STEM workers because they are our best hope to develop new technologies for clean energy, lifesaving vaccines, and the maintenance of the biodiversity that our planet still enjoys.

Given these rationales, it is hardly surprising that there is a strong consensus on support for STEM education to create more STEM workers. But there is a problem with this enterprise. What if STEM graduates don't become STEM workers?

Despite the massive governmental, philanthropic, and personal investment, only a minority of STEM grads are working in STEM jobs. Estimates vary regarding what percentage leave, with the worst numbers coming from a US Census Bureau study that found only a paltry 28 percent of STEM graduates working in STEM jobs.[2]

The exodus from STEM is not just a late-career phenomenon. Thousands of STEM graduates do all the learning that STEM education experts are continually trying to improve, earn this supposedly coveted and in-demand STEM degree, confront a supposedly wide array of job options from supposedly desperate employers, and then say, "No thanks." Some research shows that about two-thirds of recent STEM graduates choose non-STEM jobs or graduate studies in non-STEM fields.[3] Thousands of others give STEM jobs a try and then move on after a few years. Taxpayers, foundations, parents, and students may reasonably wonder what the point is of producing ever more STEM graduates if those graduates end up doing something else. If STEM education can be thought of as an investment in the STEM workforce, then the return on that investment looks quite poor.

I believe we can do better. The purpose of this book is to shed light on the puzzle of the exodus from STEM and to point to likely factors that contribute to it. Though there are growing numbers of technical workers without a college degree, and many non-STEM grads make a transition to STEM jobs, I focus here on those who graduated from college with a STEM major, as they represent the greatest investment in STEM education (public, philanthropic, and individual) and the hopes of policymakers who wish to grow the innovation economy.[4] I also focus on private employers, and not the significant though much smaller number of STEM grads who work in universities and nonprofit labs, because private employers hire the most STEM grads and complain the loudest about shortages. In contrast, the problem in universities is typically too many STEM grads chasing too few job openings, not a supposed shortage of STEM grads.[5]

To understand why so many STEM grads never take or leave STEM jobs, and thus why investments in STEM education do not bring about the desired outcomes, we must understand employers' treatment of STEM workers. Don't be fooled by the rankings of supposedly top jobs in America that put STEM jobs at the top, or the popular images of happy and well-paid STEM workers, enjoying catered lunches, offices full of games and toys, and opportunities for remote work.[6] Despite dispatches from those happily working at offices, at home, in cafés, or even on the beach, all is not well in STEM.

Of course, business is business. I understand that employers are balancing countless responsibilities while still trying to make a profit. I understand that investors are taking huge risks in putting millions or billions of dollars into companies and want them to behave in particular ways so they may get returns on their investments. But the return on investments in STEM education is important to highlight because it can be improved. If we want to end the exodus of the STEM workers we have worked so hard to create, we must ask more of employers and investors so that public, philanthropic, and personal funds are not wasted. Research that I will discuss shows that employers can *choose* to take the "high road" and treat their workers better, while still making great profits, and that investors can *choose* to ask more of companies than short-term profits.

Why focus on improving the treatment of STEM workers, and not all workers? Ideally we should expect employers to treat all workers well. But the extra educational investments, and the urgency and the valorization in the government language about how important and special STEM grads are, make their maltreatment—and their rejection of STEM jobs— particularly striking. Because if there really is a shortage, if STEM workers really are key to growing the economy, if STEM jobs really will be the ticket to the middle class for more Americans of diverse backgrounds, and if we really are going to save this planet from multiple crises, both employers and investors will have to change course.

STEM Mania

The dictionary on my Mac defines a *mania* as "an excessive enthusiasm or desire; an obsession." That might be too strong of a term to describe the consensus behind STEM education, but not by much.

On college campuses such as my own (University of California, San Diego), students with the temerity to *not* major in a STEM subject, and to major in the humanities or a social science other than economics, frequently have to justify their choice when they are asked the inevitable questions: "Why?? And what will you *do* with that degree?" Some students have told me that they almost feel ashamed because they have not chosen a STEM major.[7] It is not just at my own campus that STEM majors are rising: STEM majors have reached historical highs, while the humanities are at their low point. Even business, still the most popular major in the US, is at a low.[8]

How did we get to this place, where STEM majors are becoming the default for so many? One factor is that for years, government policy-makers, private philanthropies, and leading companies have taken strong actions to grow and improve the STEM workforce. Though most interested in the private-sector workforce, their efforts have focused al-most exclusively on STEM *students* rather than STEM *workers*. This effort fits with and may be in part driven by a commonly used metaphor: the "STEM pipeline." The pipeline represents students as a liquid, flowing forward through their schooling (the pipeline), unless some factor or combination of factors leads them to "leak" from the pipeline. Others prefer the metaphors of pathways or highways with off-ramps, but these share the idea of forward movement to some destination. In these pol-icy discussions, leaking is something that should be avoided. Policy-makers and educators try to prevent leakage and to find ways to have more and more students persist in their STEM education and graduate with STEM degrees.[9]

Many advocates for STEM education argue that leakage during school-ing is unfortunately massive, and that the American primary, secondary, and college systems are failing badly. They point to evidence that indi-cates that the US is lagging behind other nations, both big (China) and small (Finland and Singapore), in student ability tests.[10] This belief un-derlies a growing set of policy interventions designed to improve kinder-garten through grade 12 (K–12) and college education to produce more STEM graduates. These interventions focus on how STEM subjects are taught, and the reasons students might not succeed in STEM learning, might not choose to major in STEM, or might choose to leave their STEM majors for something non-STEM.[11]

There is a long history of great interest in and support for educa-tion of scientists and engineers in the US, especially since the Cold War, which was a decades-long period marked especially by competition in military technologies but other areas as well. The race to land a person on the moon was very much driven by this competitive dynamic.[12]

The pace and breadth of investment in science and engineering seemed to pick up rapidly after 2001, when Judith Ramaley, then the director of the National Science Foundation's Education and Human Resources Division, coined the STEM acronym.[13] It wasn't long before there was so much going on that the government began to investigate *itself* to learn exactly what, where, and how much it was contributing. For example, the Government Accountability Office (GAO) did an inventory in 2010 and found that the federal government was spending more than

$3 billion on 209 programs focused on STEM education. Showing how far the federal interest in STEM had moved from only a military focus, GAO found STEM education programs administered by thirteen departments and agencies—Agriculture, Commerce, Defense, Education, Energy, Health and Human Services, Homeland Security, Interior, Transportation, Environmental Protection Agency, National Aeronautics and Space Administration, National Science Foundation, and the Nuclear Regulatory Commission.[14]

The George W. Bush, Obama, Trump, and Biden administrations may have shared little in common, but one thing they agreed on was the conviction that America needed more STEM graduates. Bush was in office when the STEM acronym originated and when the bipartisan STEM Education Caucus started in Congress.[15] He signed the 2007 America COMPETES Act, which is the first time the STEM acronym appeared in a major piece of legislation (though by no means the first time Congress has supported education in these subjects).[16] The Obama administration pushed harder, with Obama speaking frequently of the importance of the STEM workforce for innovation and growth.[17] His President's Council of Advisors on Science and Technology even started an effort to produce "approximately 1 million more college graduates in STEM fields than expected under current assumptions" in order to meet demand from employers.[18] Trump declared his administration would support STEM education,[19] signed laws promoting women in STEM, and ordered his Department of Education to spend $200 million for grants in STEM education to meet employer needs.[20] While it is still early in the Biden administration, his policy appears to follow these efforts to promote STEM education for "our future STEM workforce."[21]

The federal government is not alone in public investment in STEM education. A study in 2017 found that all fifty states had some kind of program to boost STEM education.[22] An inventory looking for STEM networks, STEM centers, STEM partnerships, and STEM ecosystems found 31 national STEM organizations, 187 statewide or regional STEM organizations, and 24 STEM organizations operating at the metro level.[23] An unknown number of school districts in the nation's cities and towns have STEM education initiatives and are easy to find for any reader. For example, though my hometown, tiny Highland in the northwestern corner of Indiana, doesn't seem to promote STEM education, the nearby cities of Gary and Hammond do, and Chicago, which dominates the metropolitan area, has many public school STEM education initiatives.

A wave of nongovernmental organizations have also gone all in on STEM education. It is hard to adequately dramatize this growth, but it is apparent to anyone who attends the regular conference of an organization entitled US News/STEM Solutions. These conferences attract attendees from government, nonprofit, education, and corporate sectors. Sponsors have included STEM education purveyors iTech Exploring, Best Robotics, TryEngineering Together, and Project Lead the Way. The IT (information technology) industry association, CompTIA, contributed through its nonprofit Creating IT Futures. Also involved were the American Institutes for Research, the education funder Californians Dedicated to Education, education consultants KnowledgeWorks and Strada Education Network, and STEM-oriented corporations, including 3M, Cognizant, and Qualcomm.

And then there is philanthropy. The professional website focused on giving, Inside Philanthropy, has listed ninety-seven nongovernmental foundations that provided grants for STEM education, from A (the Actuarial Foundation) to X (the Xerox Foundation). A diverse array of corporate foundations was heavily represented on the list in 2020, including the retailer Best Buy, aerospace giant Boeing, oil company Chevron, and Farmers Insurance, as well as the more expected tech (Google, Microsoft) and pharmaceutical (Thermo Fisher and Roche) companies.[24]

The most fundamental assumption underlying these efforts is that improving STEM capabilities in America should begin, and mostly remain, focused on the STEM education pipeline producing *new* entrants to the workforce—that is, the money is directed at young people still in school. How much money? It is impossible to tally up all of it given the diverse sources at every level of government and private spending as well, but even if we could, it would not capture the investments of time and effort in getting ever more students to study STEM. Advocates of STEM education sometimes appear to assume that the more STEM grads we have, the better off we all are. It is a belief in *"the more, the better."* And students are responding—STEM majors are growing, while many non-STEM majors are in decline.

Why the Massive Commitment to STEM Education?

Understanding why so much money, time, effort, and student lives are going into STEM education requires a closer look at the four rationales for STEM education with which I opened this book: the shortage rationale, the competitiveness rationale, the diversity rationale, and the global-crisis rationale. In the sections that follow, I explain the basis and some history of each. I purposefully choose some older examples to underscore that the now-massive STEM education effort has been developing for many years. Readers can doubtless find examples like these in the news today, and it is equally likely that the STEM education effort is now what sociologists would call "institutionalized"—that is, it is taken for granted and mostly self-perpetuating. These rationales are not exclusive, and many organizations or individual advocates for STEM education will propound one or more, sometimes in the same sentence. If, for example, one argues foremost for the competitiveness rationale, one might say that employers are facing a shortage as well. But each is analytically distinctive.

THE SHORTAGE RATIONALE

The shortage rationale for STEM education refers to the idea that employers, especially businesses, want to hire STEM workers and they cannot find enough. I discuss the shortage rationale first not because it is necessarily the most important, the most common, or the strongest rationale, but because advocates often use it with the greatest urgency. How can it not feel urgent if there are jobs available, some open soon, some open right now, and employers are practically begging for qualified candidates to fill them? The urgency of the shortage rationale has often led these advocates to push not only for new STEM grads from American universities but also for STEM-educated workers from abroad.

The shortage rationale has a long history—and has long been controversial. Demographer and science policy scholar Michael Teitelbaum's tongue-in-cheek chapter title exploring the history of STEM shortage claims—"No Shortage of Shortages"—captures both the long history of this rationale and Teitelbaum's doubts. Though some of what he describes as shortage arguments might also be understood as part of the "competitiveness" rationale, much of his history relates to the availability of (what we would call now) STEM workers for job openings. As early as the late 1980s and early 1990s, the National Science Foundation predicted "shortfalls" of scientists and engineers. These predictions turned out to be wrong, but the point here is that many important people have long believed there was a shortage or would soon be a shortage, and it was urgent because the belief was that employers would not be able to fill job openings.[25]

Sometimes advocates of this shortage rationale urge policymakers to open wider the doors for permanent or temporary foreign workers.[26] These leaders, many from STEM-oriented businesses, simply cannot wait for the education system to produce STEM grads because they consider the shortage so urgent, so they call for wider immigration doors along with more STEM education. Perhaps the most prominent example is Forward.us, a lobbying group for STEM immigration and STEM education started or supported by STEM luminaries from a variety of firms, including top leaders Mark Zuckerberg (Facebook, now Meta), Eric Schmidt (Google, now Alphabet), Brian Chesky (Airbnb), Elon Musk (Tesla/SpaceX/Twitter), and venture capitalists Jim Breyer (Accel Partners) and John Doerr (Kleiner Perkins), among others.[27] The shortage rationale has always been the organization's major argument for STEM. Shortages in STEM are "dire," the Forward.us website maintained, and immigration reforms, such as allowing international students to stay in the US, would reduce them as well as boost the economy by $233 billion.[28] It quoted Schmidt with the claim that he had "spent the last 20 years announcing that the single stupidest policy in the entire American political system was the limit on H-1B visas," referring to the legal avenue for short-term STEM migrants.[29]

This isn't idle talk. For example, Microsoft pushed the administration of President George W. Bush to make policy changes allowing foreign STEM graduates of US universities to work legally in the US for longer periods than the policy had until then allowed. The lobbyist told Department of Homeland Security Secretary Michael Chertoff that such changes were necessary because "America's talent crisis has reached emergency levels. . . . With demand in fields like science, technology, engineering and math far surpassing the supply of American workers, America's employers find themselves unable to get the people they need on the job." The shortage was so bad that Microsoft hinted a threat to move operations overseas: "Microsoft has long made it top-level company priority to center its development work in the United States, and we have devoted a great deal of energy into trying to help shape the policy changes that would permit us to continue to do so. To compete globally, however, Microsoft—like other employers of the highly skilled across America—must have access to the talent it needs."[30] Microsoft CEO Bill

Gates followed up with his own congressional testimony on the urgent shortage issue, calling for more STEM education and more STEM migrants.[31] The Bush administration complied with Microsoft's demand, allowing foreign STEM grads to work in the US for twenty-nine months, up from the twelve months to which non-STEM grads were still limited. The Obama administration later extended the STEM grads' work period to three full years.

The shortage rationale isn't only advocated by tech leaders. A 2014 Business Roundtable survey of CEOs representing a variety of leading corporations in the US found that 97 percent of CEOs said "the skills gap is a problem," and about 42 percent of job openings "require advanced STEM skills." The president of the Business Roundtable, John Engler, called the situation a "crisis" and stated, "CEOs are speaking out on the issue, pursuing solutions in their own companies and urging that America develop a national strategy to prepare our workers for these STEM jobs."[32]

The shortage rationale is consistently bipartisan. Prominent Democrats have used it to justify STEM education and the need for more STEM workers. For example, the Obama administration's call for 1 million more STEM graduates mentioned impending shortages as the first reason for more investments in STEM education. It argued that in the coming years, the number of STEM jobs was going to increase by 1 million jobs. Without the education system pumping out additional STEM grads, there would be a shortage.[33] The center-right American Action Forum issued a report warning that the US was headed for a shortage of 1.1 million STEM workers.[34] In 2022, the student counseling arm of the powerful education ranking institution *US News* said that by 2030, we would need 1 million more STEM grads, explaining, "Experts suggest there are not currently enough qualified STEM degree graduates to meet employment demands."[35] The numbers change, but there always seem to be prominent advocates for the STEM shortage rationale predicting a shortage, and STEM jobs remaining open.

Many advocates have used or implied the shortage rationale by pointing out that unemployment rates for STEM workers are typically about half those of non-STEM workers, and for some fields such as software development and mechanical engineering, it can be less than 2 percent in hot labor markets.[36] Though much of this book can be read as a criticism of the shortage rationale (since I will show that employers do not treat STEM workers as if they are scarce), my goal here is not to adjudicate the debate regarding whether there really are STEM worker shortages or not.[37] Understanding the rationales undergirding commitments to STEM education is important so we can consider whether those commitments are producing the outcomes that advocates want. At the same time, it is important to acknowledge there is some evidence that might suggest a shortage.

THE COMPETITIVENESS RATIONALE

The competitiveness rationale for STEM education, in essence, states that the way to build a stronger America is to build stronger science, technology, engineering, and math, and a key way to do that is to produce more STEM grads. This rationale has been around much longer than the STEM acronym itself.[38] Advocates can use it with varying emphases that share the idea of leveraging STEM education to improve the strength of the nation. Most common in the 1950s was a national security focus spurred by competition with the Soviet Union. As early as 1954, for example, the *New York Times* learned of a deficit in the number of applied scientists and engineers graduating each year in the US (57,000 per year) compared with the Soviet Union (95,000) and on its front page warned, "Russia Is Overtaking US in Training of Technicians."[39]

Congress responded to these national security concerns with the first federal foray into education, the National Defense Education Act of 1958. The law's preamble stated, "The defense of this Nation depends upon the mastery of modern techniques developed from complex scientific principles." The law promised to "correct as rapidly as possible the existing imbalances in our educational programs which have led to an insufficient proportion of our population educated in science, mathematics, and . . . trained in technology."[40]

In the 1950s, policymakers had a relatively clear idea regarding what they wanted these new STEM (to use the current term) graduates to do. They were supposed to improve American defense technologies such as guided missiles, submarines, and radar defenses. Since then, however, the focus has shifted—or one might say the focus has been lost. In contemporary discussions, STEM graduates are supposed to move into industry or academia and be involved in unspecified but commercially viable innovations.[41] Advocates just seem to *know* we need more STEM graduates, though they do not actually know (or say) what the STEM grads are supposed to do except work in unspecified STEM jobs.

Though perhaps less urgent, the competitiveness rationale appears as prominent as the shortage rationale in calls for investments in STEM education. It is front and center, for example, in the reports from the prestigious National Academies, which include the National Academy of Sciences, the National Academy of Engineering, and the National Academy of Medicine. Congress created the National Academies in 1863 to provide evidence-based advice on pressing national issues.[42] Much of the advice related to STEM education has stressed the competitiveness rationale. Perhaps the most influential was a massive 2005 effort, provocatively entitled *Rising Above the Gathering Storm: Energizing and Employing America for a Brighter Economic Future*. Its more than five hundred pages include some of the strongest cases for investments in STEM education for national competitiveness. The first two sentences of the report's executive summary state eloquently, "The United States takes deserved pride in the vitality of its economy, which forms the foundation of our high quality of life, our national security, and our hope that our children and grandchildren will inherit ever-greater opportunities. That vitality is derived in large part from the productivity of well-trained people and the steady stream of scientific and technical innovations they produce." Following this emphasis on "well-trained people," many of the report's recommendations centered on STEM education.[43]

Congress quickly responded to *Gathering Storm*, institutionalizing the idea of STEM education for competitiveness in the America COMPETES Act of 2007.[44] Congress periodically reauthorizes the law, renewing the competitiveness rationale for STEM education. "COMPETES" is an acronym; the full name of the law is "The America Creating Opportunities to Meaningfully Promote Excellence in Technology, Education, and Science Act of 2007." When Congress reauthorized the law in 2011, it created a Committee on STEM Education to monitor efforts on STEM education and create regular "Federal STEM Education Five-Year Strategic Plans" for this goal of American competitiveness. Despite his patterns of disruption, Trump followed norms here, creating a plan and monitoring progress, and continuing the goal of using education to "encourage and prepare learners to pursue STEM careers."[45]

I do not assess the competitiveness rationale here and whether producing more and more STEM grads necessarily or even typically leads to more innovation and thus improved American competitiveness or security. I will say that advocates relying on it rarely (if ever) try to assess precisely which STEM jobs, in which STEM fields, in which contexts, actually do produce the innovation that improves American competitiveness. My point here is that advocates for STEM education commonly use the competitiveness rationale, and similar to the shortage rationale, it emphasizes the importance of STEM education to create STEM workers.

THE DIVERSITY RATIONALE

The diversity rationale emphasizes the lack of women, African Americans, and Latinos in STEM education and the STEM workforce. More specifically, it highlights the fact that most STEM majors and jobs are dominated by males, Whites, and Asians, and that this indicates a lack of equal opportunity. Advocates for diversity in STEM typically provide two main reasons why diversity is important. First, they point out that the lack of diversity means that a lot of STEM talent is not able to contribute to American innovation, making the US less competitive. Second, they stress the relatively high wages of STEM jobs and make the point that too narrow of a range of Americans are getting a chance at these middle-class jobs. Like the other rationales, the diversity rationale is often based on the idea that STEM majors will become STEM workers.

As suggested in the previous two sections, the diversity rationale fits with the shortage and competitiveness rationales. If one wants to boost American competitiveness, isn't it obvious that one should try to recruit all available talent to be educated for that goal? And if there is a shortage of STEM workers, isn't it obvious that one should not exclude anyone from STEM education? Given these linkages, it is not surprising that the influential *Rising Above the Gathering Storm* report that motivated the America COMPETES Act made recommendations for more diversity in STEM education. After calling for more Americans overall to earn STEM degrees and recommending a STEM scholarship program for this purpose, the report argued, "Increasing participation of underrepresented minorities is critical to ensuring a high-quality supply of scientists and engineers in the United States." The report explained that "if some groups are underrepresented in science and engineering in our society, we are not attracting as many of the most talented people to an important segment of our knowledge economy."[46]

More recently, the National Academies have emphasized the second part of the diversity rationale—the idea that diversity in STEM is important because it allows more diverse Americans into the middle class. For example, a 2021 "call to action on STEM education" argued that "the nation needs a cadre of talented scientists, engineers, and other STEM professionals to advance knowledge, design new technology, and drive a robust economy. The opportunity to be among that cadre should be equitably distributed across all geographies and populations of students, including people of color and women. STEM jobs are much more likely to secure living wages for those employed in them."[47]

The Congressional Research Service, charged with providing Congress with unbiased information relevant to legislation, has also identified the diversity rationale as "a central topic in the conversation about STEM education." It similarly made the connections to the need to access all talent for American competitiveness, and also to allow women and underrepresented minorities equal access to "a variety of lucrative careers."[48]

It is easy to find the diversity rationale in acts of Congress. For instance, the full name of the INSPIRE Women Act of 2017 is the Inspiring the Next Space Pioneers, Innovators, Researchers, and Explorers Women Act. That same year, the American Innovation and Competitiveness Act (a newer version of the America COMPETES Act) used all the rationales I've described thus far for investments in STEM education. It mentioned the need for more STEM workers for competitiveness, mentioned the shortage rationale ("there is currently a disconnect between the availability of and growing demand for STEM-skilled workers"), and called for broadened participation in STEM. It noted the lack of participation of women, African Americans, Latinos, and Indigenous populations, and it used the diversity rationale when it argued that "historically, underrepresented populations are the largest untapped STEM talent pools in the United States," adding that "the United States should encourage full participation of individuals from underrepresented populations in STEM fields."[49]

This is not only a preoccupation of Congress. A whole ecosystem of organizations has emerged to boost diversity in STEM, such as Girls STEM Academy, STEM Like a Girl, Girls Who Code, and Black Girls CODE.[50] Philanthropies give grants or create special STEM education programs guided by this rationale, including such well-known names as the Alfred P. Sloan Foundation, the Hewlett Foundation, the Carnegie Corporation of New York, and the Howard Hughes Medical Institute, which invested $2 billion in 2021 "to increase diversity, equity, and inclusion in STEM" over ten years "across all stages of the STEM pipeline."[51]

The diversity rationale is prominent in the academic study of STEM education.[52] The idea of the "STEM pipeline," and who "leaks" from it, has captivated researchers, and they've given much attention to the forces that lead women, African Americans, and Latinos to develop (or not develop) STEM skills in K–12 education, or to choose (or not choose) STEM majors. The centrality of diversity to the study of STEM is such that it appears in the first sentence of a comprehensive review of what academic researchers know on the topic of STEM education: "Improving science, technology, engineering, and mathematics (STEM) education, especially for traditionally disadvantaged groups, is widely recognized as pivotal to the United States' long-term economic growth and security."[53]

Not all STEM jobs lead to middle-class lifestyles because the amount of pay can vary a lot depending on the field and the location. And, as I will show in the remainder of this book, STEM jobs are not all they are cracked up to be. But similar to the other rationales, advocates forcefully argue that diversity is a key rationale for investments in STEM education, and there is no doubt that STEM workers are not nearly as diverse as they could and should be.

THE GLOBAL-CRISIS RATIONALE

My motivation for writing this book is primarily based on a less prominent rationale than the three just discussed: I believe STEM education is necessary to save the planet from a host of global crises we now face. The idea here is similar to the competitiveness rationale in emphasizing the importance of STEM education for innovation. But advocates for the competitiveness rationale tend to emphasize national defense or economic growth (where the innovations don't matter as long as they boost growth and make the US more competitive) rather than solving complex, life-threatening crises.

Climate change may be the most profound example. Nearly all scientists agree that the technological ability to generate power from fossil fuels and more than a century of carbon dioxide emissions from this and other activities have now moved us to a potentially catastrophic warming of the planet that will affect every living thing. To solve this problem— and leaving aside for now the enormous social, political, and economic challenges—we need to reduce our reliance on fossil fuels. Because we have already built a society premised on the availability of cheap energy, we need a new, cheap source of energy that does not destroy our planet, and we will need STEM workers to help us find it. There are many options available, including solar, wind, and nuclear power, but these have their own problems as well. For example, solar and wind require enormous amounts of space to generate power and huge amounts of copper for electricity transmission. If generated from fission, nuclear power creates dangerous waste and the potential for disastrous leaks of radioactive material. Then there are technological problems with the batteries to store clean energy, which rely on rare earth elements that damage the environment to extract.[54] Pandemics, plastic pollution, fertilizer runoff—there are many other problems harming life across the planet. Technological innovation is urgently needed to solve them, and STEM education is part of that.

One advocate that uses the global-crisis rationale is the federal government's Smithsonian Institution, dedicated to diffusing knowledge to the public. Its Science Education Center has promoted what it calls "The STEM Imperative," which is the idea that STEM education is crucial in complex, technological societies. The Smithsonian highlights solving "challenges our children will face" as a reason for the STEM Imperative. These challenges include how we can "thrive during times of global climate change"; how we might "balance our energy portfolio in the face of increasing global demand"; how we can improve agriculture "to minimize hunger around the world"; and how we can provide greater "access to clear water."[55]

Not all STEM students will be interested in addressing global crises. Many will care about particular kinds of intellectual problems that advance civilization in grand ways but have no obvious practical relevance, such as discoveries in astrophysics and paleontology. Some will just like engineering or scientific problem-solving on any particular issue; it may be the methods rather than the substance of STEM work that appeals. Still others may be in STEM work for the money and economic opportunity more than solving pressing global problems, and that's fine, too. Still, if we graduate large numbers of students in STEM fields, we are likely to get talented, highly skilled individuals who are excited to help resolve these global crises.

Why We Should Demand Better ROI in STEM Education

Some observers might argue that it is fine if STEM grads reject or can't find STEM jobs; at least they had the opportunity to work in STEM and likely picked up skills valuable elsewhere in the economy. In fact, the

Rising Above the Gathering Storm report made this claim when it noted that we can never produce the exact, correct number of STEM grads for STEM jobs and that we shouldn't worry about it. Its authors argued that we definitely need to have enough STEM grads, and even if they can't find STEM jobs, they can do something else, maintaining that "it has been found that, for example, undergraduate training in engineering forms an excellent foundation for graduate work in such fields as business, law, and medicine."[56]

This is technically correct but morally troubling. It is true that STEM grads who move to non-STEM careers may flourish, and their STEM education might be useful in their new line of work. But the suggestion—that we should encourage millions of students to major in STEM subjects and then not worry what happens after that because many do well—seems wrong because it seems deceptive, especially when so many STEM grads leave STEM. Maybe it is fine if they are happy. But research shows that STEM grads who do not work in STEM are significantly less likely to be satisfied, overall, with their non-STEM jobs than were non-STEM graduates. They were also significantly less likely to be satisfied with the "intellectual challenge" of their non-STEM jobs.[57] Dissatisfied and bored—this seems unfair to STEM grads.

The exodus of STEM grads from STEM jobs should be troubling to advocates of STEM education who expect to be creating workers for STEM occupations. The shortage, competitiveness, diversity, and global-crisis rationales are all about putting people in STEM occupations. These rationales are not about creating managers, physicians, lawyers, or salespeople, no matter how valuable these occupations are. When half or more of STEM grads are not doing what advocates for STEM education wanted and expected, we have a problem—and an ROI problem. We are not spending money wisely or efficiently.

The main argument of this book is that we will not get a better return on STEM education investments unless *employers* do better. For so many people to go through years of STEM training only to do something else—after they achieved their prized degree—points to employers as a problem. In the chapters that follow, I compile evidence of the employer practices that appear most likely related to the movement of STEM grads to non-STEM jobs.

I realize this sounds odd, especially given the prominence of the shortage rationale in advocacy for STEM education. How can employers be failing to attract, let alone driving away, STEM grads when they badly need them to fill open positions? Each chapter explores a particular factor that helps us understand why so many STEM grads might say no to STEM jobs, and examines where efforts to improve the return on investment in STEM education might pay off the most.

The law of supply and demand would predict that if there is a shortage or scarcity, employers would respond to that shortage by taking actions to alleviate it. These actions could take many forms. Employers can raise wages, and keep raising them until the shortage disappears. They can provide generous benefits. They can improve work conditions so that their workplace is a place where workers want to be—including women, minorities, and older workers. For the workers they already have, they can provide training so that they have the right skills.[58] They can also avoid business models that STEM grads will find morally stressful. They can find other ways to attract STEM grads that I have not considered—after all, these innovation-oriented firms are supposed to be run by very clever people. My point is that exhorting the schools to do better and better, and funding more and more investments in STEM education, will not increase STEM grads' persistence and contributions unless employers do their part as well.

Conclusion: What Drives the Practices That Can Drive STEM Grads from STEM Work?

Understanding why so many STEM grads leave or never take STEM jobs requires us to understand employers and what they do. Though I did not write this book to explain *why* employers behave as they do, I suggest some factors throughout that may lead to the STEM employment practices I detail in the next chapters.

Understanding why employers treat STEM workers as expendable, when there is a massive national effort to make more and more to alleviate a supposed shortage, requires us to understand how investors affect employers. By investors, I mean those who buy large amounts of stock in corporations and invest in start-ups, though in this book, I mostly focus on corporations because they complain the loudest about a lack of STEM workers and also have the most means to fix their perceived skills-scarcity problems.

The literature here is massive and well established, so I will only lay out the basics for why understanding investors is necessary to understand the return on investment in STEM education, and why so many

STEM grads leave STEM jobs. First, investor behavior began to change because of dissatisfaction with how corporations were being run in the period between World War II and the 1980s. This was also the time when white-collar workers (who were mostly White men) enjoyed the most job stability. Though these years were good for many workers, some economists argued that corporations were not being run well and needed to be more accountable to shareholders, the true owners. They argued that corporations should be run to increase the value of stock in the short term. The idea of "shareholder value maximization" took off, and as implemented by CEOs and their boards, it meant a lot of big changes for workers.

To make shareholders happy, corporate leaders began to do everything they could to boost the value of their stock in the short term. One strategy was to use profits to buy their own stock ("stock buybacks"), which raised stock prices but deprived their own firms—including their workers—of investment. The other main strategy was to cut costs, which investors typically rewarded, boosting stock value even more. Cost cutting meant shedding assets, such as factories, and outsourcing manufacturing to other firms in order to concentrate on "high-value" activities such as design and marketing, or pursuing business models that did not require manufacturing at all (e.g., making software). Other cost-cutting strategies included keeping the number of employees and salaries as low as possible. Keeping head counts low led to layoffs, outsourcing of jobs, and leaner, presumably more nimble firms that supposedly could better respond to increasing foreign competition and changing markets.[59]

Economists William Lazonick and Mary O'Sullivan have called this system an "ideology," a system of belief and ideals of a political nature, and thus suggest it is a part of culture.[60] The practices that it encouraged are indeed deeply entrenched culturally and appear to many observers to be self-evidently rational, especially in the US. They can be found in both private firms (which might go public, eventually seeking outside investors) and those that are already public. It leads employers to think of the supposedly scarce and incredibly valuable STEM workers as costs to be minimized, and it has created incentives for many (not all) of the employer behaviors I describe in the chapters that follow. These behaviors include maintaining low wages for STEM jobs (chapter 2); squeezing out maximum productivity through "burn-and-churn" management (chapter 3); providing unstable, precarious jobs (chapter 4); avoiding training for needed skills (chapter 5); ignoring diversity issues (chapter 6);

and using business models that don't improve the world or that make it worse (chapter 7; in this chapter I also show how venture capitalists prefer to invest in such business models, also for reasons related to their perceived likelihood of quick returns). All of these, and other employer behaviors I illustrate in these chapters, are likely factors leading STEM grads to leave STEM jobs.

In short, taxpayers, philanthropists, employers, and investors are caught in a larger system that, in the end, makes investment in STEM education popular but inefficient. But employers and investors can make different choices; they can exercise agency. Some choices they now make are not good for the national investment in the STEM workforce, and these choices need to be rethought.[61]

In the next chapter, I look more closely at the numbers—STEM grads rejecting STEM jobs, which fields lose the most STEM workers, and where STEM grads have gone when they are not working in STEM jobs. This chapter also points to the first factor that appears related to the exodus of STEM grads from STEM jobs: money.

CHAPTER 2

THE EXODUS FROM STEM JOBS

If science, technology, engineering, and math (STEM) jobs are so great, as we are often told, and if there is such a burning shortage of STEM graduates—again, as we are often told—then why do so many STEM grads not work in STEM jobs? Why do so many not enter STEM jobs in the first place? I ask these questions because the data show that, depending on how we measure and define STEM jobs, anywhere from about 30 percent to 60 percent of STEM graduates in the US do not work in a STEM job.

People change jobs and careers all the time, and even end up in jobs that are far from where their college educations would seem to direct them. But the exodus from STEM is different. Policymakers of both major US political parties, as well as philanthropies, school districts, and business leaders, all are investing money, time, and effort in STEM education with a major goal of preparing young people to work in STEM jobs. Nevertheless, huge numbers of STEM graduates are choosing not to put their degrees to work in STEM occupations despite business leaders practically begging for them to do so.

We should not just take these numbers at face value, however. We need to explore them a bit more before we can try to explain what is going on. Perhaps these numbers are just an illusion, something created by a bad definition of "STEM job." Or perhaps they are driven by one or two jobs sectors that STEM grads, for some reason, *really* hate, whereas other sectors are better at attracting—and keeping—these educated workers. We should also want to know where these STEM grads go.

It turns out that they are going, for the most part, to jobs that pay more. One might say they are going to jobs that are *better* than the supposedly great STEM jobs.

STEM Education for STEM Jobs . . . but What Are STEM Jobs?

Despite the massive public and private investment in STEM education, much of it designed to prepare students to go into STEM jobs, there is no single, official definition of STEM jobs. This is true even of the federal government, which spends billions on STEM education. The national commitment to produce more STEM graduates is based on a very fuzzy concept. Though some fields and jobs are clearly in the STEM camp, there are plenty of others on the boundaries, with no way to decide what is in and what is out.

This is because defining what is a STEM job is actually really hard to do. It's much harder than defining STEM majors, for example. Universities have little trouble dividing campuses into sciences, engineering, social sciences, and humanities. Big, broad categories such as "computer science," "physics," and "electrical engineering" will all be in STEM. The names of college majors, and even course content and requirements, are remarkably similar among universities in the US and around the world, and so deciding which educational fields are STEM and which are not is relatively straightforward.[1] Job titles and job tasks are far less standardized.

Even the label "STEM" is not standardized. The major governmental body that shapes America's investments in science, the National Science Foundation (NSF), sometimes uses the STEM acronym (after all, an NSF official invented it), but also uses "S&E," referring to "science and engineering," though the differences are obscure. NSF is idiosyncratic in counting all the social sciences as STEM, which makes sense because almost all social sciences use advanced quantitative methods (the *M* in STEM stands for math, remember), but that does not fit with most rationales for building the STEM workforce, such as those in the America COMPETES Act and related legislation.

The Department of Homeland Security (DHS), meanwhile, has its own distinctive list of STEM fields. It needs a list because employers successfully lobbied DHS to allow international STEM grads to work for three years in the US rather than the one year allowed for non-STEM graduates. This criterion put the burden on DHS to decide what was STEM and what was not to see who would get the three years of access to the US labor market. Because universities benefited from more international students (who typically pay full tuition[2]), the list has expanded beyond what employers demanded and now doesn't fit what most people think of as STEM.

For example, Pomona College and then the Massachusetts Institute of Technology (MIT) were able to get "quantitative economics" onto the DHS list, and then other individual universities lobbied to have their economics programs recognized as STEM-worthy and thus eligible to have their foreign economics graduates stay in the US and work for three years.[3] A critical investigation by Bloomberg News found that New York University was able to get a bewilderingly large number of programs included in the STEM extension, including Classical Civilization, Classics and Art History, Journalism, Linguistics, Bioethics, Construction Management, Drama Therapy, and even something called "Tonmeister Studies," which offers training in supervising music production and broadcasting.[4] DHS's official STEM list would provide poor guidance for counting who is and who is not in STEM to assess the return on investment in STEM education.

The US government has struggled to define STEM jobs because the project is something of a chimera. It can't be done because there really is not an either/or, STEM/non-STEM distinction to make. In other words, it's a false dichotomy.[5] STEM jobs are really part of a continuum, with jobs varying in the amount of technical (STEM) content—and this is true even with jobs with the same occupational titles because jobs vary between firms and even within firms, so that some have a lot of technical content and others do not despite similar titles. Some of these jobs may have traditional STEM occupational titles, but for entry-level workers they may end up having a lot of clerical and administrative work yet become more technical with more experience.[6] Jobs also change over time regardless of the level of experience, becoming more technical in some cases, so that (for example) jobs in marketing or sales may require STEM skills today when they did not in the past.

Some jobs may not have titles that most of us would know or understand unless we work in the relevant industry and yet require a high level of STEM skills. For example, in the city where I live (San Diego), biotechnology and pharmaceuticals are major employment sectors. I have a neighbor who has a PhD in biochemistry, but though formerly her title was "senior scientist" (definitely STEM), more recently she has held various jobs (manager, director, vice president) in "regulatory affairs." She helps drug companies navigate the Food and Drug Administration's complex approval process. Another neighbor has a PhD in microbiology but most recently has held positions in "quality assurance" or simply "quality." He helps companies run the trials that determine whether their treatments work and under what conditions. Both neighbors' jobs require highly advanced knowledge in the life sciences, but both jobs also involve a lot of work that is not actually doing lab science. Neither would likely show up in lists of STEM jobs.

Policymakers in the federal government know about this STEM-jobs continuum. NSF reports have discussed, for example, the many STEM graduates who do not work in STEM occupations but nevertheless report that their jobs are related to their STEM degrees or that their jobs require college-level STEM expertise.[7] In the Obama administration report calling for one million more STEM graduates than higher education would normally produce, the emphasis was on educating workers for traditional STEM occupations. But that report noted that there were many other "STEM-capable" workers who were also valuable.[8] The Trump administration sought to build basic "STEM literacy" for all Americans as well as to train STEM "practitioners."[9]

However, the major investments of the government and other funders in STEM education, and the four rationales for STEM education I discussed in chapter 1, tend to be focused on filling the traditional STEM occupations, not the wider, growing range of jobs requiring "STEM-capable" people. Obama's effort called for one million additional "scientists, engineers, mathematicians, and technicians in STEM occupations."[10] The majority of Congress's STEM programs and STEM education dollars target STEM learners at the college level and beyond.[11] Similarly, the focus of business leaders on foreign workers with STEM degrees reinforces the idea that employers are looking for workers with technical STEM skills to fill technical STEM jobs. If employers are lobbying for more access to foreign "STEM-capable" managers and salespeople, they are doing so very quietly.

Which STEM Workers Are Most in Demand?

The focus on STEM *education* puts attention on creating a supply of STEM workers, but another way of thinking about the return on the investment in STEM education is to think about demand. In which STEM fields are employers hiring the most? Here there is a clear winner: jobs dealing with computers—especially software and the internet, often referred to as IT (information technology) jobs. In 2019, the year for the most recent data, NSF counted 7.5 million STEM graduates working in STEM occupations, and 3.8 million of them were working as "computer and math scientists" (don't be distracted by the "math scientists," a category that includes statisticians, modelers, and even actuaries; they amount to a small part of this category). This category is the 800-pound gorilla in the world of STEM employment, accounting for *more than half* (50.6 percent) of all STEM jobs in the US.

Even the agglomerated megacategory of "engineers" (which would include electrical, mechanical, civil, chemical, and even computer hardware and software engineers, so the 3.8 million computer-related workers is not complete) is only 1.9 million employed, or about 25 percent of all employed STEM workers.[12] The dominance of computer-related occupations is likely to become even more pronounced. NSF projected this category to grow the fastest of the STEM occupations (13 percent between 2019 and 2029), dwarfing growth projections for all the other categories (engineers only 4 percent, life scientists 5 percent, and physical scientists 5 percent).[13]

This may not be surprising if we think about it. Perhaps every business in America uses computers in some way, and most have at least a website. Larger or more advanced businesses have more advanced needs in these areas. The rise of the internet and software as key parts of the infrastructure of American commerce created a massive demand for workers with expertise in computers and IT. One study found that between about 2002 and 2012, jobs in the internet sector increased by 634 percent, and in second place were jobs in software (562 percent). In third place in this growth were jobs in life science research (300 percent), which is also explosive growth, but starting from a much smaller base of jobs.[14]

News media and others may refer to these jobs as "tech," but we can think of them as a band of jobs that cuts across every sector. The job market data firm Burning Glass issued a report showing that the vast majority of STEM jobs were both IT jobs and outside what Burning Glass considered to be tech. In 2018, there were 6.2 million job postings for IT jobs outside tech firms, an increase of 65 percent from 2013. Job postings in tech had grown 40 percent in the same time period but only reached about 740,000. Major sectors hiring IT workers were firms in professional services, finance and insurance, manufacturing, health care, and educational services.[15] These firms are much less likely to need engineers, life scientists, and chemical scientists.

The training firm General Assembly, which specializes in training workers in coding, software engineering, and user experience design, provides more insight into how IT dominates STEM. It boasts major corporate clients in media (Bloomberg, NBCUniversal, Disney), professional services (Booz Allen Hamilton, Deloitte), insurance (Aetna, Liberty Mutual), banking (Citibank, American Express), and consumer goods/retail (Walmart, Procter & Gamble).[16] Another report found that firms as diverse as airlines (Delta) and banks (US Bancorp, JPMorgan Chase, and Capital One) were top employers of software developers.[17]

The Exodus from STEM Jobs by the Numbers

We have seen that though STEM jobs can be a broad category, best understood as a continuum rather than a binary of STEM and non-STEM, the investors in STEM education and the rationales that guide them simplify this situation by emphasizing education for what we might call "traditional STEM occupations." We've also seen that though there are many of these, computer-related jobs are the dominant category because employers in a variety of sectors need these workers. Of central interest here, however, is the exodus of STEM grads. Who is leaving? And are the numbers really that bad?

In the study of STEM education, scholars, policymakers, and educators often talk about a pipeline that "leaks." A "leak" implies the unintentional loss of a small amount. But the number of STEM grads leaving STEM occupations does not look like a leak, like a small, accidental loss. It looks more like a like a major break and a gushing flow.

As figure 2.1 shows, using the traditional STEM occupations as defined by NSF and using the National Survey of College Graduates 2017 data (a very hot job market), well over half of STEM graduates do not work in STEM occupations.[18] These numbers have been consistent since early in the first decade of the twenty-first century, varying only by a percentage point or two. This is a huge amount of loss. If you are losing almost two-thirds of something that you said over and over was valuable and scarce, you were losing it for decades, and you said it was just an accident, a leak, you'd likely get some incredulous stares.

We might think these numbers are driven by one or two fields that

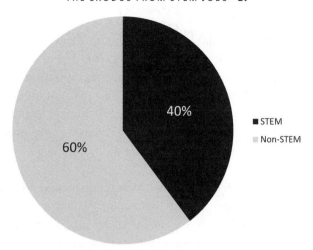

FIGURE 2.1 STEM graduates in STEM and non-STEM occupations. (Data for 2017 from National Survey of College Graduates; STEM and non-STEM occupations as defined by National Science Foundation.)

Note: "STEM graduate" defined by field of major of first bachelor's degree.

STEM grads really seem to hate working in, but that's not the case. Although fields do vary in the amount of exodus, the numbers are bad no matter where we look. Engineering looks the best at retaining STEM grads, with a bit more than 50 percent working as engineers. But that obviously means that engineering is losing almost half the students who toiled for years to learn the theories and skills of an engineer to do engineering. Computer and mathematical sciences, where employer demand is the greatest, are actually a bit worse at showing persistence, with numbers just around 50 percent staying to work in these occupations. Physical and related sciences lose about 60 percent of their grads from the occupations for which they were trained. But the real disaster—from the perspective of STEM education policymakers hoping for more scientists—is in the biological, agricultural, and life sciences. Only about 20 percent of students who major in these subjects work in life science occupations.

A reader might reasonably protest here. "Sure, some STEM grads leave STEM, but it is older folks who do that, looking for a new challenge." However, the exodus from STEM is not only a story of older workers leaving STEM. There are many points of failure of the STEM pipeline, but a significant one is right at the point of graduation. Research by B. Lindsay Lowell and Hal Salzman and their colleagues followed STEM majors after graduation and found that 45 percent had taken a non-STEM job, while 20 percent were in graduate school but no longer studying STEM. This means that immediately after earning a STEM degree, their research showed that about 65 percent of STEM graduates moved out of STEM.[19]

A reader might protest some more: Surely these numbers vary by gender and ethnicity, as sex and race discrimination in STEM are well-known problems. The numbers do vary, as I show in chapter 6, but focusing only on Whites and males still shows an exodus from STEM occupations.

Another possible objection is that these numbers may be padded by masses of astronomy and paleontology majors, fields that are important for advancing civilization's march of knowledge (and longtime favorites of mine—I'm not picking on them) but, along with other basic science fields, do not have clear applications to any dominant business models. But this also appears wrong. While it is true that majors in the basic sciences are more likely to opt for non-STEM opportunities right out of the gate, it is also the case that the more applied STEM fields—and the ones supposedly facing shortages—also experience an exodus right after graduation, including those working in computer fields and engineering. Policy researchers Hal Salzman and Beryl Lieff Benderly's review of the data show that "colleges graduate 50% more computer science and engineering students than the number from their cohort who are hired into those occupations, and in sciences, colleges are graduating nearly double the number of science graduates than are hired into science jobs."[20] Other researchers also find high percentages of computer science and engineering majors not working in STEM jobs. A Census Bureau report, for example, found that overall, only 52 percent of engineering majors worked in STEM, about the same as computer science, statistics, and math majors.[21]

Surely those leaving STEM are the weaker students—those who could not handle the pressure and intensity of work that required math and science, or whom employers reject because they perceive these graduates to be low achievers and poorly qualified. But this seems wrong, too. Lowell and Salzman's research shows that STEM grads with the highest GPAs are no more likely than the average to take a STEM job out of college. STEM grads leave STEM at about the same rate regardless of demonstrated ability.[22] In fact, as we will see in chapter 5, many of these best students leave STEM a few years later, when their skills start to become out of date.

An additional objection presents itself: How can we expect people who are eighteen to twenty-two years old (the typical age range for college students in the US) to know what they want to do for the rest of their lives? It is common for college grads to change their interests and do something else. I agree—it *is* common. But I argue that we should especially care that so many are deciding that STEM work is not for them.

The reasons we should especially care more about the exodus from STEM jobs are several, and I discussed them in the first chapter: The US is investing billions in creating more STEM workers, and doing so for some seemingly urgent and compelling reasons. If there is a shortage of STEM workers, we should be greatly concerned about them leaving STEM. If STEM jobs are key for American competitiveness, bringing more diverse people into the middle class and solving planet-destroying problems, we should be greatly concerned.

Moreover, the exodus from STEM appears to be *worse* than the normal changing of minds would suggest. As Anthony Carnevale, Nicole Smith, and Michelle Melton have shown, both at the points of graduation and ten years after graduation, STEM workers leave at higher rates than those in other fields. Whereas their data show that 56 percent of STEM grads worked in STEM immediately after graduation, 62 percent of business majors were working in business immediately after graduating, 61 percent of those majoring in healthcare fields worked in healthcare, and a (relatively) whopping 84 percent of those majoring in education worked in education. STEM looked unimpressive for keeping graduates in the field later on as well in this study: 46 percent of STEM majors were still in the field ten years later, compared with 53 percent of business majors, 66 percent of education majors, and 72 percent of healthcare majors.[23]

No matter how you slice the data, it appears that employers are failing to attract and retain a lot of people who have learned STEM skills and knowledge, and could be working in STEM jobs, including more than half of those with STEM degrees. Apparently, a lot of jobs are more appealing than STEM jobs.

When STEM Grads Leave STEM, Where Do They Go?

To fully understand why STEM grads do not work in STEM jobs, we also need to know which jobs they are choosing. The answer may surprise those who think that STEM jobs are great because they pay so well: many

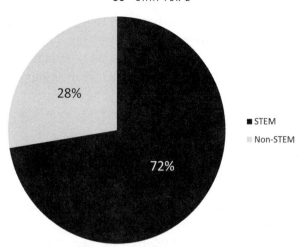

FIGURE 2.2 STEM graduates in occupations requiring STEM expertise and not re-quiring STEM expertise. (Data for 2017 from National Survey of College Graduates.)
Note: "STEM graduate" defined by field of major of first bachelor's degree.

STEM grads leave STEM jobs for higher-paying jobs. Whereas a great number of these jobs actually require STEM expertise, they are not the jobs that policymakers, business leaders, and educators mention when they call for more and more STEM education.

The smart people who run the National Survey of College Graduates had the great idea to put a question on the survey asking respondents whether their jobs require college-level STEM expertise. This question allows us to see that many STEM grads are rejecting the traditional STEM occupations that the funders of STEM education aim to fill, but these grads still claim to be using college-level STEM skills.

The survey consistently shows that America loses more than a quarter of its STEM grads to jobs that do not require STEM expertise (figure 2.2). The numbers vary greatly with majors. About 15 percent of engineering grads claim to no longer use STEM expertise, around 25 percent of computer and math scientists say the same, just a bit larger share of physical scientists turn their back on use of STEM expertise, and about 40 percent of biological, agricultural, and environmental life sciences grads leave both STEM occupations and the use of STEM expertise.[24]

This might appear to be a much better return on investment to STEM education, but we need to first know where these STEM grads are going to understand the ROI, and why they are not working the traditional STEM occupations that are supposedly facing severe shortages. First, we need to acknowledge that some STEM grads leave STEM because they cannot find a job in STEM.[25] About 7 percent of those who earned a STEM degree in the previous four years are what the NSF calls "involuntarily out of field," meaning they have a job that is out of their field of degree but they want one in that field.[26] This is a number we would reasonably expect to be lower if there really is a shortage. Other researchers argue that a far higher percentage cannot find jobs in the field of their STEM degree, where the number may be as high as 30 percent even in the high-demand IT industry.[27]

More important for explaining the exodus from STEM jobs is STEM grads choosing to pass up traditional STEM jobs. What jobs would be better than the supposedly great, supposedly in-demand, supposedly essential-for-America STEM jobs? The short answer is: jobs that pay more. Some researchers examining school-to-work trends, as well as persistence in STEM careers, have argued that this pull factor is crucial for understanding why so many STEM grads leave STEM or never take a STEM job.[28]

For example, to get a clearer picture of movement in and out of STEM, I and a colleague examined NSF data on the top ten occupations for STEM grads in four categories: (1) those whose job was in the NSF's category of traditional STEM occupations and who also said that their job required college-level STEM expertise; (2) those whose job was in the NSF's STEM occupations but who (for whatever reason) did not think their job actually required a STEM degree; (3) those who were *not* in the NSF's list of STEM occupations but who said that their jobs did require college-level STEM expertise; and (4) those who were not in the NSF's list of STEM occupations and who also said that their jobs did not require a STEM college degree.[29]

The results show that one big story on the exodus from STEM is the move to medical occupations, with "diagnosing/treating practitioners" being the top choice of those who are not in STEM jobs. STEM majors in healthcare jobs earn about 40 percent more per year than STEM majors in STEM jobs.[30] They likely show up in both categories of leavers (those who say their jobs require STEM expertise and those who say their jobs do not require it) because of a quirk of NSF question wording. Medical diagnoses would seem to require some knowledge of life sciences, but the NSF's survey offered respondents options to say that their jobs required "technical expertise" in "engineering, computer science, math, or the natural sciences" and also "some other field" (e.g., "*health*, business, or education"; emphasis added). Several other medical occupations show up in both lists (see table 2.1).

We may argue about whether or not medical professions are really STEM or are not STEM, and whether they use STEM expertise or something else (such as the survey's mention of "health expertise"). But the pattern is that STEM majors move into medical professions at high rates, their salaries go up about 40 percent on average when they do this, and the pattern of movement persists despite an absence of voices saying we need more STEM education to create more physicians, nurses, and pharmacists. And if they did so, pushing broad "STEM education" to create more health practitioners would be a very inefficient way to increase that supply. First, the push should be for education for physicians, nurses, and pharmacists, not generalized STEM education. Second, any demand for more physicians should first focus on what appears to be a very broken medical profession. Scholars and other observers have pointed to the American Medical Association's efforts to restrict the number of practicing physicians to maintain high status and salaries twice as high as in other developed countries.[31]

Another non-STEM destination for STEM grads is management of various types. This profession is prominent in the category of STEM grads who are not in STEM occupations but claim to use STEM expertise on their jobs. I am quite ready to consider many of these jobs as STEM occupations in themselves,[32] and no doubt they are crucial to the innovation economy. Many observers would argue that this is a good thing—wouldn't we want STEM experts to manage STEM workers? But again, the advocates for more STEM education have been calling for more technical workers to fill traditional STEM occupations such as software developer—these positions are where the shortages are, we are told—and not *managers* of software developers (more on this important issue later in the chapter).[33]

Other prominent occupations receiving STEM grads are business related. For example, "accountants, auditors, and other financial specialists" shows up on both the STEM-expertise list and the non-STEM-expertise list. In the latter list, some other business-sounding occupations are prominent ("other administrative"; "other marketing and sales occupations"; and "insurance, securities, real estate and business services").

What many of the non-STEM jobs for STEM grads have in common is they are better paid than STEM. The evidence also suggests that

TABLE 2.1. Top ten occupations for STEM graduates who leave/stay in STEM, by two definitions of STEM

Occupation definition	STEM	STEM	Non-STEM	Non-STEM
Expertise definition	STEM	Non-STEM	STEM	Non-STEM
% STEM graduates	38.2%	2.2%	33.7%	26.0%
1.	Computer engineers—software	Computer support specialists	Diagnosing/treating practitioners	Diagnosing/treating practitioners
2.	Software developers—applications and systems software	Other computer information science occupations	Top-level managers, execs, admins	RNs, pharmacists, dieticians, therapists, PAs, NPs
3.	Electrical and electronics engineers	Computer system analysts	Other management-related occupations	Other management-related occupations
4.	Mechanical engineers	Network and computer systems administrators	Teachers: Secondary—computer, math, or sciences	Top-level managers, execs, admins
5.	Civil, including architectural/sanitary engineers	Software developers—applications and systems software	Engineering managers	Accountants, auditors, and other financial specialists
6.	Computer system analysts	Medical scientists	Other midlevel managers	Other administrative
7.	Computer support specialists	Web developers	Computer programmers*	Other marketing and sales occupations
8.	Chemists, except biochemists	Database administrators	Accountants, auditors, and other financial specialists	Sales—retail
9.	Other computer information science occupations	Computer engineers—software	Computer and information systems managers	Insurance, securities, real estate and business services
10.	Biological scientists	Biological scientists	RNs, pharmacists, dieticians, therapists, PAs, NPs	Health technologists and technicians

Note: The occupations listed are based on averages from four NSCG survey years (2003, 2010, 2013, 2015). The 2003 survey had a few differences and categories only used in that year are excluded. Data analysis in Skrentny and Lewis, "Beyond the 'STEM Pipeline,'" 14. RNs: registered nurses; PAs: physician assistants; NPs: nurse practitioners.

* The National Science Foundation (NSF) does not consider "computer programming" to be a STEM or "science and engineering" occupation. In contrast to other computer occupations, NSF sees it as in decline. Table LBR-A, in National Science Foundation / National Science Board, *The STEM Labor Force of Today: Scientists, Engineers, and Skilled Technical Workers* (Alexandria, VA: National Center for Science and Engineering Statistics, August 2021), https://ncses.nsf.gov/pubs/nsb20212/u-s-stem-workforce-definition-size-and-growth#growth-of-the-stem-workforce.

employers are not offering the wage increases we would expect if they were facing massive shortages, either.[34] Moreover, non-STEM careers in healthcare, management, and professional services look even more attractive with education beyond a bachelor's degree.[35] If money is what motivates you, there is far more of it to be had for those pursuing degrees in business (MBAs), law (JDs), and medicine (MDs) than advanced degrees in STEM. Thus, a lawyer will typically earn 50 percent more than a PhD-level scientist, and a physician will make twice as much.[36]

Many readers might reasonably protest here—after all, almost 75 percent of Americans believe that STEM jobs pay better than non-STEM jobs.[37] Many readers will know STEM workers who are living the dream—bought a house, maybe even retired early. How can I say that STEM wages are too low to retain STEM grads when there is so much trumpeting, in the media, government, schools, and elsewhere, of the great wages in at least some fields of STEM?

I do not deny that STEM jobs may be tremendously lucrative and a major upward move for many workers. At tech giants, salaries can be very high for STEM workers—software engineers at Google, for example, could make more than $300,000 a year in 2022.[38] Some STEM occupations may see sudden spikes in demand and sky-high wages, at least over the short term. This is likely to happen when a new technology or subfield bursts onto the scene and becomes hot. This happened with the rise of e-commerce in the 1990s for some developers and engineers. It happened again with artificial intelligence (AI) in the 2010s, as individual workers with this particular STEM expertise could pull in $500,000 to $2 million per year—even working at a nonprofit.[39] Fresh PhDs could make an annual salary of $300,000 to $500,000 straight out of graduate school, and one superstar AI expert, who was the subject of a legal battle over intellectual property between Google and Uber, earned from Google an eye-popping $120 million in incentives.[40]

There are two other reasons for impressively high STEM pay. Sudden spikes in wages can also occur when there is more money to be made in a particular sector. Wages of petroleum engineers, for instance, tend to shoot up during periods of higher oil prices.[41] In addition, STEM wages, like other wages, vary regionally. In Silicon Valley they tend to be very high, creating higher real estate prices and thus more pressure for rising wages.[42]

But these are special cases, and if they were the rule, we would not likely see so many STEM graduates leaving STEM jobs. My argument about STEM jobs failing to retain STEM grads is about overall patterns and averages, not special cases. On average, STEM wages are very good, better than many jobs, and certainly way better than most jobs for people without a college degree, but the data show that many other jobs simply pay better. The reason for this is that employers have set wages for STEM jobs lower than some non-STEM jobs—including non-STEM jobs at their own firms. STEM grads can see that they can boost their take-home pay if they move to non-STEM jobs, sometimes just across the hall.

Employers Have Incentivized Moves Away from STEM

The lower wages of STEM jobs relative to some other jobs are not simply a fact of life. Employers *choose* to keep STEM wages low relative to some other jobs. After all, the setting of wages for particular jobs is one of the most basic things that employers do. In setting and keeping wages in STEM jobs relatively low, employers incentivize STEM graduates to leave STEM, exacerbating whatever shortages they perceive to exist.

We know employers have discretion on the wages they give for every job they offer, and this discretion is the premise of a growing research literature on employers who choose to take the "high road" and treat their employees well, as investments for current and future productivity, rather than employers who choose the "low road," who see their employees as costs to be minimized.[43] The sociologist Jake Rosenfeld studied processes of wage setting by employers, noting that they tend to copy each other ("mimicry"), and then through inertia, wages tend to stay where they are for given jobs. They might change pay for equity, to equalize some jobs, or to respond to worker mobilization (such as union demands).[44] But at the end of the day, employers decide how much to pay people, at least in the private sector.

That means that employers are deciding to pay STEM workers lower salaries than those earned by attorneys, physicians, and workers in business of various types. We might think it is reasonable for employers to pay bachelor's-level workers less than professionals with advanced degrees (JDs for attorneys and MDs for physicians), but this is not the whole story.

Many employers choose to pay their *own* non-STEM workers more than their STEM workers. We can see this in the pay of managers. Even where STEM workers are supposed to be the most scarce—the tech sector—employers typically pay managers more. Although there are some highly paid technical STEM workers, as previously discussed, and STEM entrepreneurs and early joiners of start-ups who have hit it big, most STEM workers will toil under the supervision of managers who are more highly paid than they are.[45]

For example, the Congressional Research Service, the organization responsible for giving high-quality, unbiased facts to members of Congress, used Bureau of Labor Statistics data to show that STEM managers made much more than did scientists and engineers, with an average wage of $144,000 while the more traditional STEM occupational titles averaged between $83,000 and $96,000. STEM managers also had the highest rate of wage growth, growing at 2.5 percent a year between 2012 and 2016, whereas traditional STEM occupations had wage growth between 1 percent and 2.4 percent, depending on the field.[46] Other sources consistently show the pay premium for managerial work over technical STEM work.[47]

Given that employers typically choose to pay their STEM workers less than some non-STEM workers, even at their own firms, what can STEM workers do to boost their salaries? As Rosenfeld argues, one thing they can do is mobilize and fight for higher wages, perhaps by forming a union. Some are taking this step, but this is very difficult to do, as I discuss in later chapters.

For most STEM workers, there are two major ways to raise their wages. One of these, increasingly common for all workers given employers' preference for hiring from the outside (as we will see in chapter 3), is to change employers, bargaining with the new employer for more pay. They can also take a new offer back to the original employer if they don't really want to move. Employers don't like being pitted against each other, but they contribute to the practice by hiring so often from the outside rather than from within.

Some of the biggest and wealthiest companies in Silicon Valley deliberately tried to short-circuit this process, and they violated American antitrust law to do so. Adobe, Apple, Google, Intel, Intuit, Lucasfilm, and Pixar—none struggling, none hurting for profits—made a secret agreement not to poach each other's employees. A Justice Department investigation found that the companies had promised not to give offers if employees at another company in the agreement applied for a job, and to never start any bidding wars for the services of even a highly skilled worker. In other words, they agreed to limit workers' ability to negotiate and bargain for higher wages. In 2015, a federal judge ordered the firms to pay $415 million in restitution to more than 64,000 workers who were parties to the case and whose wages had been held down by the agreement.[48] While this may look like a one-off situation, it does reveal even thriving STEM employers' desire to keep wages down and willingness to take even illegal actions to make them stay down.

More commonly, employers have the law on their side as they limit workers' ability to bargain. For example, the legal enforcement of "covenants not to compete," sometimes called "noncompete agreements," prohibits workers from using their skills at competitor companies—in some cases, even if they were fired. Such covenants or agreements are illegal in California, which is why the Silicon Valley employers tried to keep their agreement secret, but they are common in other states. A study of tech workers bound by these covenants in other states found that these workers tend to stay at the same companies for longer than those who are free to negotiate with others, and thus they experience lower wages throughout their careers as a result.[49] A report from the US Department of the Treasury during the Biden administration concluded that employers' limits on workers' bargaining power led to an overall (not only in STEM) wage decrease of "roughly 20 percent relative to the level in a fully competitive market."[50]

The other major way to raise one's wages is to get promoted at your current employer.[51] In non-STEM jobs, workers have routinely moved up career ladders, taking on more responsibility while earning more pay. These opportunities may have declined over the years as firms laid off workers and flattened hierarchies, but are still there for many employees.[52] In STEM jobs, where we often hear of a scarcity of STEM workers, we might reasonably expect employers to use job ladders and salary scales to incentivize STEM graduates to remain in STEM work while moving up and increasing their pay. These employers would leverage employees' common desires for more money, more power, more fancy titles, and more prestige to create a technical STEM track to advancement.

But it turns out that this is usually not the case. Though many firms do indeed maintain a technical track for advancement and promotion to retain STEM workers, we do not see much evidence of it in the aggregate wage data, with managers typically making more, and quite a bit more, than technical STEM workers. If STEM workers regularly enjoyed promotions to higher-paid technical jobs, we might expect to see the salaries to be more similar. Researchers Lotte Bailyn and John T. Lynch identified the crux of the issue: "For most engineers . . . there is no satisfactory way to combine day-to-day involvement in technical engineering problems with an increased span of responsibility and concern. Faced with this dilemma, some engineers opt for scope by turning to management, but then deprive themselves of the unambiguous and immediate gratifications obtainable from solving concrete technical problems."[53]

Readers might reasonably protest here: Who better to manage technical workers than people who understand the technical issues? As I discuss in chapter 4, some STEM workers have moved into contract work because they did not respect their managers. But a closer look reveals problems with this approach.

First, by promoting from their own bench of STEM workers to fill managerial positions, employers incentivize moving *away* from STEM. Movement from more purely STEM work to management is actually *expected* by some employers. This means that employers' job ladders contribute to their own perceived STEM worker scarcity problems.

Second, there is a morale problem. Some engineers have reported that staying in engineering eventually begins to feel like *failure* because of these culturally embedded norms of movement—promotion!—to management. It is an odd system where students are trained in STEM subjects for many years, encouraged to love STEM subjects, hired for their passion for STEM, and then expected to leave it for bigger payouts. One interviewee told researchers Bailyn and Lynch of having "enjoyed technical work very much," but after a promotion to management, "Now I am sad all the way to the bank."[54]

Third, in addition to missing work on technical challenges, some STEM workers also dislike the tasks of management that are very different from technical work. One who made the move complained of having to make presentations, explaining, "It's not my favorite part of my job. Personality-wise I tend to be, and I guess a lot of engineers tend to be, more introverted than extroverted." Another identified the challenge of communication for engineers: "We weren't trained as engineers to be communicators. Some people are very good at it—it's a skill. It's more a natural one. You could improve it with learning I think or practice, but you don't tend to get a lot of practice."[55]

Researchers Hal Salzman and Leonard Lynn interviewed engineers and engineers who went on to earn MBAs, and found similar struggles in moves to management. The logic of their argument is not limited to engineering and would extend to other STEM workers: "An engineering education tends to reinforce the notion that there are 'right' answers to every question and these answers can be systematically determined by following one rule or another. There is little room for emotional intelligence and not much patience with ill-defined problems."[56]

Fourth, promoting STEM workers to be managers can hurt the overall organization. Social scientists long ago studied "the Peter principle," or the idea that in organizations people are promoted based on their performance until they are incompetent at their position, where they then stay. The Peter principle may be at work in some STEM worker moves to management. Executives in STEM-oriented firms often choose their managers from those who excelled at some task *other* than management. One study found that high performance at some task unrelated to management is actually *negatively* correlated with managerial ability. This finding suggests that most employers of STEM workers would be wise to allow promotions to better paying but more fully technical STEM positions—in line with their STEM skills—rather than moving them away from technical jobs.[57]

The Cultural Dynamics Keeping STEM Worker Pay Lower Than It Could Be

Employers do not typically complain of a scarcity of managers, and the federal government does not spend billions of dollars a year to graduate more managers, which would suggest that managerial skills are more common than STEM skills. So why do employers pay their supposedly scarce STEM workers less than their managers? Why don't they pay like a team in the National Basketball Association, where the players make far more than the coaches and general managers do?[58] Economists typically argue that pay corresponds to skill levels—"human capital."[59] But this idea does not appear helpful in distinguishing the skill levels of STEM workers with their managers—who is to say one is more skilled than the other?

Rosenfeld's ideas of mimicry and inertia are more helpful in understanding why employers pay STEM workers less than they do their managers, or even why they are paid less than other business occupations, or attorneys or physicians. It is fundamentally a cultural process. Rosenfeld shows that about 75 percent of employers used surveys of other firms' wages for particular jobs in the last year, and 20 percent were looking at such data on a daily basis. In a process typical of institutions, wage levels become baked into the culture of employment and are maintained and reenacted over and over through this mimicry and then inertia for paying the "going rate."[60]

STEM workers accept as normal that they are paid what they are paid and that managers are paid more. They likely look at the starting salaries of liberal arts majors and feel no equity concerns because STEM workers are paid more at the entry level—in fact, they probably think they "have it good" and may feel sorry for those poor literature and philosophy majors. Employers mimic each other on STEM pay, so it is rare for any to get out of line even without overt collusion. Employers also use their power to resist unions and maintain the superior pay and positions of managers—again, despite the supposed scarcity of STEM skills.

I saw this dynamic when I visited a Southern California tech start-up that had developed an app that was becoming popular. The executive with whom I spoke complained that he could not keep his UX designers (responsible for creating a user-friendly interface on the app)—they kept leaving for higher pay. His response, however, was not to raise pay. Despite his UX designers leaving, he did not think he should raise his wages any more than he already had, which ensured that they paid less than the STEM workers who did the "back end" of the app, such as engineering the app's interface with the cloud, and of course the managers at the firm. Showing both the inertia and mimicry dynamics that Rosenfeld identified, this executive showed me pay surveys from business support firms that provide salary data to justify his views. These showed typical salaries for various occupations. He explained that he chose to outsource his UX designing to a low-cost country in order to avoid raising pay. At no point did he say he could not afford to pay more for this job—he just did not want to.

Conclusion: STEM Grads May Reject STEM Jobs for Better Pay

I am definitely not arguing here that employers pay STEM workers terribly, and I'm not arguing that STEM is a lousy way to make it to the middle class. We can easily find comparisons where STEM looks great relative to non-STEM jobs. The Congressional Research Service I discussed earlier in the chapter showed that STEM workers (understood as traditional STEM occupations, plus STEM managers) had a mean annual wage in 2016 (a booming economy) of about $94,000, while the mean for all occupations (including jobs for those without college) was only $50,000. STEM salaries ranged from a high of $96,000 (engineers) to a low of $83,000 (life scientists). Computer occupations were in the middle at $88,000.[61] This looks impressive. My argument here is that the numbers for STEM jobs should be even more impressive if there really is a shortage and we really do want our STEM grads to work in the traditional STEM occupations.

To assess what we are getting for our national investments in STEM education, I've tried to simplify things, focusing on what advocates of STEM education typically say they want and on how the government has allocated its investments. The rationales for STEM education emphasize creating college graduates in STEM subjects who work in STEM occupations so they can mitigate shortages, innovate to boost national competitiveness, take middle-class STEM jobs (especially if from diverse backgrounds), and (my hope) innovate to solve crises facing the planet. Not every STEM education advocate thinks in these terms, but many of the most prominent do. The federal government has focused its efforts on college-level STEM education and creating workers in what I've called traditional STEM occupations. Policymakers have shown little interest in investing in STEM education to create managerial talent, businesspeople, or healthcare providers, three major destinations for STEM graduates who leave STEM.

The evidence shows that STEM grads have options, and many, if not the majority, are rejecting traditional STEM occupations. I have argued here that a big reason is money—but this is not the whole story. Why, besides wages, aren't STEM jobs attractive enough to keep STEM grads in them? Why else might they leave for something else? What's wrong with a life devoted to technical work related to science, technology, engineering, and math? My goal for the next chapters is to shed some light on these questions.

CHAPTER 3

BURN AND CHURN

How Management Strategies Can
Drive Away STEM Workers

In chapter 2, we saw that science, technology, engineering, and math (STEM) graduates leave STEM jobs in great numbers—or never take a STEM job in the first place. They do the hard work to earn their STEM degrees but then turn their backs on traditional STEM occupations. Many appear to leave for higher pay. Some move to management, some move to business, some move to medicine or other professions. But this desire for higher pay is not likely the only factor contributing to the exodus from STEM and calling into question the returns on the huge national, philanthropic, and personal investments in STEM education in the US.

I will argue in this chapter that another likely cause of the exodus from STEM is the way employers manage their STEM workers. Too often, they treat STEM workers as if they are a dime a dozen, easily replaceable, and not at all scarce. Employers often will burn through their STEM workforces, working them hard until they leave—and then demand that the education system produce more to keep the burn-and-churn process going.

Moreover, we cannot assume that those who continue to work in STEM are happy. If STEM jobs are so great, we might wonder why some workers in these jobs are taking the major step to unionize, thereby emulating workers in manufacturing, food processing, teaching, and government. Some employees at Google, a giant firm with a near monopoly on internet search and one of the largest market capitalizations in the world, saw the need to unionize and succeeded in 2021. Those leading the effort were a minority, to be sure, but significant enough that—according to the National Labor Relations Board—Google violated labor laws by spying on employees and firing union organizers. Workers formed a union at the online crowdfunding platform Kickstarter, also despite efforts to squash the unionization drive, and there have been attempts to unionize employees of video game makers such as Rockstar, Epic, BioWare, and Activision Blizzard. Issues motivating these unionization efforts included an issue that is the focus of this chapter: overwork (e.g., eighty-hour workweeks). Other motivating factors are the focus of subsequent chapters, such as layoffs, second-class treatment of contractors, discrimination against women and minorities, and how firms choose to make money.[1]

My point here is not to say that STEM jobs are terrible. My goal is to look for clues about why STEM grads would reject these jobs. I take at face value employers' claims of STEM worker shortages and then examine employers' behavior to see whether what they are doing regarding STEM workers makes sense if there are such shortages. I focus on tech employers and computer-related or information technology (IT) occupations for two reasons: because tech employers have been the most forceful in claiming that educational (and immigration) failures are hurting them by not providing enough workers with the right skills, and because computer-related occupations constitute about half of all STEM occupations. Tech firms may provide the best test of an argument that employers are driving STEM graduates from STEM. We should see the happiest STEM workers in tech because—if STEM workers really are scarce—it is tech employers who should be working the hardest to keep them happy. Where possible, I will refer to other sectors, but the focus here is on those working for big tech firms.[2]

The media image of skateboarding, foosball-playing, happy-go-lucky STEM workers enjoying life on the corporate "campus" or doing relaxing remote work in sweatpants or beach resort wear, may be accurate for some, but it does not capture the grueling work schedules that many will face—or leave STEM to avoid. A darker interpretation of those apparently fun-filled offices is that they are designed to keep workers from going home. As Allison Arieff, an architecture and design journalist who has focused on corporate offices, has commented, "Work-life balance is not eating three meals a day at your office, going to the gym there, having all your errands done there."[3] The same can be said for remote work that is more than eight hours a day.[4]

Happy Are the STEM Workers? The Survey Evidence

Those pushing to get more Americans to work in STEM often seem to assume that STEM jobs are especially great jobs and that STEM workers find their work especially satisfying. But is this true? The most common way that sociologists, psychologists, and economists have explored job quality is to measure worker attitudes toward their jobs through surveys. Researchers ask respondents to report on how they personally feel about their jobs. Relying on these is a lot easier, and more feasible, than trying to define and measure job "quality" in some supposedly objective way, and when survey responses from hundreds of people form a pattern, that pattern is likely communicating real information about jobs or the kinds of people who choose these jobs.[5]

Studies of job satisfaction tend to find strong majorities of people reporting that they are very or somewhat satisfied with their jobs or occupations (the exact terms vary). Social scientists believe such findings likely overstate how widely appealing jobs are. People who don't like their jobs have probably already left them—a "survivor bias" whereby only the happier ones remain in particular jobs or occupations. It may also be difficult for people to admit that they don't like what they are doing for forty or more hours a week, and so they inflate their satisfaction. For comparison, it might be similar to asking someone if they have a happy marriage: although divorce is common, the celebration and expectation of happy marriage are the norm, and it might be hard to admit, even to oneself, to being only somewhat satisfied, or even dissatisfied, with a spouse. It may be telling that when social scientists ask whether people would like for their children to have their jobs, where there are some real stakes added to the question, respondents typically report less satisfaction.[6] In addition, we might question whether someone who says they are "somewhat satisfied" with their job is really feeling positively. (More on this later.)

Another reason to be cautious about data showing high job satisfaction relates to what workers expect from their jobs. As I discuss in chapter 4, the 1980s marked a turning point when management practices changed, and mass layoffs and wage stagnation became more common in the US.[7] If people *expect* jobs to be awful, then they are more likely to say they are satisfied because, well, what else is there? People might feel lucky, and satisfied, because they have a job that they do not despise. This attitude may be especially prevalent among those who are more likely to expect discrimination at work, such as women and African Americans.[8] In fact, studies show that women tend to be more satisfied with their jobs than men.[9] However, it would be unreasonable to conclude from this finding that women have better jobs than men do.

With these cautions clearly stated, it is time to look at some data, with the expectation that supposedly scarce and valuable STEM workers will be pretty happy in their jobs because employers will be doing whatever they can to retain them. Even simple, descriptive statistics could reasonably be expected to show, emphatically and clearly, the superior satisfaction of STEM workers. However, I wish to argue that the data invite glass-half-full/glass-half-empty interpretations. The basic finding is that *yes*, STEM workers seem satisfied according to these surveys. On the other hand, it is not clear that they are satisfied enough to stick with their jobs. More important, these supposedly coveted STEM workers are not more satisfied than non-STEM workers, who are presumably more plentiful and less valuable and thus employers have less incentive to make happy.

A picture of STEM job satisfaction comes from a random sample that captures all workers, including all STEM workers of a great number of types and varieties—*and* allows comparisons with non-STEM workers. With the National Science Foundation's National Survey of College Graduates, we are also able to examine a variety of STEM occupations as well.[10]

The results show STEM workers as mostly satisfied with their jobs—but we can interpret the results positively or negatively. For example, in every major category of STEM jobs—"biological/life scientists," "computer occupations," "mathematical scientists," "physical scientists," and "engineers"—between 40.9 percent (computer occupations) and 45.5 percent (mathematical scientists) of respondents report being "very satisfied" with their jobs. Very few—between about 1 percent (mathematical scientists) and 2.4 percent (physical scientists)—report being "very dissatisfied." Of those saying they were "somewhat dissatisfied," those in computer occupations were at the high end of the range (8.3 percent) and mathematical scientists at the low end (5.9 percent). All of that looks great to those putting money, time, and effort into STEM education.

We can look at these same data in a more negative light, however. For instance, we see that between 45.9 percent (biological/life scientists) and 49.1 percent (computer occupations) are only "somewhat satisfied." This means that nearly half of STEM workers are finding something wrong with their jobs, and it is workers in computer occupations, which make up about half of all STEM workers and who are supposedly in the shortest supply, who seem the least enthusiastic. That's not a ringing endorsement for employers who are supposedly almost begging for workers. If you work an eight-hour day and you sleep eight hours, that means that a third of your life is spent working—and for about half of STEM workers, working means doing something they are only "somewhat satisfied" with. If someone said they were only "somewhat satisfied" with their spouse, you might feel a bit sorry for them.

A reader might ask, "Compared to what? Surely job satisfaction in STEM is higher than for those poor non-STEM workers." Given the huge push for the education system to create more STEM workers for eager employers facing skills scarcity, we would reasonably expect STEM workers to report being very satisfied at higher rates than non-STEM workers. However, this is not the case. College graduates in the broad category of non-STEM jobs do not look much different in terms of job satisfaction from those in STEM jobs. Indeed, though the differences are small, it is non-STEM workers who have the highest percentage reporting being "very satisfied"(46.2 percent) and the lowest in the squishier "somewhat satisfied" category (43.6 percent).

Overall, these data tell us a story: non-STEM workers look comparable to STEM workers in job satisfaction, and nearly half are only "somewhat satisfied" with their jobs. There may be some employers giving their STEM workers some pretty amazing jobs over their non-STEM colleagues, but not enough to show up in the job satisfaction data.

How the Hiring Process Fails to Match STEM Workers to STEM Jobs

I take a glass-half-empty view of the STEM job satisfaction data, but only because of the endless hype about these jobs, how great they are, and how students should aspire to them. Still, these survey data provide only a blunt instrument for understanding what STEM work is actually like. To understand why so many STEM grads leave or never enter STEM employment, we must explore more descriptive accounts and begin with the start of any job—the job search. What we see is job seekers confronting—and doing their best to navigate—what is often a broken hiring process, even for the employers seeking to hire for STEM jobs.

First, let's examine how STEM workers might try to get a job. It is important to understand that for a variety of reasons, some of which I discuss in this section, employers—not just in STEM—prefer to hire from the outside to fill vacancies. One survey of talent acquisition leaders found that only 28 percent saw internal candidates as an important source of workers for new openings. As management scholar Peter Cappelli noted, the focus on hiring from the outside is so significant that, according to the US Census, a majority of the people who started a new job in the previous year were not even looking for a job. As Cappelli puts it, "Somebody came and got them."[11] According to Cappelli, all of this job placement occurs without any serious analysis by firms or their organizations about whether hiring from the outside is better than promoting from within.[12]

That "somebody came and got them" makes it sound easy to get a new job (just wait until a job comes to you!) and for some people, it is easy. But for many workers, including STEM graduates, including those in tech, seeking work for firms based in tech *hubs* (that is, concentrations of STEM-oriented companies, especially in the top innovation centers—Boston, San Francisco, San Jose, Seattle, and San Diego[13]), significant effort is required to appeal to employers. These STEM workers continually cultivate their attractiveness to possible future employers—their "employability."

According to anthropologist Ilana Gershon's study of the matching of workers to jobs in Silicon Valley, job seekers increasingly thought like entrepreneurs, as if they were each their own independent business. The workers tended to view the hiring process as if they were establishing a business-to-business contract, rather than being taken in and developed as a loyal and productive employee for a long relationship. Workers, in effect, would build their personal employability brand. They typically did this online, and not just with a single social networking website such as LinkedIn.[14] Human resources professionals and "career coaches" (an occupation that owed its existence to the imperative of building employability[15]) advised those aspiring to tech careers to build a consistent personal brand *across* platforms to send a strong, consistent message about what kind of worker one was and could be. Software developers, for example, had opportunities to show expertise on tech-advice websites such as Stack Overflow, where users who supplied helpful answers to posted questions earned reputation scores, plus gold, silver, and bronze badges, with those points determined by user votes.[16] These sites signaled skill levels but also built workers' network ties, as did other sites including LinkedIn, Github, Facebook, and Twitter.[17]

We might question why, if jobs are (supposedly) so plentiful for STEM workers, they would put so much effort into building their own brand and employability. One important reason is that employers' process for filling positions has many flaws, and these flaws make it difficult for them to fill positions—a self-inflicted wound, we might say, but one that also harms workers.

The problem begins with the job ads. Too often, ads for jobs have too many skill requirements listed. It is a problem that does not only afflict hiring for STEM jobs. Hiring managers—those who identify the need to hire, define the job requirements, and are likely to be managers of the new employee—have become increasingly demanding and uncompromising regarding the skills job candidates should have. Management scholar Peter Cappelli has done insightful research into this process, describing the ways that hiring managers "find it hard to resist including in job descriptions the experiences and skills that will ensure a successful candidate can step right into the job and do everything needed," and therefore "pile all the credentials and expertise into the job description to minimize the risk that the candidate will fail, making it virtually impossible to find anyone who fits."[18]*

Though common in many industries, this tendency may be especially pronounced for STEM jobs, and especially for those in software. Software may be a unique case, and not just because it is such an outsized presence in STEM work. Variation in coding ability may have a huge impact on productivity, so that a brilliant coder is worth much, much more than an average one. As Cappelli and others note, some research indicates that the best software developers are ten or more times more productive than the lowest performers—such that someone of that caliber is known as a "10-X Programmer."[19] Whether true or not, what matters is that there are employers who *believe* that star coders are major boons to their firms. They therefore offer very high starting salaries to land these top talents. The problem is that hiring managers have trouble predicting exactly which potential employees will be so outstanding as to be worthy of those high wages. Given their uncertainty about which applicants really are going to be so amazing, employers try to ensure that they get the super talent by demanding that applicants have a lot of qualifications.

They may demand college graduates from top universities but then also demand a variety of skills and experience in the hope that the amazing performers will make it through this stringent process.

In other words, according to Cappelli, the normal process wherein high skill requirements for a job come first and drive the high wages offered for that job is reversed: ads for jobs that will have high wages get loaded with skills demands. When employers then cannot find applicants with these complicated combinations of skills and experience—what some observers describe as a search for a "purple unicorn"—they may complain there is a shortage of qualified workers.[20] They may continue their futile search for the coveted purple unicorns because their accounting processes do not calculate the costs of *not* hiring someone, whereas they know—to the penny—what the wages and benefits are when they hire someone, and they greatly fear hiring and paying loads of money to the wrong person.[21] Frustrated employers who can't find workers may then complain of STEM worker shortages where none may exist—and demand that more money be invested into producing STEM graduates and that more STEM-educated migrants be allowed in.

Cappelli sketched out this process in 2001, but Gershon's more recent analysis found little had changed. As one recruiter told Gershon, "In the old days . . . if I was looking for somebody that had A, B, and C and they're smart, and they could pick up E and F, they'd get hired. Over the last ten years, five years it's gotten much, much more . . . they better have A, B, C, D, E, and by the way, F and G would be nice too. So it's a lot harder specs to get people hired. . . . A lot of them have an idea of 'I only want people with good pedigree. I only want people who have done a certain type of technology. I only want people from A, B, C, D, E, F, G, H, I, J companies. I only want people who've worked at a start-up before. I only want people who—and it's highly illegal but—who are youthful.'"[22]

This all sounds bad for the STEM job seeker, but we are not done yet. The challenges are made worse by the increasingly common process of firms using software and algorithms to sort through job applications. Firms can program this software to search for particular qualities or keywords and disqualify others. It sounds efficient, but it is prone to error. Candidates may list past jobs accurately but inadvertently use a job title that the software is not programmed to handle. The machine then jettisons the whole application without a human being ever laying eyes on it. The software can replicate and worsen biases, kicking out promising candidates, especially women and those from minority backgrounds, while also remaining blind to applicants who might be excellent at the job but lack some specific (but irrelevant) characteristic, or have some "fatal" keywords in their applications.[23]

Given this set of compounding problems, it is not surprising that firms complain that they can't fill positions. But wait, there's more—next is the interview itself. Some evidence suggests flaws here as well in the search for STEM workers. One study showed that what would seem to be a virtuous practice of meritocracy—having job interviewees solve technical problems *during* the interview—actually may be counterproductive to the goal of finding new employees. The study compared interviews where subjects solved computer science problems on a whiteboard with interviewers watching and measured their stress levels and "cognitive load" (basically, the amount of stuff in your working mind at the same time), and compared this process to interviewees solving the same problems but doing so privately. The results showed that the public problem solvers failed 62 percent of the time, whereas those working on the problems privately (as they would most likely do when actually working on the job) failed only 36 percent of the time. Thus, job applicants may fail a portion of a job interview that does not replicate real-world job conditions.[24]

And then there are the outside parties who are part of the hiring process. About 40 percent of US companies (overall, not just those who hire STEM workers) use outside recruiting firms to fill positions. Cappelli could comment that "someone came and got them," referring to the ways workers often changed jobs, because of the large presence of recruiters. The use of recruiters is significant because it means that some job openings will be invisible to job seekers, including workers hoping to move up at the firms doing the hiring. The involvement of recruiters is premised on the idea that the best person for a job will be found outside the hiring organization and not through the internal promotion of an existing employee.[25]

Recruiters come in many forms but are often also staffing agencies, a business model pioneered by ManpowerGroup in 1948.[26] Recruiters that also work as staffing agencies recommend particular workers to employers, and if one of those recommended workers gets hired and stays on the job for a period of time (for example, six months), the employer pays the recruiter a finder's fee.[27]

It may seem odd for employers to pay someone just to hire someone, and that they do so might suggest that employers are responding to a scarcity of workers. But employers perceive several benefits in using recruiters that have little to do with a scarcity of skills. First, given that a lot of new employees already have jobs, one appeal of recruiters is that they create some distance between the hiring firm and the firm that is being poached. Having the recruiter do the dirty work, so to speak, allows some plausible deniability regarding the raiding of another firm's human resources ("It wasn't us who did it—it was that darn recruiter!"). Second, hiring through a recruiter rather than posted ads avoids signaling to competitors what skills a firm is seeking to employ, and thus where it has deficiencies. A third reason is office politics: hiring managers might want to avoid their own human resources (HR) department because it might have different priorities (such as following legal requirements).[28]

But there are also downsides to the use of recruiters that impact STEM workers. Recruiting removes from contention the firms' own employees, making job ladders shorter or nonexistent. It also ensures that firms will not see the wide range of available talent, only those who caught the recruiters' attention. Finally, recruiters might simply use the same lists of irrelevant qualifications that make the jobs ads so bad.[29]

In summary, those arguing for the production of more STEM graduates for the nation's employers should encourage—or demand—that those employers scrutinize their hiring procedures. Their reliance on unrealistic requirements, badly written job ads, poorly performing application sorting mechanisms, unnecessarily stressful job interviews, and recruiters (who keep hiring obscure and insular) may be screening out excellent candidates—including workers already at their own firms who are looking for a promotion that might keep them in STEM.

How Managers May Drive STEM Workers
Away by Stressing Them Out

If there is a scarcity of workers in traditional STEM occupations, we would reasonably expect managers to do what they can to keep those workers happy—to manage the workers in ways that take into consideration needs and concerns, in ways that make jobs enriching and maybe even enjoyable, and in ways that can at least avoid making them unnecessarily stressful or painful. This matters because, as I describe in this section, research shows that how employers manage their workers affects worker attitudes toward their job, their stress levels, and their decisions to leave their jobs.

Despite their supposed scarcity, STEM workers do not appear different from their non-STEM counterparts regarding their reasons for leaving a job. They both leave for reasons that management controls at least
in part. For example, the National Survey of College Graduates showed
that nearly identical percentages of workers in both STEM and non-
STEM jobs give the same reasons for leaving a job in the last two years
and in similar frequencies (the survey allowed respondents to choose as
many reasons as they wanted from a list). "Pay, promotion opportunities" topped both lists, with about 60 percent giving this as a reason. But
for both STEM and non-STEM workers, the second most common factor,
and another that management controls and where we would find stress
as a factor, was "Working conditions (e.g., hours, equipment, working
environment)." About 40 percent mentioned this as a reason they left.[30]

If the "working conditions" reason for changing jobs was related to
stress, it would hardly be surprising. The American Institute of Stress
(there is such a thing) has reported that work is the most common cause
of stress in Americans' lives. One survey asked what causes work stress,
and 39 percent of survey respondents listed "workload," ahead of "interpersonal issues" (31 percent), "juggling work/personal lives" (19 percent),
and "lack of job security" (6 percent).[31] Similarly, according to a report by
the National Institute for Occupational Safety and Health, 40 percent of
Americans in one survey described their job as "very or extremely stressful," and 26 percent in another survey responded that they are "often or
very often burned out or stressed by their work."[32]

Other research sheds light on how stressful workplaces relate to
workers' intentions to stay at a job or to leave. Management scholars
Matt Ferguson, Lorin Hitt, and Prasanna Tambe's survey of 3,500 full-
time workers found even higher numbers—59 percent—of those who
reported being stressed at their jobs. Among respondents who said they
were highly stressed at work, 46 percent planned to leave, far more planning an exit than among those who reported moderate stress (25 percent
planned to leave) or no stress (only 18 percent planned to depart).[33]

Similarly, researchers Donald and Charles Sull and their colleagues
examined 34 million online profiles from a sample of leading, mostly
for-profit companies to identify those that had the highest rates of
workers leaving. They also analyzed 1.4 million reviews of the companies on the employer review site Glassdoor to determine which topics
were correlated with rates of workers leaving. The researchers found
that "toxic corporate culture" was ten times more powerful than salary

considerations as a predictor of leaving.[34] This corporate culture included what the Sulls and their colleagues have called the "The Toxic Five Culture Attributes." First, workplaces that were *disrespectful*, or that showed "lack of consideration, courtesy, or dignity for others" led workers to leave. Second, being *noninclusive*, especially on the bases of sexual orientation, disability, race, age, and gender, was a significant problem (as we will see further in chapter 6), as were places that excluded workers because of "cronyism and nepotism." Third, *unethical* workplaces—that is, those with "unethical behavior," "dishonesty," and "lack of regulatory compliance"—incurred high rates of attrition (as we will see further in chapter 7). The two remaining aspects of a toxic work culture are, along with disrespect, particularly germane to this chapter. Employers who maintained, fourth, *cutthroat* cultures ("backstabbing behavior and ruthless competition") and, fifth, *abusive* cultures ("bullying, harassment, and hostility") saw workers leave at extremely high rates. Cutthroat workplaces garnered such descriptors as "dog-eat-dog," "Darwinian," "throw one another under the bus," "stab each other in the back," and "sabotage one another."[35]

This research showed STEM-oriented sectors well represented in the list with highest attrition rates during 2021. This may not be so surprising considering that the researchers also found that the factor "high levels of innovation" was 3.2 times more likely than compensation to contribute to attrition. Though apparel retailing topped the list of occupational fields with 19 percent attrition, followed by management consulting (16 percent), the internet sector was third (14 percent), and other STEM sectors that were at or near the top half of the list included pharmaceuticals/biotech (10 percent), aerospace/defense (9 percent), data and analytics (9 percent), and semiconductors (9 percent). Adding to the indication that these attrition rates are *management* problems is the finding that the data showed attrition could vary greatly between firms in the same sectors. For example, Netflix had an attrition rate of 14.2 percent, compared with fellow media company WB's 6.2 percent; and in aerospace, SpaceX shed 21.2 percent of workers, compared with Boeing's 6.2 percent.[36]

How employers manage their workers, then, is key to understanding why they might leave a job. Although these statistics do not capture decisions to leave STEM work specifically, we know that thousands of STEM grads reject STEM work, and management decisions seem to be at least a likely factor. Since employers of STEM workers are benefiting from extra public and private investments in STEM education, we might reasonably expect them to be more attuned to the stress of their STEM workers than others. But STEM workers are often stressed out, some especially so. Part of the problem is a phenomenon social scientists call *overwork*.

Increasing workloads are likely part of the reason college-level American workers in all sectors may be stressed. Research on the number of hours Americans spend working has found Americans increasingly working longer hours. Around 1970, a hundred-year trend of shrinking work hours reversed for workers with college degrees and advanced degrees. It wasn't that managers started demanding longer workdays, though that undoubtedly occurred in some cases, but that they organized compensation so that working long hours started to pay off for workers. Put simply, they incentivized overwork, and many workers responded by overworking. Putting in long hours may signal to managers ambition that may lead to higher earnings, promotions, or protection from layoffs. Feelings of insecurity, which may drive some of this apparently voluntary overwork, have also increased since the late twentieth century (I explore these dynamics in the next section, related to performance reviews). Working long hours may also develop more workplace skills and richer, more diverse personal networks, further incentivizing working longer and harder.[37]

Employers appear to respond positively to overwork even if there is no evidence it leads to greater productivity.[38] This perception is apparent in remote work as well—one study found that workers who come into the office are promoted at higher rates even when the employer explicitly allows remote work.[39] Perceived effort just seems to pay off. This may be because of employers' use of the "passion paradigm," a preference for workers who display passion for their jobs, as I discuss in the next section.

These survey data and studies of work hours do not single out STEM workers, but the supposedly scarce STEM workers are not immune from these trends—and stress and long hours may be especially pronounced in STEM.[40] The Sulls' work also showed high levels of innovation as a major factor leading workers to leave. The Sulls and their colleagues argue that continual innovation requires long work hours at a rapid pace, which is difficult to sustain as it eats into personal lives.[41] Though not linking their findings to innovation, management scholars Erin Kelly and Phyllis Moen have argued that work hours have gone up in STEM jobs as well as the professions. Even for occupations where the hours worked are similar to past levels, the *intensity* of the work has gone up.

This finding was especially true in the software development occupations Kelly and Moen studied.[42]

As most STEM and professional workers will readily understand, measuring work hours is not an exact science because it is unclear when work actually starts and stops. Even before the COVID-19 pandemic turbocharged the move to remote work, some jobs came with an expectation that workers will respond to an email or a text at any time.[43] In that case, one may not be working, but nevertheless "on" or "on call," with greater expectations of multitasking along with more appearances, either in person or on a screen, and so not entirely relaxed and away from work, either.

Software development is prime terrain for these patterns because of this sector's sometimes unrealistically short timelines for product development and a tendency for salespeople to oversell what software can do. These factors put great pressure on STEM workers to actually make the software deliver on the promises in the stipulated time frame. Project managers on tight budgets are then pressured to hide hours worked to keep projects under budget, adding more stress to the work environment.[44]

The bottom line here is that work hours, work intensity, or both have gone up in the US, including and perhaps especially for workers in STEM jobs. Consequently, many workers feel stressed, and work stress is related to moving to another job. In a search for why so many STEM workers leave STEM, we will want to know what employers are doing to create or mitigate this stress. We will also expect to see employers of STEM workers especially motivated to guard these presumably precious resources.

If STEM Workers Are Not Passionate, Employers Manage Them to Act as if They Are

There are two common ways employers use to maximize worker productivity, roughly analogous to ways employers view skills and training (as I discuss in chapter 5). They can either "buy" (or employ) job applicants who arrive already willing to put in grueling hours, or they can "build" those workers—make them willing to put in those hours—through their management techniques. These strategies are not mutually exclusive— why leave anything to chance?

Regarding the buy strategy, employers can base hiring decisions on their perceived "passion" inherent in the job candidate instead of or in addition to skill or experience. Sociologist Lindsay DePalma has called this the "passion paradigm," understanding it as a coherent ideology of work. In this view, work is not just something that pays the bills. Instead, both parties—employers *and* employees—assume that the employees should love what they do. From the perspective of both, if that passion for the job is not there, something is wrong with the match, and they should go work somewhere else or do something else. An absence of passion in a worker is especially a problem from the employer's perspective as it indicates that the employee will not work hard and might not mind "coasting."[45]

Sociologist Erin Cech's research powerfully shows how the passion paradigm shapes the thinking of employers. In a survey experiment, she showed business leaders job applications that were similar in skill but differed in the job applicants' stated motivations (such as desire for promotions, desire to work for the particular company, and passion for the work). She found that those who were rating the applications were most likely to prefer job applicants who stated that they were passionate about the job. Raters regarded the passionate applicants as more reliable and hardworking. Notably, however, those rating the passionate applicants highly were not more likely to offer them higher salaries—they expected passionate work but did not want to pay for it.[46]

The passion paradigm is common throughout the American workforce, including in the hiring of supposedly scarce STEM workers. Gershon found it among employers in Silicon Valley, sometimes explicitly stated. For example, a manager told her "he would much prefer choosing the not-so-talented person to work on his project as long as he or she was passionate about the work" because "this is what guarantees that the employee will work the long hours necessary to get the job done." Unlike skills that could be taught, Gershon explained, that manager believed it was not possible to "make someone deeply committed to tasks if they didn't feel committed from the outset."[47] The premium on passion has been so strong that some firms, such as online retailer Zappos, have actually paid workers to quit on the theory that workers who would take the cash offered for leaving are not passionate enough about working at the firm. Amazon has also made this offer to employees.[48]

Turning now to the second strategy, some employers try to *build* passion in their workers, or at least coax behaviors that resemble passion. This is the "burn" part of the "burn-and-churn" management that characterizes so much management in STEM, and especially the tech sector. The burn is a major source of the stress that workers say they feel. Journalist Dan Lyons's scathing attack on the management consultants who push these kinds of techniques likened workers to "lab rats" on which managers should experiment. The guiding compact, he wrote, was that "employees can (and should) be underpaid, overworked, exhausted and then discarded."[49]

Sociologist Ofer Sharone's study of a major tech firm (kept anonymous) offers valuable insight into how employers use management techniques to induce STEM workers to act as if they are passionate about their jobs.[50] The engineers there willingly (or apparently willingly) put in an average of 67 hours a week—either 13.4 hours each weekday or 9.5 hours every day of the week. The firm fit the stereotypes of superficially "fun" tech employers, as it offered open spaces filled with arcade games, table tennis, and free snacks. There was no formal dress code, and the engineers personalized their offices like dorm rooms. But they were not working long hours because they just loved being at work. Most of the toys sat unused, and workers stayed secluded in their offices, even emailing each other from their self-imposed seclusion rather than going over to see their coworker in person. Many others toiled for long hours at home, choosing a remote option well before the COVID-19 pandemic began.

The workers did not see themselves as part of a team, either, whether working at home or in the office. In other words, they were not working so many hours because managers got them to think of themselves as grinding away for the greater collectivity, which may occur in start-ups when workers strongly identify with the new company and its products. In fact, the workers tended to view themselves as individuals competing *against one another*, rather than working together to succeed or to defeat other companies.

The overwork was not a response to simple material incentives, either. Managers did not coax passionate overwork by simply offering more money. Interviews showed that money was not the engineers' primary motivator.

Finally, this was not a case of the firm selecting employees who were passionate to begin with and just couldn't stop themselves from doing STEM work. They were not motivated to work long hours because they found the work enjoyable to do. That is, they did not want to work the long hours, even though they did so. From the outside, it may have looked like passion, but it really wasn't.

Instead, managers coaxed the grueling work hours through a management technique that scholars and practitioners call by several names: *forced ranking*, *stack ranking*, or *forced distribution ranking*. Sharone himself called it "competitive self-management" to highlight its effects on workers. Despite the varying names, this is a management technique that combines freedom with powerlessness. On the one hand, employees have considerable freedom to decide their hours, including when they work and for how long, and they can also typically set their own deadlines for deliverables. That sounds like a lot of freedom. However, they exercise this freedom with the knowledge that managers will grade them, ranking their performance in regular reviews that determine the projects they work on, their specific tasks on those projects, their pay, and their promotion possibilities. Moreover, managers will put each and every worker in the ranking, with no ties or duplications, so there *definitely* will be some workers rated as poor performers, some as middle-of-the-pack performers, and some as top performers. Small wonder, then, that the workers who were managed this way considered their coworkers competitors rather than colleagues.

We might credit Jack Welch, CEO of the venerable STEM employer General Electric, for this miserable strategy with its unnerving nickname of "rank and yank."[51] Welch developed the strategy in the 1970s out of frustration with managers rating nearly everyone in the middle. This was the easy solution because both high and low rankings usually required justification (and thus more paperwork).[52] The forced ranking system received a lot of positive buzz and quickly became widespread beyond STEM. One study found that in 2012, about 60 percent of Fortune 500 firms were using forced ranking.[53]

Sharone's study captured the anxiety that forced ranking produces in many workers and explained why they felt compelled to work long hours: to avoid being ranked in the bottom of the distribution. In interviews, employees revealed that they feared any score lower than an eight on a ten-point scale because to them, being in the middle wasn't just being average, it was a mark of mediocrity. Employees believed that to get the coveted eight or above, they needed to tell managers that they could do any assigned work and that they could do it quickly. Saying that they needed a lot of time for a task risked appearing slow, unskilled, or unmotivated—and then having *other* employees claim that they could do it quickly. Workers also learned—or at least believed; it does not matter whether it was true or not—that choosing the most difficult and complex part of any software project would lead to more visibility and more manager trust to handle the most challenging and important assignments in the future, which would, in turn, show how important they were to the firm. In short, choosing short deadlines and difficult projects made a higher score more probable—and long hours a certainty.

This thinking process was not always obvious to the workers themselves. In interviews, workers had trouble explaining why they worked so hard and for such long hours. As one responded:

> When you get a good review score, you know you are doing a good job. It's competition with yourself and implicit competition with your peers. Because if you get an eight you did better than x percent. It's really covert, I'd say, that if there is any, I [long pause], I'm having a really difficult time answering your question actually, um. I think part of it is, I am having a hard time articulating what my motivating factors are. Why do I work hard, why am I here so often, what keeps me here. I'm having a difficult time articulating, and I think the reason is that most of the factors, most of the motivation is really a covert kind of subtle thing. If I am not working many hours it's not like someone comes in and says, "Hey you are not working enough hours." Right, there are subtle sort[s] of pressures that I feel, and I don't know if it's self-imposed or it's external.[54]

This company was able to manage employees so that they worked *as if* they cared, *as if* they loved the work, *as if* they were passionate, when in fact they were being managed—one might say manipulated—to feel and act as they did.

Despite its apparent success in getting workers to work longer, managers across the US are moving away from forced ranking as a method to coax something that at least looks like passion from employees. Evidence supporting its use has been mixed, with some studies showing improvements in performance but also increased perceptions of organizational injustice and dysfunction, as well as employees sabotaging one another.[55] There is also evidence that forced ranking is a major source of stress. Some observers argue from a neuroscience perspective that ranking and assigning numerical ratings to performance impacts workers like a physical threat from a wild animal, creating a "fight or flight" response, hijacking the brain's executive functions, and impairing judgment.[56] Consequently, some high-profile firms, both in technology and outside it, have moved away from forced ranking systems, including Microsoft, Adobe, Accenture, Cargill, ConAgra, Gap, Intel, Medtronic, and General Electric itself. There seems to be no obvious replacement, but most of these firms are turning toward more frequent and less formal feedback.[57]

Moves away from forced ranking will not mean that long hours are on their way out for all STEM workers, however. Management scholar Jeffrey Pfeffer argues that long hours have become a taken-for-granted practice, a part of the culture, in many jobs. Employees themselves have come to see working long hours as a signal of toughness and strength, particularly in Silicon Valley, and necessary for advancement into hard-to-get management positions.[58] Journalist Dan Lyons noted that T-shirts emblazoned with the slogan "9 to 5 Is for the Weak" could be seen in Silicon Valley, and that tech leaders who have given talks on the danger of overwork reported being met with "incredulous gasps" and critiques that they are not being ambitious enough.[59] But employees' embrace of this "passion paradigm" may occur because employers cling to it even if they jettison the performance reviews. Whether they use forced ranking or not, employers can continue to reward the workers who appear to work the hardest and the longest and leave behind those who prioritize work-life balance. Employees cannot change that culture by themselves even if they want to.

It is important to emphasize here that the passion paradigm's relationship to overwork is found in STEM despite the supposed scarcity of these workers—they are not always coveted or coddled. It's also not something found only in struggling start-ups or firms that have lost market share and are panicking before their stock price plummets. On the contrary, journalists seem to delight in showing that even the richest or most dominant firms can burn and churn through their employees.

AMAZON: CULTIVATING RELENTLESS AND OBSESSIVE "AMHOLES"

The online retailer and technology company Amazon was one of the first targets of journalists seeking to expose a toxic workplace in a firm with massive wealth and near monopoly power. Amazon has tried to both "buy" and "build" passion in its employees, using a variety of means, including forced ranking.

For example, when hiring, Amazon has tried to screen out dispassionate employees. In its early years, CEO Jeff Bezos told shareholders the following:

> It's not easy to work here (when I interview people I tell them, "You can work long, hard, or smart, but at Amazon.com you can't choose two out of three"), but we are working to build something important, something that matters to our customers, something that we can all tell our grandchildren about. Such things aren't meant to be easy. We are incredibly fortunate to have this group of dedicated employees whose sacrifices and passion build Amazon.com.[60]

Not content to only try to screen out the dispassionate, Amazon has also sought to coax passion in employees whom it had already selected for passion. It is easy to see how Amazon's "Leadership Principles," displayed proudly on the company's website, could lead to overwork. What the principles share is a sense of limitlessness, "the more, the better," so passion is implied. There are no apparent reasons to ever think one has done enough for the firm. Notably, there are no principles that emphasize how valuable workers themselves are to the firm—instead, the firm must be paramount to the workers.

Some principles suggested a kind of mania or mental illness. For example, "Customer *Obsession*" (emphasis added) meant that employees should "work vigorously to earn and keep customer trust." Similarly, "Insist on the Highest Standards" was about "relentlessly high standards" that "many people" will think are "*unreasonably* high" (emphasis added). Absolutist language also came up a lot, especially the word *never*. For example, "Ownership" means employees should "never say 'that's not my job.'" Another principle, "Deliver Results," stated that leaders "rise to the occasion and never settle." The principle "Learn and Be Curious" was not a reference to a playful state of mind. It was a 24/7 job: "Leaders are never done learning and always seek to improve themselves." The principle of "Frugality," while avoiding absolutist language or a maniacal approach to work, seemed to be a directive for overwork: "Accomplish more with less. Constraints breed resourcefulness, self-sufficiency, and invention. There are no extra points for growing headcount, budget size, or fixed expense."[61]

In 2015, the *New York Times* published a profile of the company with a headline calling Amazon "a bruising workplace." It claimed that employees were encouraged to attack one another's ideas and enabled to provide secret feedback about one another to managers. Culling workers was so common that a former HR director called it "purposeful Darwinism." Workers complained of being fired after dealing with a variety of personal health challenges, from miscarriages to cancer. One employee reportedly said, "Nearly every person I worked with, I saw cry at their desk."[62]

According to the *Times*, "Amazon uses a self-reinforcing set of management, data and psychological tools to spur its tens of thousands of white-collar employees to do more and more." One former marketer for the firm, Amy Michaels, called it a "continual performance improvement algorithm" run on the staff. The result was long hours and the loss of work/life boundaries, so that employees were working Thanksgiving and Easter as well as vacations, nights, and weekends. One (male) manager who worked eighty-five or more hours a week and rarely took vacations warned a young mother that her family responsibilities would likely limit her promotions because she could not work the hours that younger (childless) coworkers could provide. Around Seattle, the kind of worker who fits in with this combative and obsessive work culture earned a derisive nickname: "Amhole."[63]

The *Times* account attributed part of the strife to the forced ranking performance review system, which Amazon embraced with gusto. In a long, tense meeting called the "Organizational Level Review," managers debate their rankings of employees and who will be pushed out. The meeting starts at the lower levels, and once those layers are dispensed with, the managers of those lower levels leave the room, knowing that they could be the next ones on the chopping block.

The *Times* reporting, like the cases described in the next two sections, concentrated on the negative and gave disproportionate space to unhappy workers. It is certainly a more mixed picture if one samples workers randomly, with many denying that things are so bad, or even claiming to be quite happy to toil in the *Hunger Games* atmosphere at the firm. For example, a review of comments at the job review site Glassdoor showed a more mixed picture of worker satisfaction with Amazon.[64] The point here is that Amazon has sought to attract passionate workers and to use management tools and culture to coax passionate effort, and the result is a lot of stress among workers who supposedly are scarce. "Passion" at Amazon can mean long, hard work and little accommodation of personal or family needs, and these expectations are likely to drive away workers and make any labor scarcity problems worse. These family-unfriendly strategies can also limit diversity at the firm (an outcome discussed in chapter 5).

UBER: "ALWAYS BE HUSTLIN'"

Management scholar Jeffrey Pfeffer's study of how overwork erodes health and literally kills people described a case that showed, in tragic fashion, the stakes of dehumanizing management of STEM workers.[65] Joseph Thomas, an Uber employee, died by suicide after only five months of working for the company that (along with Lyft, its competitor) created the business model of connecting drivers to riders via their smartphones. Thomas, however, was not a driver—he was an experienced, in-demand software engineer who earned $170,000 a year at Uber. He also was not a beginner, joining Uber after leaving his job with the business-oriented social network LinkedIn, and he was not desperate for a job, having turned down an offer from Apple.

Whether staying at LinkedIn or taking the job at Apple would have been better for him we cannot know, but he attributed great pain to his choice to take the job at Uber. A married father of two, Thomas reportedly confided to his wife, Zecole, that his decision to move to Uber "ruined our life." He sought therapy and was advised to leave the company, but he allegedly said, "I cannot do it, I cannot think." He complained that the company's managers laughed at him, criticized his engineering skills, and led him to feel "stupid." He told a friend in a text message, "The sad thing is this place (Uber) has broken me to the point where I don't have the strength to look for another job." After a few months in this condition, he took his own life. His surviving spouse told reporters that her husband had also said to her that he was "broken."[66]

Had he been able to last until six months, his family might have had access to $720,000 in workers' compensation, and so Zecole Thomas sued Uber to release the compensation. She argued that the case was bigger than her husband, explaining how the desire for passionate workers was destroying lives: "The way many of these companies work is they want you to love your job more than your families, with breakfast, lunch and dinner and places to sleep at work," and noting that "people in IT want to have families, too."[67]

The conditions Thomas complained of were not unique to his expe-

rience. Investigations of the company's practices by BuzzFeed News and
the *New York Times* provided plenty of evidence of stress and overwork.[68]
BuzzFeed's interviews with employees (who insisted on anonymity because of fears of retaliation) revealed "impossible workloads, around-
the-clock emergencies, fear of management, a total erosion of work-life
balance, and a pattern of public humiliation at the hands of higher-
ups." Workers complained of "panic attacks, substance abuse, depres-
sion, and hospitalizations."[69]

In addition to long hours, Uber's management team created what one
worker described as "asshole culture." The company's original fourteen
core values (derived from Amazon's but infused with assertiveness bor-
dering on bellicosity) included such items as "Champion's mind-set,"
"Superpumped," "Be an owner, not a renter" (which encouraged total
buy-in to the mission of the company), "Meritocracy and toe-stepping,"
"Always be hustlin'," and "Principle confrontation."[70] What this meant
in practice, according to one employee, was, "You've got to be a certain
assholeish type of personality, otherwise you're considered weak. . . .
Either you are an asshole, or you are considered not valuable."[71]

Two managerial decisions nurtured the competitive, toe-stepping,
always-hustlin' culture. Neither was unique to Uber. First was the promise of riches from company stock, offered as an option to employees.
One employee told BuzzFeed, "You're just so invested that you can't walk
away from it . . . the equity is in the millions for some people." The longer workers stay, the more they could make if the company would go
public.[72] Note the emphasis here is on *could* and *if*. Workers had no control over these decisions and what the valuation would be. But the fact
that it could be truly massive riches led to a lot of forgiveness regarding
working conditions.

Second, like Amazon, Uber relied on forced ranking, and it used these
rankings to determine who stayed at the company, received raises, and
received promotions. The high stakes of the scoring, plus the uncertainty regarding how those scores were assigned, led to stress and anxiety that drove employees to avoid actions that might make them appear
uncommitted to the firm. Predictably, this behavior led to overwork and
at least the appearance of passion. Offered an invitation to an Uber re-
treat in upstate New York? Better go to *all* worker retreats. Told you are a
bad fit because you are leaving before 7:00 p.m.? Better work until mid-
night. Worried that your managers don't like you and might give you a
low ranking? Better socialize with them, go drinking with them, and not

do anything to attract any critical attention.[73] This is a rough ride for a lot of people, and it is not how we would expect a firm to treat workers who are supposedly scarce and valuable.

FACEBOOK: PLEASE DON'T ASK ABOUT OUR ENGINEER'S AT-WORK SUICIDE

Meta Platforms, formerly and more popularly known as Facebook, despite years of a near monopoly on social media, has also managed its workers to display passion through overwork. Facebook also has its own controversies related to STEM worker suicide.

In September 2019, Qin Chen, an engineer from China working on a temporary (H-1B) visa, died by suicide while actually working at the company. The location and dramatic nature of the death—leaping from a fourth-floor window of an office building—suggested that the source of his anguish was work related. News reports stated that Chen, a thirty-eight-year-old married father of one child, was working on core activities of the company. Specifically, he did "advertisement engineering," which is central to Facebook's business model of gathering data on users so the company could sell targeted ads. The unit was known as a high-stress place to work, and there were rumors that a manager bullied Chen. Around the time of his suicide, Chen was especially stressed because of a low performance review, and he was worried that his status on the temporary work visa made him vulnerable to being forced to return to China, since the H-1B rules required an employer to sponsor the worker. Details of Chen's death were sketchy because Facebook sought to cover up the incident.

Another engineer, Yi Yin, spoke out about the incident, arguing, "We need the truth," and demanding that Facebook conduct "a fair investigation on what on earth had happened." He added, "I really want people to be aware of the H-1B abuse and also the PSC system," referring to the "performance summary cycle," a forced ranking technique that included peer reviews. Rather than using the incident as an inspiration for soul-searching and better treatment of employees, Facebook fired Yin, apparently for speaking to the press about Chen's suicide, and forced him to pay back his signing bonus of $39,000.[74] Both Chen's suicide and the firing of Yin led to significant anti-Facebook blowback on social media, especially in China.[75]

Despite the apparent cover-up, the Chen suicide put a spotlight on

Facebook's managerial strategies. Like all companies, Facebook has changed over the years. When the company was young and growing rapidly, it was able to coax long hours and passionate overwork from employees through a management style scholars call "normative control," which creates a group norm of overwork for all workers toiling together, sometimes with a kind of siege mentality that is common in start-ups. Using normative control techniques, managers generate the passion to work long hours by getting employees to see themselves as part of the larger collectivity—like a team or an army—and associate their own well-being with the well-being of the firm.[76]

An account of Facebook's early years from a former employee, Antonio García Martínez, revealed Facebook's normative control techniques. In a book and also an article in *Vanity Fair*, Martínez described how long and hard Facebook employees worked, especially when encouraged by founder Mark Zuckerberg to rise up to defeat Google's attempt at social media, the short-lived Google Plus, that directly challenged Facebook on Facebook's turf. Martínez compared Facebook to a cult and to a totalitarian country such as North Korea to explain why thousands of employees worked tirelessly toward the company's goal of getting every single human being onto Facebook—and preventing Google from doing something similar.

Propaganda signs pushed ever more effort from workers already indoctrinated into the collective. This indoctrination began when employees had their first day of work, called the "Faceversary," that the firm celebrated annually at workers' desks with colleagues and balloons. The firm treated leaving the company almost as a death, quickly removing ex-workers from an employee-only Facebook group, and, according to Martínez, "almost instantly, someone would add you to the ex-Facebook secret groups." Even before a "lockdown" that founder Mark Zuckerberg ordered to defeat Google Plus, employees worked long hours. As Martínez explained, "This culture is what kept 23-year-old kids who were making half a million a year, in a city where there was lots of fun on offer if you had the cash, tethered to a corporate campus for 14-hour days. They ate three meals a day there, sometimes slept there, and did nothing but write code, review code, or comment on new features in internal Facebook groups."[77]

Martínez's account, published in 2016, does not give attention to performance review strategies, but by 2017 at least, forced ranking was a regular part of Facebook practice to make employees behave as if they had passion. In the Facebook practice, managers *and peers* would give grades to employees twice a year, in February and August, placing every employee in a category. There were seven categories, with the highest grade being "redefine," as in redefines the position (in a good way), and to the lowest being "does not meet" (expectations), a rare ranking that indicated the employee would be fired immediately.

As in other firms, this system would make employees work hard (which may look like passion) but also make them anxious. As with other STEM workers, they worked nights and weekends to boost their chances of a high score. As one Facebook engineer told CNBC.com, "If you're up for promotion, and it's based on whether you get a product out or not, you're almost certainly going to push that product out. . . . Otherwise you're going to have to wait another year to get that promotion." The inclusion of peers in the review process could lead to paranoia and phoniness. Workers complained of a "popularity contest" infused with fears of anonymous complaints. As one former employee explained, "You have invisible charges against you, and that figures mightily into your review. . . . Your negative feedback can haunt you for all your days at Facebook." Worse, coworkers and managers could be unforgiving if your personal life became too important for you. One employee going through a divorce was slammed for not attending team-building events outside work. Another facing a serious health problem took vacation time to handle it rather than medical leave, at the advice of a manager. She explained, "I was afraid that if I told too many people or took too much time off, I would be seen as unable to do my job." Both of these individuals later left the company. Not surprisingly, employees tended to present themselves as happy go-getters when posting on Facebook's social media platform to impress colleagues and managers. As another former employee explained, "There's so many people there who are unhappy, but their Facebook posts alone don't reflect the backdoor conversations you have with people where they're crying and really unhappy."[78] As another ex-employee stated, "There's a real culture of 'Even if you are f---ing miserable, you need to act like you love this place.' . . . It is not OK to act like this is not the best place to work."[79]

Conclusion: STEM Workers Are Valuable and Supposedly Scarce, but Employers Don't Treat Them That Way

Some important caveats must be emphasized as I conclude. The analyses in this chapter are mostly of software workers at tech firms. This is only one part of the innovation economy, though it is enormously wealthy, impactful, and demanding (regarding the desire for more STEM grads). STEM workers in the life sciences, or in chemicals, or some fields of engineering, may have a slower, more family-friendly pace owing to slower product cycles. New drugs or treatments for illnesses or disabilities need to be extensively tested and then approved by the government. These processes can take years. It is also the case that when nontechnology firms—retail chains, trucking companies, and so on—employ STEM workers to manage software in logistics or inventory management, payroll, or web interfaces, they may be shielded from some of the pressure to be passionate in the sense of overwork, at least at the same level as seen at Amazon, Uber, and Facebook. Finally, readers likely know of, or may be themselves, examples of STEM workers who love their jobs, possibly even at major computer and software firms like those profiled here. Some readers might find this chapter's negative portrayal of STEM work to be misleading or inaccurate.

At the same time, aggregate data show that STEM workers, including the half of them who work in computers and IT, appear no happier than workers in non-STEM jobs. I have sought to make the case that employers do not seek out, hire, and manage STEM workers as though they are a scarce, valuable commodity. If you were worried about having enough STEM workers, you would likely be concerned that your recruiting and hiring processes might have unrealistic expectations and drive away good candidates. You'd likely also be concerned that your desires for "passionate" employees might lead to management techniques that squeeze that passion out of them in ways that stress them out to the point of leaving. You'd likely be worried that employees sometimes cry at their desks. You'd be embarrassed and seek reform when your workers have reputations that lead people to call them "Amholes" or describe your firm as having "asshole culture." And you'd treat it as an urgent and serious problem if your valuable workers were taking their own lives by suicide—especially if it involved leaping from your own office buildings. Employers could do far better if they were serious about respecting national, state, philanthropic, and personal investments in STEM education.

So why is burn-and-churn management so prevalent in STEM? Although I have not designed this book to be a study of causes, it would appear that investor demands (discussed in chapter 1) make an impact. As long as shareholders put short-term profits above all else, and employers believe that maintaining high stock prices is their goal, employers may be incentivized to avoid making risky bets on different (even if better) recruitment practices and to continue to demand passion and expect overwork from their STEM workers and tolerance of heartless workplace cultures. Venture capitalists will similarly want to see a start-up's profits as soon as possible, and not workers who are well cared for, especially if the start-up promised stock options.

It is a paradox that employers in the same sectors where complaints of worker shortages are the loudest are so willing to push them so hard that they leave in tears—if they are not fired first. Leaders at Netflix, another high-profile employer of STEM workers admired for ruthlessness in its management style, like to think of their workforce as akin to a pro sports team, in which players are regularly cut from the team.[80] But in high-level competitive sports, there is a massive *over*supply of eager participants, vying for a scarce position. Leaders of tech companies say the opposite—that they are facing a severe *under*supply of workers, and these companies supposedly compete with one another to attract the workers but then too often manage them as if they were plentiful. This suggests a major disconnect between an education policymaking establishment that is dedicated to ensuring that the US graduates enough STEM majors to satisfy employers and employers who see it as their right to burn and churn right through those STEM graduates, requiring ever more STEM majors to graduate.

CHAPTER 4

THE PRECARIOUSNESS OF THE STEM JOB

We saw in previous chapters that employers do not seem to manage science, technology, engineering, and math (STEM) workers as if they are scarce and valuable. Though much of the investment in STEM education is premised on the idea of placing graduates in good, rewarding jobs in STEM, we saw that on the whole, STEM workers are no more satisfied than non-STEM workers, and many experience high-stress, burn-and-churn management, inefficient recruitment, and pay scales that encourage them to move out of STEM work.

But perhaps employers are making up for these issues in other ways, doing their part to boost the return on investment in STEM education. One might reasonably assume that employers would at least make jobs stable and secure for those who excel on performance reviews and are willing to stick it out and handle the stress. Despite the supposed scarcity of workers, however, STEM workers appear to have followed the trend of the overall American workforce toward precariousness and insecurity.

The case studies in chapter 3 included stories of workers being let go, or leaving on their own, because managers deemed their performance inadequate. The possibility of being fired is certainly part of job security. But sometimes workers lose their jobs for reasons completely unrelated to their performance. Sometimes large numbers of workers, including top performers, lose their jobs as part of corporate cost-saving measures. These job losses usually come in batches and may seem to come out of nowhere, a total surprise, or they may be part of a regular culling. Some workers are never fully employed to begin with—they may perform tasks for a firm but are paid on a short-term contract, rather than as a full-time employee. These situations are the focus of this chapter.

I use the term *layoffs* here to refer any situations where an employer lets a worker go without regard to that worker's actual job performance. Human resource specialists might distinguish between a layoff, whereby workers *might* be called back to work, and downsizing or "reductions in force," which occur when there is no intention of refilling a position.[1] In the past, a layoff could refer to a potentially short period of not working for a specific company, but such is rarely the case.[2] It is unusual to hear of laid-off workers getting rehired or expecting to be rehired. Layoffs, understood here as any shedding of workers unrelated to individual performance, can happen for a variety of reasons, such as a downturn in the overall US economy, a decline in a particular product line offered by a firm, or even because investors pressure a firm to eliminate head count as a means of cutting costs, boosting share price, and increasing dividends in the short term.

The point here is not that we need to be concerned that there are masses of unemployed, unwashed, shivering STEM grads sleeping under bridges. There may be a few, but the truth is that most unemployed STEM grads find new jobs without spending years or even many months unemployed. As I showed in chapter 1, grads in almost all STEM fields enjoy unemployment rates lower than the average of non-STEM grads, with engineers and software workers having the lowest unemployment rates (but higher than some non-STEM professionals, such as lawyers and dentists). I am not arguing that we have to worry about laid-off STEM grads starving, as they probably won't be. But that doesn't mean that there isn't a big problem here.

I want to make the case that STEM workers do not enjoy better protection from layoffs than other college-educated workers do. A simple statistical comparison of layoff probabilities is not possible, unfortunately, as comprehensive data are not available to compare these categories. But I will argue that employers who might claim that there are overall shortages in STEM skills also will easily discard their supposedly scarce STEM workers—or keep them working in precarious positions of contractor status. The ax can come down at any moment, and often does. The result is an endless series of positions throughout many careers, particularly in information technology (IT) jobs, which are especially important in the discussion of STEM jobs because they constitute about half of all STEM jobs.

Moreover, losing one's job can be disruptive and harmful, especially for older workers or workers with young children. Consider the website TheLayoff.com, which I learned about from an engineer in his fifties who was laid off—out of the blue, with no warning—from a profitable division of a major engineering firm. The site described itself as "a simple discussion board for all of us who would like to learn more about the rumors or possibility of job cuts in our company." It explained its reason for being in the following way:

> The workforce reduction process is inherently secretive and plagued with rumors. Companies release little or no details while planning such resource actions. On the other hand, the lives of each of us may be greatly impacted by these top-secret decisions—hence all the anxiety that workers may experience.[3]

The sites listed the main companies being discussed, and companies that employ STEM workers were prevalent in the discussions—tech companies, oil companies, chemical companies, telecommunications, and on and on. No sector is immune, and no jobs are immune. That includes STEM jobs. Despite the billions that the US invests in STEM education, employers regularly throw those dollars away and ask for more workers.

STEM Jobs as Part of a National Trend toward Employment Insecurity

To understand the level of security of STEM jobs, we must first understand the level of security of American jobs in general. It is not very high and has been in decline for decades. Work in America has traditionally been insecure, especially for women and ethnic minorities. From the end of World War II into the 1970s, employment was relatively secure, at least for White men with college degrees or union membership. There is a national nostalgia for these "good old days" of secure employment that was actually only about a thirty-year exception (mid-1940s–mid-1970s), a blip that benefited only some workers, in a long history of precarious employment.[4]

One can see a shift in employer attitudes as America approached the end of the twentieth century. In the late 1970s, the Conference Board, an organization of businesses, conducted surveys that showed that firms designed their employment practices to achieve a goal of stable and loyal workers. Ten years later, the Conference Board began to set employment practices with contrasting goals: reducing costs and improving performance in the short term. By the mid-1990s, the surveys showed that more than 66 percent of businesses had turned away from offering employment security, and only 3 percent said they still offered it.[5]

One could also see the shift in employer actions, not just attitudes. As management scholar Peter Cappelli has shown, firms shed workers during the economic downturn of the early 1980s, but the real sign that something different was going on was that layoffs continued even after the economy picked up. The period of 1993–95, during President Bill Clinton's first term, was a period of economic *growth*, yet the rate of job loss was the same as during the contraction of the 1980s. By one measure, about 15 percent of all workers were let go not because they were bad at what they did or because they failed a performance review but because managers decided it was better for the firm if those jobs were eliminated.[6]

Research examining hundreds of firms and their managerial job descriptions in the period from 1986 to 1998 found that firms became "flatter" as they eliminated intermediate-level manager positions.[7] Companies called it "restructuring" or "reengineering," and the impetus came from many sources, including new managerial strategies that gave lower-level workers additional responsibilities (thereby supposedly making some higher-level workers unnecessary) and computerized information systems that required fewer managerial controls. One 2006 survey of Americans with college degrees showed that they felt less secure and less loyal to their employers than they had in the past, and they believed the situation would get worse in the next twenty to thirty years.[8]

Layoffs can happen everywhere, in STEM and non-STEM jobs, in small companies and the Fortune 500. Large corporations may be especially prone to layoffs, however. Though the 1990s rounds of layoffs, when the term *downsizing* became popular, were driven by a variety of factors unique to that period,[9] increasingly it was investors driving the layoffs. Activist investors sometimes insist on cost cutting, and the firms begin to see workers as costs to be minimized rather than assets to target for investment. This happened at the venerable conglomerate General Electric Company (GE), America's largest manufacturer, when activist investors at Trian Partners, a hedge fund, decided the GE stock was underperforming and began to push cost cutting. Trian demanded $2 billion in cuts. To meet this target, GE executives laid off workers.[10] Activist investors have shown their power at many employers of STEM workers, even ousting CEOs at Procter & Gamble and Microsoft; fighting to break up Motorola, eBay, and Yahoo; and forcing consolidation at chemical giants Dow and DuPont.[11]

Layoffs have several negative effects. First, as indicated by TheLayoff .com's reason for existing mentioned in the opening section of this chapter, laid-off workers are more likely to suffer stress, poor health, and even earlier deaths.[12] But the damage is not limited to those sent packing. The workers who remain may have their workloads increased because whereas layoffs typically dismiss people, actual tasks performed by them may still need to be done, and so the remaining workers get those tasks added to their plates—while also having their anxiety heightened as they wonder if or when they will be next to be jettisoned.[13] One study found that workers in all industries were 3.5 times more likely to leave a job because of concerns about job insecurity than because of dissatisfaction with compensation.[14] This anxiety can lead to paranoia and behaviors that might hurt the firm's performance (as we will see later in the chapter).

One strategy that firms use leads to layoffs but does not actually eliminate the job: *outsourcing*. When firms outsource, the job goes somewhere else, to another firm, sometimes in another country, especially to India, China, and countries in Eastern Europe and Latin America.[15] For years, managers targeted outsourcing in jobs they believed were peripheral to the firm's core competencies or profit centers (the rise of remote work appears likely to expand the range of jobs affected). Sometimes the contractors work alongside full-time employees at the same work site—but they are no longer employees of the firm.

Management scholar Gerald Davis called this process "Nikefication," after the athletic apparel firm. For Davis, Nike was not special, just a firm that symbolized a common practice of outsourcing that focused the firm on one, or just a few, high-value competencies. Nike sells clothing, but it is not an athletic apparel manufacturer. Nike *designs* athletic apparel— shoes, clothes, hats—and *markets* athletic apparel, but it then has the athletic apparel manufactured by other companies in countries such as Vietnam and China where costs, especially labor costs, are lower.

While Nikefication is far worse for less-educated workers involved in manufacturing, it also makes college-educated STEM workers more vulnerable to layoffs. By shedding whole divisions and focusing on core competencies, Nikefication shortens job ladders, creating fewer promotion opportunities.[16] Though Davis chose an apparel company, Nikefication is common in the innovation economy as well. To pick a few examples, Apple is known for putting on every tangible product that it was "designed in California," but the company actually makes almost no tangible products in California or the US (more on this in chapter 7). It's not just an issue for tech, either. About 60 percent of drug manufacturing is outsourced,[17] and about 80 percent of the chemicals used in drug manufacturing come from one country—China.[18] Unlike the big conglomerates common in the middle of the twentieth century that would happily and purposefully add diverse divisions, corporations in the twenty-first century may suddenly sell off or dissolve divisions, creating instability for everyone whose job is connected to those divisions. Even worse for STEM worker job security, from the CEO position on down, firms increasingly filled their number of promotion openings on their shrinking job ladders by bringing in people from *other* companies (as I discussed in chapter 3).

This is a problem with self-reinforcing dynamics because as firms cut positions through layoffs and outsourcing and then hire from the outside for the remaining positions, they send signals to existing employees that they will not get chances to move up and they should not plan or hope for such opportunities. Some still do, which is why many STEM workers can boost their salaries by moving into management or (more rarely) moving up on a technical track. But the trend has been for job ladders to shorten, which in turn makes workers less likely to work for promotions internally and more likely to leave for a better opportunity elsewhere.[19]

The sense that one could lose one's job at any time, even if performing well, that there are fewer opportunities to advance since job ladders have been shortened, *and* that employers fill the remaining openings with outsiders has led workers to think more exclusively about their own interests, their own employability, rather than any shared future with a firm. One author called these developments "the end of loyalty."[20] There is more to say on the pernicious effects of layoffs and other management practices on worker thinking and feeling, as we will see in the next section.

Insecure Employment Is Especially
Common in Some STEM Jobs

I argued in the previous section that—despite their supposed scarcity—STEM workers are not immune from these dynamics and the resulting job insecurity. But there is some evidence that STEM workers actually may be *more* vulnerable to layoffs than workers in other sectors. The National Survey of College Graduates shows that 21 percent of STEM workers say they changed jobs because they were laid off or "terminated," while only 16 percent of non-STEM workers chose this response.[21] There is also evidence that IT workers—the most prevalent STEM workers in the US—are especially vulnerable. In testimony to Congress, social scientist Hal Salzman presented data showing that about 100,000 IT workers were laid off each year from 2005 to 2015, comprising 13 percent of all layoffs in the US—non-STEM and STEM. According to Salzman, this IT layoff rate is "over four times the size of its share of overall employment."[22]

The pharmaceutical sector also sheds STEM workers with regularity. For example, the workforce data company Revelio Labs showed that leading pharmaceutical companies laid off thousands of scientists between 2009 and 2019 (Pfizer) or between 2014 and 2019 (Novartis and Merck).[23] Scientists and engineers working on new drugs or medical devices are especially vulnerable to having their world rocked, such as when clinical trials or Food and Drug Administration approval do not go the way that they expect, as products are found to be unhelpful or even dangerous.

Some STEM sectors are especially prone to severe boom and bust cycles related to rising and then swiftly falling demand. As demographer Michael Teitelbaum has shown, the booms tend to create short-term boosts in salaries, which is a great thing for STEM workers—until there is a bust, when large numbers of STEM workers with similar skill sets are suddenly looking for work at the same time.[24]

The energy sector, for example, which hires thousands of petroleum, nuclear, and other engineers, is especially susceptible to booms and busts. When prices are high, oil companies ramp up their research and development efforts and hire more scientists and engineers. When prices are low, hiring is frozen and layoffs are common.[25] The nuclear power sector tends to hire more when oil prices are high and nuclear energy appears less costly, but high-profile nuclear plant failures (e.g., Three Mile Island in the US, Chernobyl in Ukraine, and Fukushima in Japan) can lead to hiring busts.[26] STEM workers with expertise in clean energy—"cleantech"—such as solar and wind power have faced booms and busts based on emerging and then expiring federal subsidies.[27]

Another STEM sector with insecure employment attributable to booms and busts is aerospace. This insecurity exists because aerospace is tied to national defense and security, and demand here grows and shrinks with the rise and fall of geopolitical threats and the ensuing changes in the politics of defense procurement. Though the public may associate California with the tech sector, it is also home to major defense contractors that hire loads of scientists and engineers. Northrup Grumman, Lockheed Martin, Raytheon, General Atomics, and General Dynamics NASSCO, to name just a few, all have headquarters or major outposts in California—and they were hit hard when the Cold War ended in the early 1990s.[28] When I first came to the University of California, the senior faculty still discussed with notable emotion the early 1990s, when the contraction of this sector across the state led to plummeting tax revenues and a massive financial hit on public institutions.

The boom and bust cycles may be exacerbated by employers and the signals they send to students. When employers loudly proclaim that their sector is facing severe shortages of STEM workers when there are not really shortages, or continue doing so when there was a shortage but it disappeared as students responded (with a lag of a few years while they earn their degrees), a glut of STEM graduates is the likely result. New entry-level workers can be crushingly disappointed when the demand falls and hiring freezes—or layoffs—begin.[29] As Carrie McClelland, a professor at the Colorado School of Mines, told the trade publication *Inside Energy* in 2015, following a crash in oil prices, "I think the demand has already leveled off even though the number of students continues to increase, and we're going to see a lot of students that end up with a petroleum engineering degree but have to go find a job in a different industry."[30] The lesson of job insecurity can come before a STEM career has even started.

Layoffs may have harmful effects for STEM workers still on the job and their overall organizations. When Blind, a workplace chat app, anonymously surveyed almost six thousand "tech professionals" in 2021 about whether they were worried about layoffs, it received wildly varying answers, depending on the company and the survey year, but indicated high levels of worry, and some workplaces were hotbeds of insecurity. Overall, in 2021, nearly a third said they were worried. PayPal, Dropbox, and IBM all were in the 70 percent to 80 percent range of being worried about layoffs, but the numbers and companies at the top and bottom of the list vary from one year to the next.[31]

Another problem for STEM workers created by layoffs relates to the kinds of specific technical expertise that are required to do these jobs combined with the regular practice of working on project teams. Erin Kelly and Phyllis Moen's study of a tech firm in the Midwest described a manager who saw a "fear-based" behavior among employees where they would not ask for help on tasks, even if they were feeling overwhelmed. The reason was that these workers worried that managers would not recognize their uniquely valuable contributions if others were involved. Working alone was therefore a strategy to show one was special, a unique contributor, and thus should be protected from a layoff. More pernicious for the overall firm—but perhaps logical from the individual employee's point of view—was a tendency that Kelly and Moen found whereby some employees hoarded their unique skills. That is, when they were only ones left at the firm with expertise in a particular software or system (as a result of the firm having laid off the other experts), they might avoid training others. Though having more people around with needed expertise could obviously help the firm, it could also make some of those experts seem redundant and thus a potential target for additional layoffs. Kelly and Moen described how "Hayward, a developer and dad who described a specific program he had written as 'his baby,' seemed to put up with very long hours and calls at any hour because being the sole expert on this program meant his job was protected." Hayward was not unique: a survey of more than nine hundred IT workers and managers found a correlation between feeling insecure about one's job and a reduced tendency to help coworkers.[32]

A culture wherein employers and employees alike take for granted that layoffs will occur and are actually routine, combined with the stress-inducing performance reviews I described in chapter 3, has led many STEM workers to say that they feel insecure. The American Enterprise Institute surveyed almost 1,400 STEM graduates and found that 52 percent believed that feeling "replaceable" described STEM work either very or somewhat well.[33] This is not what we would expect to see in jobs where there is supposed to be a shortage of skilled workers.

Social scientist Carrie M. Lane's interview study of the tech sector in

Texas sheds light on how STEM workers' thought processes connected to feelings of insecurity. Workers might start their careers with a sense of loyalty and shared destiny with their employer but then show a range of reactions after life-disrupting layoffs. This change could be seen in the comments of an engineer at a telecommunications firm who struggled with self-doubt regarding whether he did something wrong to cause his layoff. He asked himself, "Was it the fact that I wasn't working seventy hours a week?"[34] But he also saw his attitude toward work and employment change, as any semblance of loyalty to his employer began to dissipate. Speaking of his employment relationship after being laid off, he explained, "Things are changing—I've got to do these things, you've got to pay me. But if somebody else tells me to do the exact same thing and they pay me more, I'm going to go away. . . . I have changed. I am a changed man. I'm not loyal to anyone. I'll sell my soul to anyone but the devil as long as the price is right."[35]

Lane found that workers weathered the transitions by learning to give in to market forces, which they assumed to be the dominant explanation for the firms' behavior. Then they looked with annoyance at workers who had not (yet) given in—who still expected firms to invest in workers and take care of them. The more workers accepted a culture where sudden, life-changing layoffs were normal and to be expected, the more established that culture became. Younger workers, therefore, who never thought stable employment was even possible, sometimes had the emotional advantage of never having had higher expectations of employers. They (like many of the readers of this book) were likely to take all of this for granted—that they would have to manage their careers by continually enhancing their employability until they retired. Lane also found that some workers considered themselves independent contractors—even though they were employed full-time—because few expected to stay with a firm much longer than any one-year contractor would.[36] They thought periods of unemployment were to be expected, and being unemployed was normal, even if also disruptive and stress inducing.[37]

Though I've separated the layoff discussion from harsh management practices featured in chapter 3, layoffs are part of the burn-and-churn management strategy found in STEM employment. It really is a cluster of practices coming together to make STEM (and non-STEM) employment unstable and to guarantee the rapid churn, if not the burn. The recruiting firms I discussed in chapter 3 have also contributed: the more companies hired from the outside, the more recruiting and staffing firms rose to meet the demand for outside hiring, thus spurring even more demand as their services improved and became taken-for-granted parts of bringing in workers.[38]

Constant job change is now the norm in STEM, and especially in IT jobs. Workforce churning and "job-hopping"—a term that puts a positive, happy-go-lucky spin on constant disruption because it suggests that the workers are in control—is indeed most common in tech hubs like California.[39] For example, a 2019 survey of software developers by the community-advice platform Stack Overflow found that more than half—about 56 percent—of those developers had changed jobs within the past two years.[40] Management scholars Matt Ferguson, Lorin Hitt, and Prasanna Tambe discuss a 2012 survey of employers that found that employers in IT were almost 10 percent more likely than average private-sector employers to report an increase in voluntary turnover (37 percent to 28 percent), and 14 percent more likely to report that top performers left (46 percent to 32 percent).[41] A 2018 analysis of thousands of résumés by the employment-support firm LiveCareer showed that software developers had the highest number of jobs in the last five years—an average of 2.8 jobs, equal to food and beverage servers, and higher than administrative assistants, registered nurses, and store managers, all of whom had an average of 1.9 jobs in the last five years.[42] The rise of IT skill certifications signaling measurable levels of skills achievement with some IT-related products contributes to the movement by making it easier to signal competence to outside employers.[43]

From the 1940s to about the 1980s, a person who moved from one employer to another with great frequency could be seen as flaky, easily bored, unwilling to commit to projects or missions, or—worse—someone who does not get along well with other workers. Some employers still regard job-hopping negatively.[44] But increasingly, constant job change can be strategic for workers and not a sign of problem personalities or workforce disruptions and turmoil.

In Ilana Gershon's study in Silicon Valley, for instance, her interviewees, who "had an average of four jobs from 2004 to 2014," believed that job-hopping was "essential for crafting a successful career."[45] Job-hopping could signal valuable experience or knowledge, especially in STEM jobs. At the same time, there was a danger in how this constant change could fit (or not obviously fit) together. Firms doing the hiring tend to assume that each job taken was part of a strategy under the control of the job-hopper. If the jobs were not connected coherently, it could hurt the applicant's personal brand—and thus their employability and job opportunities.[46]

Some workers may be happy with these new arrangements. It certainly is not boring to always wonder where one will be working next year or even next month, and continually moving around creates new challenges that many people find exciting. My point is that not all workers are like this, and many, especially older workers with families, may crave—even need—stability. For these people, sudden layoffs that force them to quickly seek a new job will seem like an ax falling from the sky, apparently randomly. Proponents of greater investment in STEM education to create more STEM workers might consider insisting that employers that benefit from this investment treat these graduates better. Finally, everyone thinking of going into STEM, especially for computer and software firms, should be fully aware of the sometimes tumultuous environment into which they will be plunging. Their skills may be scarce, but they should not count on employers treating them like they are scarce.

Free Agents or Second-Class Citizens? Contract Workers in STEM Jobs

Being a STEM worker does not always mean one is a STEM *employee*. And this distinction matters—a lot.

What's the difference? Throughout this chapter, I have mostly referred to workers as if they are "employees." In US law, *employee* is a legal term, referring to a specific set of duties and rights. Having employee status obligates a worker to pay income taxes on earnings that the employer reports on a specific form at the end of the year (the W-2). Employee status comes with wages, of course, and maybe stock options, but typically for jobs that require a bachelor's degree also includes benefits such as health insurance or company matching of the employees' contributions to retirement savings (the 401[k]). In US law, employees also have many legal protections. They are entitled to unemployment insurance when they lose their jobs; they are covered by the Fair Labor Standards Act, which governs minimum wage and overtime rules; they can sue employers for discrimination under the Civil Rights Act of 1964, the Americans with Disabilities Act, and the Age Discrimination in Employment Act; they are covered by the Family and Medical Leave Act; and their right to organize is protected by the National Labor Relations Act.[47]

But many STEM workers are not STEM employees. They are *contractors*. As such, they may work at a firm with earnings reported at the end of year on a different form (the 1099), and with no taxes taken out. Instead, they are expected to pay "estimated taxes" directly to the Internal Revenue Service (IRS) at quarterly intervals throughout the year. By law, these workers are on contracts that typically specify a deliverable, but the number of hours they work, as well as the place where they work, is up to them. In return, they forgo the legal protections enjoyed by those with employee status. I mention the federal income forms because they often serve as shorthand to describe a worker's status at a company: "Those workers are 1099s (contractors), not W-2s (employees)."

Complicating the picture, some workers are both contractors *and* employees. This happens when they work for staffing firms. These staffing firms form contracts with companies that, for example, might want short-term assistance for a large task, typically beyond the scope of a single independent contractor. Companies might also contract with a staffing firm when they, for a variety of reasons, do not desire full-time employees for specific tasks. In these cases, the workers may perform specific job tasks at a particular company, but they are employees of another firm, a staffing firm that places them at the work site, pays their salary, and usually produces a W-2 for taxes.

Nevertheless, these workers are similar to independent contractors. In both cases, companies use the workers for some specific skill or to perform some specific task, usually for a predetermined period, after which the relationship ends with a separation that is not a firing or a layoff. It's just the end of the contract. These workers contracted through staffing firms may also work alongside and with official employees, despite being of different statuses. And although some contractors enjoy the contractor status for reasons I explain later in this chapter, others might believe it is a second-class status and feel excluded, disrespected, unvalued, and insecure.

"SHADOW WORKERS" AT "BLACK SITES": WHY MANY CONTRACTORS WANT TO BE EMPLOYEES

In many cases, contractors toil in the hope that they will be moved to employee status.[48] Media reports in recent years have put a spotlight on these workers and tended to expose the use of contractors as an injustice. They describe the contractor status as something like indentured servitude and second-class citizenship, to be escaped as soon as possible.[49]

Moving to permanent employment may be especially challenging for foreign contractors, who typically work on H-1B temporary visas. Workers on these visas may be employees or contractors. Major tech firms can hire highly skilled foreign employees on H-1B visas, pay them very well, and sponsor them for green cards. But the same firms may also use H-1B visas for entry-level, low-paid IT contractors placed on-site by India-based firms such as Infosys and Wipro.[50]

These sometimes unhappy and badly treated workers, and the business practice of using them to hide the number of workers actually on a project, make the contracting practice look nefarious, and news media have seized on this framing. CNBC's article on contractors referred to "Silicon Valley's Dirty Secret: Using a Shadow Workforce of Contract Employees to Drive Profits." The *New York Times* referred to "Google's Shadow Work Force," highlighting a precarious, disadvantaged, even stigmatized work experience. Bloomberg published an article focused on "Apple's 'Black Site'" where some contractors doing a project for Apple (developing its Maps app) were actually employees of a firm called Apex Systems, working in a nameless building away from the company's glamorous main headquarters.[51]

KQED, Silicon Valley's public broadcaster, referred to contractors in tech firms as the lower part of a "two-tiered caste system" and appeared to have little trouble finding workers to support that characterization. None were willing to share their names. Though afraid to be identified, these contractors were not afraid to talk. They said they felt "less than everyone else" and aspired to employee status—and they worked extra hard to make that happen.[52] One Google contractor who wished to transition to employee status was let go after she experienced sexual harassment and had rebuffed those advances (her complaint was found to have merit, but she was no longer able to work at Google).[53] Workers at Apple's alleged "black site" complained of a "culture of fear" and managerial monitoring that one worker found "super dehumanizing and terrifying."[54]

The inequalities also may take the form of daily embarrassments and indignities. For instance, contractors at some firms must wear badges that denote their contractor tier. The contractor badges symbolize a lower tier because firms may have restrictions on where contractors can physically move at work and what facilities they can use. Work sites will have several "no-go zones" for contractors, such as recreational facilities or shuttles. Other perks, such as invitations to office parties or even access to security information in the event of a mass shooting (as occurred at Google's YouTube division), can be limited. For the aforementioned Apple contractors, the work site was six miles from Apple headquarters and had so few bathrooms that lines formed at lunchtime, even for the men's room.[55]

The issue of contractor status became more urgent during the COVID-19 pandemic when working from home became a key way to prevent rapid spread of the deadly virus. KQED reported on the experience of a data analyst named Ben Gwin who officially was an employee of HCL Technologies, a staffing firm, but who performed work at the Pittsburgh office of Google and had been assigned there for a year and a half. Gwin, a single dad, did not have work-from-home privileges equal to Google's official employees, and he feared becoming ill. When he asked to work from home, the responses took a pattern that is common in contractor work: no one took responsibility. HCL said Gwin's working from home would violate Google policy, and Google said he should ask HCL. Gwin complained, "This will be one of the more stark examples of the tiers and the classist system that is implemented at our building," and he worried that if workers like him became ill with the virus, they would face the difficult choice to either stay home and not receive pay or go into the office and possibly infect others.[56]

As Gwin's story shows, whereas contractors may enjoy greater freedom, they also bear greater risk. For contractors, sick time may not be compensated, even for those who are employed by staffing firms. It may be simply lost time, as the worker worried about COVID-19 showed. Managing the transition times between jobs can also be challenging, especially if project end dates have to be changed. In addition, for some contractors, the need to upgrade skills when no employer will train you, or tell you what skills to pick up yourself, creates distinct pressures. Finally, for the independent contractors, getting clients to pay—that is, to live up to their end of the contract—is not guaranteed and can lead to stress, lack of payment, and terminated contracts.[57] In response to these difficulties and other mistreatment, some STEM contractors have mobilized to fight for better conditions, even attempting to form unions or guilds.[58]

WHY COMPANIES USE STEM CONTRACTORS
RATHER THAN STEM EMPLOYEES

Researchers have shown that employers prefer to use contractors for some STEM work, and in doing so they are following a trend. It is generally understood that short-term or "alternative" work arrangements are growing nationwide, though they have long been common in Silicon Valley.[59] What is important here is that STEM workers are supposed to be valued and scarce, but here again we see them treated as expendable.

Though there is little recent research on the specific numbers of college-educated STEM workers—my focus in this book—who toil in contractor status,[60] anecdotal evidence suggests that the use of contractors is a very big deal in tech. For example, the *New York Times* acquired an internal document from Google that showed that the firm contracted with 121,000 workers globally. Though most of these were not STEM workers, it was nevertheless a massive number that suggested that contractors were not just filling niche roles. In fact, Google had more contractors than full-time employees (who numbered 102,000). Most other tech firms have similar ratios, according to OnContracting, a firm that helps contractors and staffing firms find positions at firms looking for short-term labor.[61] OnContracting's head, Pradeep Chauhan, has claimed that there were 1,000 staffing agencies in Silicon Valley alone.[62]

The are several factors that appear to push or pull employers toward the use of STEM contractors. Academic studies have identified short-term skills needs driven by product cycles as a major incentive to use contract workers, sometimes for short durations. This finding could explain why employers in tech, where product cycles are more rapid, are more likely to use contractors than employers in the life sciences and chemicals, where product cycles are slower because of safety regulations. Firms may need extra help during crunch time to meet a deadline, or specific skills such as quality assurance or technical writing that are crucial for a specific period but not needed throughout the year.[63] Google spokespersons have explained why the tech giant has used contractors, echoing these studies. For example, Google said it needed short-term contract workers for sudden spikes in work activity, or if a regular employee had to go on leave for some reason.[64]

Yet these explanations do not fully explain the use of STEM contractors, who may work for the same firm all year or even over multiple years. Hiring contractors may be deeply intertwined into the business model of these firms because full-time employees can be time-consuming and expensive to "onboard" (i.e., to orient and train) and then later let go.[65] Firms may prefer contractors also because the more employees a firm acquires, the less nimble it becomes, and having too many employees can make a firm unattractive to investors (as explained in chapter 1).

Social scientists Stephen Barley and Gideon Kunda have called this the "budgets and headcount" explanation for tech firms' use of contractors. At firms they studied, top-level managers starting a new project would create sharp limits on the amount of money that could be spent on the project and the number of full-time employees who could be assigned to it. If managers needed more people, they were to use some of their budget to hire contractors. An advantage to keeping the number of employees low—by using contractors instead—was that it made the firm appear to be more productive because financial analysts used a valuation formula that calculates productivity by dividing revenues by the number of employees. Contractors may be invisible in this formula, so productivity per employee appeared higher than it actually was.[66] This valuation calculation could affect both corporations and emerging firms. As social scientist Lilly Irani has written about tech start-ups, "Hiding labor is key to how these startups are valued by investors, and thus key to the real winnings of entrepreneurs."[67] This process could also make STEM workers into losers.

The pressure to hire contractors may be even greater if a firm expends substantial funds for a few superstar STEM workers. The windfalls that go to these talented, happy few put downward pressure on wages and commitments to hire other workers, leading to the use of more contractors. This is an example of what some scholars have called "winner-take-all" markets.[68]

Barley and Kunda identified two other reasons why firms have brought on contractors rather than provide more full-time employment opportunities. One reason, which fits with the idea discussed in chapter 3 that many employers are not sure how to assess the skills of their STEM workers, also contributes to the precariousness of STEM work: Hiring contractors could be a way to screen workers, creating what amounts to a trial run. If the firm liked the workers, it could hire them full-time. If it did not like them, it could simply cut ties at the end of the contract and look for someone else, having saved itself the hassle and expense of bringing on a new employee.

A final factor leading firms to bring on contractors was that sometimes firms had work that needed to be done but no employees could do the work and there were no incentives for workers to develop the needed skill. This situation might occur if it involved knowledge of a "legacy" technology—one that is no longer being developed and on the way to being phased out but still in use in some crucial areas.[69] These contractors might be a rather happy lot, especially if they are older and winding down their careers. They have a valuable skill, firms will pay top dollar for it, and they do not have the stress of having to learn new skills.

POSSIBLY INSECURE, BUT ALSO POSSIBLY APPEALING: WHY SOME STEM WORKERS PREFER TO BE CONTRACTORS

I have included contractors in this chapter on the precarious quality of some STEM jobs, but a fair analysis must acknowledge that working on a contract basis rather than working as a full-time employee definitely has its appeals to many STEM workers. First, for some, being a contractor pays better than being an employee. For example, a software developer in Silicon Valley, Anton Anismov, told CNBC that he can make more money as a contractor than as an employee, and he was better able to build his network of contacts, and learn more skills, as a contractor. Anismov explained, "As a freelancer, I can choose to work hourly. . . . I would say you can earn two times more."[70] Well-paid contractors like Anismov tend to have some scarce and in-demand skill set, like the legacy tech experts described in the previous section, or expertise in some new, cutting-edge tech, and they can often name their price and choose the projects that interest them the most.

Even without access to superior pay, many choose contracting because work as a contractor allows them to be less invested in office politics, personalities, or even the fortunes of the firm. Why care who stabbed whom in the back if you will be there only a short time, and you are not really a part of the organization anyway? Why worry about layoffs or failed products if your stay at the company is by definition short term? Relatedly, others choose contracting because they cannot tolerate being in an employee relationship with an incompetent manager who has the power to fire them at any time (a dynamic I discussed in chapter 3). A software designer told Barley and Kunda that some bosses in Silicon Valley were "egomaniacs who just happened to stumble into a bunch of

money. . . . It's the Beverly Hillbillies story. They were shootin' at a rab-
bit, struck oil, and now they think they are a genius." Another compared
her manager to the incompetent managers in the *Dilbert* comic strip and
said, "It's almost prophetic. I mean, they hire people to be managers that
you'd say 'Why in the world is this person leading?' They just don't have
the skills." A quality assurance technician who had been laid off was still
angry about her incompetent manager: "To have a person like that say,
'You have been tagged and you don't have a job anymore,' was just too
much. This bozo is telling me I don't have a job anymore and he's still
working?"[71] The clear, time-limited relationship in contracting lessens
the pain of being managed by a bozo.

There are other appeals to the contracting life. For many, contracting
means constantly learning exciting new skills and working on a greater
variety of projects. For independent contractors with in-demand skills
(not those working for staffing companies), work as a contractor can provide great flexibility and control over their work—and thus their lives.[72]
These high-level contractors can be sought-after data scientists, or even
chief financial officers and CEOs who run a firm for a while during some
crucial phase. Highly specialized staffing firms such as Beeline and Cat-
alant exist to help tech firms find and land this elite contractor talent.[73]
In short, though for some workers being a contractor rather than an
employee means a life of indignities and exploitation, for others it can
mean high salaries and a lot of freedom.

Conclusion: STEM Is No Protection
from a Precarious Work Life

Being a STEM worker does not mean a stable work life. Just like other
workers in the economy who are *not* continually lauded as the keys to
national competitiveness or who are supposedly not in short supply,
STEM workers can be laid off at any time, even scientists working on
lifesaving medical treatments. There is evidence that STEM workers in
IT are actually *more* likely to be laid off than non-STEM workers. STEM
grads who invested years of hard work into their specialized expertise
are also likely to face both booms and busts in their job opportunities.
Many work on contracts, which can mean a life in the shadows, charac-
terized by instability, disrespect, mistreatment, and struggles to become
full-time employees. Whether they work as employees or contractors, the

precarious and unstable work environment makes STEM workers prone to hop from job to job, adding to the cycle of employer–worker mutual distrust and disloyalty.

Why are layoffs and the use (and exploitation) of contractors such common experiences for STEM grads? Perhaps more than some of the management practices I described in chapter 3, layoffs and contractor use are traceable to investors' preferences and demands for high stock prices in the short term. As long as shareholders and the venture capitalists who invest in start-ups demand nimble, low-asset firms that can make quick profits, and as long as they consider employees to be costs that weigh down firms, we are likely to see employers treat the supposedly scarce STEM workers as if they are expendable. Although I cannot prove a direct causal impact, I am suggesting that this precariousness is why some STEM grads do not work in STEM and instead pursue jobs in management, medicine, and other professions, lowering the return on the national, philanthropic, and personal investments in STEM education.

Management scholar Gerald Davis made this point in a way that struck me as especially trenchant and memorable. In discussing the corporate pattern of outsourcing, which is related to layoffs, he wrote, "If education is thought of as an investment, then corporate hiring practices help define the payoff for that investment. And if companies are quick to replace skilled workers with lower-cost replacements, then the alleged skill gap is likely to become a self-fulfilling prophecy. Who is going to invest in developing a skill when the payoff depends on the arbitrary actions of corporate employers?"[74] If policymakers, philanthropies, and individuals are going to keep investing in their education, especially in STEM, they can reasonably ask for better employer behavior.

CHAPTER 5

TRAINING AND THE STEM-SKILLS TREADMILL

When educators, policymakers, philanthropists, and business leaders discuss and fund science, technology, engineering, and math (STEM) education, the focus is usually on the education of young people. Are our elementary schools teaching the right skills? What about the high schools—does a high school diploma signify a level of STEM know-how? And especially important: are universities teaching the right skills for STEM grads to join the workforce and contribute as STEM workers? Sometimes there is a panic as policymakers or advocates look at a competitor state, China, or education standard bearers such as Finland and Singapore, and they see masses of STEM graduates who show high levels of competence. What about *our* students, they ask: are they sticking it out in the STEM majors so the US can compete with rising economic powers across the globe?[1]

The focus on young learners, however, neglects an equally important topic about STEM education: the skills training of *existing* STEM workers. Are the folks who already earned STEM degrees, and are already on the job, getting the education they need to continue to contribute? Or do many leave the field because their training has become obsolete?

If we care about the return on investment of the national commitment to STEM education, and we want to know why so many STEM grads leave or avoid STEM jobs, we should care about how long that STEM education is useful to grads. We need to know if—and how—it is updated so its usefulness can be extended through an entire career. If employers are concerned about STEM-skill shortages, we should expect them to be taking the lead in reskilling STEM workers as knowledge advances and new skills are needed.

The issue of education that continues through the career is especially important in STEM because of what I like to call the "STEM-skills treadmill." The idea highlights a dark side to innovation: we all love innovation for the improvements in products and processes that it brings to us, but innovation means change, and especially for STEM workers, the change might be that their old skills and knowledge are no longer needed.

As technology progresses, skills may become obsolete again and again throughout a STEM worker's career. The contrast can be stark with much basic science knowledge, which typically builds on foundational laws and principles. The more applied sciences and engineering can become useless. It is easy to laugh when I open my desk drawer and see floppy disks on which my doctoral dissertation resides—no longer retrievable. In the few decades since I did my doctoral work, we moved from floppy disks to zip disks, to CD-ROM burners, to external hard drives connected by the standardized serial computer interface known as USB; then firewire (which had a moment of usage), then USB-2, and then USB-c. More recently, many students and workers skip these local data storage devices altogether and instead store data "in the cloud"—that is, on multiple remote servers that can be accessed through the internet.[2] Meanwhile, my printer no longer physically connects to any computer I can buy. Did I actually say "printer"? The satirical newspaper–turned–online news site the *Onion* knows about the STEM-skills treadmill—when Steve Jobs passed away in 2011 and Tim Cook took over, it ran an article with the headline, "New Apple CEO Tim Cook: 'I'm Thinking Printers.'"[3]

The treadmill is a metaphor that highlights why training has its own chapter in this book—there may be no career progress or advancement occurring even when workers train. That does not mean training is useless. It's more like the opposite: some workers must train just to keep their jobs, just to stay in place, like runners sprinting on a treadmill but not moving forward. It also implies that even more work is needed to actually move forward in a STEM career (the treadmill metaphor works less well in this case, though perhaps we can say that moving forward requires getting on a different treadmill). Making this pressure worse, as I show in this chapter, is a long trend toward employers pulling back from training their own workers.

Academic survey research on skills training highlights some of these stakes in the matter for STEM workers, revealing that whereas training adds to job satisfaction and may be intellectually stimulating, it can be a major problem when employers do not accommodate it. One study showed it can then be correlated with increased work-family conflict, including in technical occupations.[4] Training for new skills is related to conflict because unless employers allow workers to train during their normal workday, employees must train for new skills on their own time, taking their time and attention away from their families. Project-based occupations—common in STEM jobs that create new products—commonly lead to pressures for especially rapid upskilling, leading to more stress that spills out into family life. In short, employer-provided training is likely to be a key factor in retaining STEM grads in technical jobs.

These ideas are crucial to understand as a factor in the return on investment in STEM education. It certainly seems unwise to spend billions of dollars and countless hours of effort to help young people master STEM skills and knowledge that are only useful for a few years. As I will discuss in this chapter, research shows that STEM careers are often very short, and that shortness is linked to skills becoming obsolete. If the burn-and-churn management or insecurity of employment don't force STEM grads to leave, then the constant pressure to reskill or upskill may be what finally pushes them out.[5]

The Big Picture on Training: What Are Firms Doing? What Should STEM Workers Expect?

American workers seem to have given up on the idea of employer-provided training—even though they realize how hard it is for them to do it themselves. The Pew Research Center asked American workers their views on who had the responsibility to provide work-related training. Workers seemed to accept that they must take responsibility for their own skills and education, as 72 percent agreed that "a lot" of the responsibility is on "individuals themselves" to manage this, and 22 percent said that they had "some" of the responsibility. The workers seemed to let employers off the hook, as only 49 percent said employers had "a lot of" the responsibility (39 percent said employers have "some" responsibility).[6] But when they asked Americans reasons for not training to update their skills, the answers pointed to the value of employer-provided training. For example, 57 percent said that the main reason was time—they could not take time off from work or other responsibilities; 45 percent said they could not afford training; and 25 percent did not believe the right training was available.[7]

These barriers to self-training appear to be significant. One comprehensive study of skills training found that employers pay for about 84 percent of skills training in the US, also suggesting that workers have a hard time doing it themselves.[8] Moreover, the study found that training declined in the US by almost 30 percent between 2001 and 2009, suggesting that employers were pulling back or barriers to worker self-training were worsening, or both. The decline hit every sector of the nation's economy, across occupations—including the supposedly scarce STEM workers—as well as education levels, age categories, length of time on the job (so even those with seniority had less training), genders, and ethnicities.[9]

A 2015 report by the President's Council of Economic Advisers highlighted that decreasing number of employers embraced responsibility for training their workers. It showed that the percentage of workers receiving employer-paid training declined steadily, from 19.4 percent in 1996 to 16.7 percent in 2001, 12.4 percent in 2004, and 11.2 percent in 2008. "On-the-job training" also fell in those same years, from 13.1 percent in 1996 to 11.7 percent in 2001, 8.6 percent in 2004, and 8.4 percent in 2008.[10] Employer spending did not pick up after the US climbed out of the Great Recession and came to full employment in the 2010s, either. Adjusting for inflation, spending on training barely changed between 2008 and 2018.[11]

In short, the big picture on training in the US is one of decline. Employers say they want workers to have up-to-date skills, but they are less and less likely to pay for them. But what about training of STEM workers specifically? Where there is supposedly a severe skills shortage, we should see not training declines but increasing employer efforts to train workers in the needed skills. STEM workers should look different and should buck these downward trends.

One way to check for this is to look at data collected by the National Science Foundation's National Survey of College Graduates (NSCG). The survey asked college grads whether they trained to improve their skills and knowledge in their occupational field.[12] In my research with a colleague using data from 2003 to 2015, we compared workers who said their jobs required college-level STEM expertise with non-STEM workers, and used this broader understanding of STEM because many jobs outside

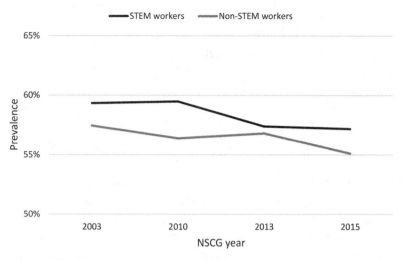

FIGURE 5.1 Percentage of currently employed college graduates who reported taking skills-related training in the past twelve months, by National Survey of College Graduates (NSCG) survey year. (Data analysis in Skrentny and Lewis, "Beyond the 'STEM Pipeline,'" 11.)

traditional STEM occupations may have workers running on STEM-skills treadmills just as the traditional STEM occupations do. The data show (figure 5.1), first, that despite the NSCG's very conservative measure of skills training (emphasizing formal training in workshops or seminars) and declining employer investments in training, majorities of American workers report doing skills and knowledge training for their occupations. We also see, however, a decline over time, which is very small but is a trend consistent with other research. This decline occurred despite tightening labor markets in the 2010s. Finally, regarding STEM workers specifically, we see that the workers using STEM expertise were training more than non-STEM workers, which is good news for the return on investment in STEM education, but the difference is just a few percentage points.[13]

In other words, if employers are facing a dire scarcity of STEM workers, the data on training don't show them doing much more to alleviate it than they are doing for presumably plentiful non-STEM workers. The data consistently also show that workers at for-profit firms—where leaders complain the loudest about not being able to find the skilled workers they need—are also the *least* likely to report skills training.[14] That is, for-profit employers are simultaneously the biggest complainers about skills gaps and the ones doing the least to help themselves. Whether one is a supposedly scarce STEM worker or a supposedly plentiful non-STEM worker, it is increasingly up to individuals to identify a skill set to learn, find the time to do the training, possibly after work hours, and pay for it themselves.[15]

Why the Training Decline Is a Big Problem for STEM Workers: The STEM-Skills Treadmill

If we care about the massive educational investments to create more STEM workers, we should care that STEM workers are not bucking the downward trend of firm-provided training. This is because the skills treadmill can be especially challenging for those who have to know technologies inside and out, and not just as users of new technologies. STEM workers might have the degree related to their job, but if they do not know the new technology and skills that have become necessary to do their job—as it is in their current moment, which might be very different from what they studied in school—they become unqualified by standing still.[16]

It is not hard to find examples of huge innovations that rocked the worlds of some STEM workers. The internet was obviously a huge development for anyone who worked with computers, as internet connection became a—if not *the*—key function of the personal computer. Perhaps less appreciated is how much Apple's iPhone changed computing. Suddenly, the iPhone and its imitators made the internet available all day, anyplace, to anyone willing and able to spend a lot of money—which turned out to be billions of people. This development changed internet usage for consumers but also changed jobs related to the internet, where website design now had to be responsive to radically disparate screen sizes and shapes and could take advantage of new features such as geolocation. As a commentary in *Wired* magazine put it in 2014, "Smartphones, tablets, and the mobile apps that populate such devices have forever changed the approach to web development as we knew it."[17]

It is hard to predict new changes that will change a huge chunk of reality "as we knew it." In computing, it could be the metaverse—Facebook was so convinced of this coming hugeness that it picked "Meta" as its new name to suggest the company's new orientation toward it. In transportation, it could be electric vehicles replacing those powered by fossil fuels. Artificial intelligence appears on the verge of changing everything.

I'm uncomfortable making any predictions as they will look dated very soon and could be wrong. But it is safe to predict that more transformative technologies will emerge, and the STEM grads who work most closely with that technology, or whatever is impacted or even rendered obsolete, will have the biggest adjustments to make.

It is not only advanced STEM workers who face a rapidly moving skills treadmill. Technical workers without a bachelor's degree, whose skills may be narrower than a college-educated STEM worker, can be affected, too. Though I focus this book on graduates of four-year colleges and universities, a training effort that occurred at Foothill College, a community college in Silicon Valley, powerfully captured the pressure of the STEM-skills treadmill. As explained by social scientist Chris Benner, Foothill College formed a partnership with a local semiconductor company. The company needed new technicians to work some very expensive equipment—more than $1 million per machine. In two years, thirty-five trainees undertook Foothill College's highly specialized curriculum. The company chose not to hire any of them. The reason was not that the training failed but that the market and technology had changed. The firm no longer needed workers with the skills that the workers had just obtained. The people who did the training, and those who organized the curriculum, had wasted their investment in STEM education—and the employer took no responsibility. Leo Chavez, the college's chancellor at the time, lamented:

> The message we get from the private sector is "I want you now, get the skills as fast as you can . . ." That job lasts 90 days or 9 years, and then they are right back where they started. . . . [Industry] has been yelling and screaming at education recently that we're not providing sufficient numbers of people. Finally I said, it's not just a pipeline issue. What you're asking me to do may in fact be antithetical to my own values, and that is give you a crew of 25–35 year olds who you can burn up, use up and discard. Maybe part of the problem is not that we're not filling the pipeline, but that you're flushing the toilet too many times.[18]

The idea that workers have skills that become obsolete (*obsolesce* is the verb that appears in these studies) has been around a long time. Some economists who studied the issue took a big-picture view and explored whether new technologies reduced *overall* employment, without asking what happened to specific workers whose skills were no longer needed.[19] Others looked at whether training kept pace with innovations and change (without asking how this affected workers' lives). These researchers quickly established the commonsense idea that although innovation put pressure on workers, the workers' skills did not become obsolete as long as training kept pace. For instance, in the 1980s, a study of both Japan and the US found that the faster technology changed, the more training occurred.[20] Accordingly, workers in fields with fast-moving skills treadmills still tended to have long careers because training and upskilling were widely available. Older workers did tend to retire, however, if an especially sudden burst of change rendered their skills obsolete.[21]

The STEM-skills treadmill received a lot of attention during the late 1990s when the internet was transforming nearly every industry, as well as creating new ones—and employers nevertheless seemed to turn away from their training commitments. During the Clinton administration, the Commerce Department's Office of Technology held hearings across the country on the supply and demand for information technology (IT) workers. Its 1999 report on "the digital workforce" emphasized the "strong need to focus on upgrading the skills of the existing work force"—and not just in Silicon Valley. It quoted "a Mississippi academic official" who criticized the mindset "that when you finish school, you stop," and warned that "you don't do that in information technology. It's changing so much." An academic leader from Arizona similarly pointed out that the rapid evolution of technology meant that the skills taught in school are not likely to be the skills that employers need—even at the time of graduation—because college curriculum designers could not keep up.[22] A congressional committee focused on diversity in STEM similarly noted in 2000, "we must remain cognizant of the continuing need for the retraining of workers currently in the workforce. It is recognized that individuals in today's workforce will likely change the type of work that they do several times over the course of their careers."[23]

The National Research Council reported in 2001 that, based on advice from IT professional associations and job placement specialists, IT workers needed to spend 1.5 to 2 hours per *day* in some kind of training to maintain relevant skills. Not doing this would lead to a decline in employability.[24] In 2013, the magazine for the Institute of Electrical and Electronics Engineers concurred on this figure for engineers and IT workers, stating that "an engineer or IT professional today would have to spend roughly 10 hours a week studying new knowledge to stay current (or upskilling, in the current lingo)."[25] Major authorities on STEM education, including the Accreditation Board for Engineering and Technology (responsible for giving accreditation to US schools of engineering) and the National Academy of Engineering, continue to maintain that engineers *must* embrace lifelong learning in order to keep their skills up to date.[26]

Keeping up on a STEM-skills treadmill can be especially challenging if one is a contractor rather than an employee because contractors have even less access to whatever firms are providing. When contract tech workers in Seattle formed an organization, WashTech, to fight for better work terms with Microsoft and Amazon, one of the issues in dispute was that permanent employees had more access to company-provided training for upgrading skills than did the long-term contractors, or "permatemps," as they were sometimes called.[27] Some contractors manage their training by engaging in "stretchwork," or the bridging of established competencies to new ones that contractors claimed to have in order to get a gig but are actually learned just before or while working in what can be a high-pressure context (more on this in the next section).[28]

Do STEM Workers Really Want Training, and at What Points in Their Careers?

Survey data show that STEM workers value training as a lifelong practice, and it is a key component of what makes a good job. When the job-search platform Indeed surveyed "tech workers," they found that about 90 percent considered "learning and education" to be top characteristics for jobs, similar to pay, benefits, flexibility, opportunities for advancement, and working for a company with an ethical reputation.[29] A Pew Research survey found that although this thinking was not limited to STEM workers—54 percent of all respondents said that "training/ skills development throughout their work life will be essential"—this response increased to 63 percent for those with a bachelor's degree or more, and "computer/IT" workers had the highest proportion, agreeing that training was "essential" (66 percent). Relatedly, when asked about traits important for success in today's economy, "access to training to keep skills up to date" was said to be "extremely important" by 33 percent, and 49 percent said it was "very important."[30]

The NSCG data show that college-level STEM workers can expect to be training for most of their careers. NSCG survey results for STEM-expertise

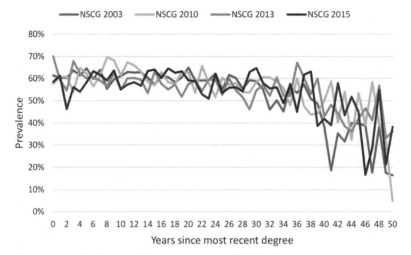

━━ NSCG 2003 ━━ NSCG 2010 ━━ NSCG 2013 ━━ NSCG 2015

FIGURE 5.2 Proportion of STEM workers who reported taking skills–related training in the past twelve months, by years since most recent degree and National Survey of College Graduates (NSCG) survey year. (Data analysis in Skrentny and Lewis, "Beyond the 'STEM Pipeline,'" 12.)

workers (anyone who reported that college-level STEM expertise was necessary for their job), and focusing on those who reported that they did training to improve their skills and knowledge in their occupational field, showed nearly lifelong learning (see figure 5.2). Tracking years since the worker obtained their most recent degree with the prevalence of training, we see that training prevalence hovers around 60 percent and hardly declines at all for the first thirty years after the degree. Even forty years after the degree, near retirement, about 50 percent of STEM workers were still engaging in skills-related training.[31]

One of the more striking findings about the STEM-skills treadmill is that it moves so rapidly that skills learned in college may not provide much advantage in keeping skills up to date. We can see this in NSCG data, which include not only workers in STEM-expertise jobs who have STEM degrees but also those with non-STEM degrees who moved into STEM later in their careers.[32] Although a STEM degree is necessary for many if not most STEM jobs, it is not absolutely necessary for all, and many non-STEM graduates have moved into STEM jobs, especially those related to computers and software, by obtaining advanced training from other sources. What is interesting is that this did not seem to put them behind. STEM workers without degrees were no more likely to train than STEM graduates—that is, they all appeared to be running on the same treadmill.[33]

Management scholars John J. Horton and Prasanna Tambe similarly found significant support for the idea that the STEM-skills treadmill puts all STEM workers in the same boat (to mix metaphors a bit) with a creative study designed to show how STEM workers respond when a specialty suddenly becomes obsolete. They took advantage of a rare occurrence: a sudden, measurable point when a particular software went into freefall. In April 2010, Steve Jobs announced that Apple would no longer use Adobe's Flash software for multimedia. The STEM worker response showed that those with formal technical education had no advantage in reskilling over those without it.[34] In other words, once a STEM job is obtained, and everyone is on the STEM-skills treadmill, all workers appear to be similarly affected and are equally likely to train for new skills.

One of the more comprehensive and thorough analyses of the challenge of maintaining STEM skills also found strong evidence of a faster skills treadmill in STEM jobs, even linking it to the departures of STEM workers from STEM and thus lowering the return on investment in STEM education. Economists David J. Deming and Kadeem Noray examined job postings in two ten-year periods—the 1980s and 2007–2017—and found that the job task requirements of STEM jobs changed faster than non-STEM jobs. For younger STEM workers, this faster pace of change was less of a problem. Though even recent STEM grads can be out of date, as discussed earlier, the recent grads were still most likely to have the latest, most in-demand skills. Employers rewarded them, too. At this early career stage, they were able to earn higher wages than workers in non-STEM jobs. Deming and Noray also found that when technology changed more rapidly (as measured by changing skills demands in job ads), the wage premium for younger STEM workers was highest. Their earnings averaged about 25 percent more than the earnings of workers in non-STEM jobs.[35]

But there were more concerning results. First, Deming and Noray found that older workers' earnings did not show a wage premium like that of the younger workers, suggesting that employers were not valuing experience.[36]

Second, the story here was not that all STEM jobs had skills treadmills that moved at the same rate. Whereas STEM jobs overall may have faster skills treadmills than non-STEM jobs, within STEM, some job skills requirements changed more rapidly than others. The jobs that changed the most rapidly were in computer science, engineering, and tech-intensive business jobs (e.g., jobs focused on logistics and market research). These jobs also had the highest earnings right out of college, but earnings advantages declined very quickly over time as the skills learned in college became obsolete. Software jobs had the most rapid skills turnover, so anyone working closely with software is likely on the fastest treadmill.

Third, and most concerning for the return on investment in STEM education, workers in these fast-changing fields apparently get tired of being on the skills treadmill. It is precisely *these* rapidly changing jobs that workers are most likely to abandon the soonest. Moreover, it is workers who have the highest academic ability (as measured by test scores) who tend to leave these jobs at the youngest ages. Though high-ability students may be initially attracted to STEM majors and careers, they begin to peel away and do something else as their earnings advantages decrease over time.[37]

To be sure, everyone who works with technology is on a skills treadmill to some extent since technology is always changing (and, one hopes, improving). My point here is that STEM workers are on the fastest skills treadmills, especially those working with software, and changes can disrupt the very core of their jobs. If we are serious about investing in STEM education to produce STEM workers, we shouldn't ignore them after they earn their degrees. For STEM workers especially, education and training are lifelong commitments.

Employers Want Cutting-Edge STEM Skills, So What Training Are They Providing?

We've already seen that employer-provided training is on a downward trend, but this does not mean employers have left the training space completely. What may be surprising given that employers of STEM workers complain of shortages and skills gaps is that much of the training that they do provide is not designed to mitigate these skills gaps. This is because many firms see training to be most valuable if it is related to pushing their own products, increasing their market share, or attracting new workers rather than keeping relevant their supposedly scarce STEM workers. At the same time, there are some firms—scholars sometimes call them "high-road" firms because they appear to "take the high road," to do the right thing—that are training their own workers to keep up with changing technology. They see training as a smart investment, but in part because these STEM employers have no other choices but to train.

THE MOST COMMON FORM OF EMPLOYER TRAINING: ONBOARDING AND INCULCATION

Employers commonly provide training at the point of hiring so the workers can get acclimated to their new home away from home. There is the process that human resource specialists call *onboarding*, which goes beyond the signing of paperwork and understanding benefits. Typically, it will also include some specific training about employer "culture," or the set of expectations, rules, and values that every employee should adopt or at least understand. On top of that will be specific skills needed to excel at that particular employer—use of a unique software, for example, or use of some technical equipment if there is a lab involved.[38] This company-specific training may also be in decline,[39] but it is still common.

An elaborate example of this firm-specific training is provided by tech giant Apple. Apple University, begun in 2008, is quite high-concept (like Apple itself). According to the *New York Times*, "Steven P. Jobs established Apple University as a way to inculcate employees into Apple's business culture and educate them about its history, particularly as the company grew and the tech business changed." Students of Apple University— that is, Apple employees—learn about key business decisions made at Apple, the company's distinctive strategies of management and communication, and of course Apple's hallmarks—design and engineering.[40]

What is distinctive about this onboarding/inculcation training is that none of it is expected to translate to any general skills that could be used at other firms. This onboarding training will likely help a STEM professional perform better if they understand in a deep way what a company is about, but it will not help them run on the skills treadmill. It is not surprising that an alumnus of Apple University told the *Times* that Apple University education didn't make "much of a difference" after he moved to another company.[41] Training as part of onboarding is widespread and important, but even the advanced form done at Apple is not going to help a midcareer worker struggling to keep skills relevant.

MAINTAINING AND EXPANDING PRODUCT
MARKET SHARE BY TRAINING NONEMPLOYEES

Some major firms, especially in tech, are investing in training initiatives that appear designed to help not employees but customers. They train customers or others to use the firm's products—that is, they are training for market share, not to upskill their own workers. Firms using this training strategy provide technology for other businesses or other organizations, not directly to consumers.

For example, the internet networking conglomerate Cisco has had a great number of training opportunities listed on its website. What tied them together is a focus on Cisco's own products. At the time of this writing, Cisco has a "Learning Locator" designed for users to "find Cisco-authorized training around the world." Cisco listed some courses as "popular," including "Developing Applications and Automating Workflows Using Cisco Platforms" and "Implementing and Administering Cisco Solutions." The site also listed a series of "certifications" to signal competence in Cisco technologies, such as "CCNA" (or "Cisco Certified Network Associate").[42]

Cisco is by no means alone in training endeavors targeting business or other enterprise consumers and not employees. Oracle, makers of business software, has "Oracle University," which is very different from Apple's Apple University. Oracle's foray into training provides a range of courses for products and certifications and boasted of "2.2 million Oracle Certified Professionals in the global workforce."[43] Microsoft has offered a range of training opportunities and certifications, such as "AI Engineer," designed to help "AI Engineers use Cognitive Services, Machine Learning, and Knowledge Mining to architect and implement Microsoft AI solutions."[44] Illumina, a global life sciences company that makes equipment for genome sequencing, has similar training initiatives. Its customers include research institutions (such as universities), biotech and pharmaceutical companies, and hospitals. Illumina has an Illumina Training Center that has offered a range of courses such as "Illumina DNA Prep Training."[45]

Employers are not designing these impressive offerings to help incumbent workers on STEM-skills treadmills; they appear designed to increase and reinforce market share by enabling people to use their products. Their training is relevant to STEM employment in that these courses and certifications can help trainees signal to *other* employers who use these products that they have competence in these specific skills—which may, of course, fall out of date and need to be recertified to demonstrate competence with upgraded technology.[46]

TRAINING AS RECRUITMENT TOOL—OR LAYOFF GIFT

Some large firms provide training to their own STEM employees, but they do so mainly as an employment perk. They believe that many STEM workers like the technical challenge of learning new skills and will see upskilling as stimulating and enriching and not a burden. Firms might promote this training as career development but also as optional and fun.

For example, Google has pitched training as a perk, framing it as something similar to personal fulfillment through hobbies: "Lifelong learning is inherently Googley. That's why we offer extensive opportunities for personal and professional development. Whether it's onsite coding or cooking classes, degree programs, or the guitar lessons you've been meaning to take, we'll support you in doing what you love."[47]

Other firms, including those in life sciences or energy, may promote training as a perk and with an emphasis on experiential learning, not the targeted transfer of skills for job security with the firm. For instance, the pharmaceutical company Pfizer (which has laid off thousands of STEM workers, you'll recall from chapter 4) has said, "We'll foster your learning and encourage your development. We'll listen to your aspirations and fully support your requests for job-rotation assignments, experiential action projects and short-term project roles."[48] ExxonMobil, the oil company, similarly tells prospective engineers that they can "discover world-class career development through a range of assignments in one of the world's leading technology and innovation companies."[49] The software company Adobe has boasted that "Adobe employees are the brightest of the bunch, so around here the learning never stops. Grow your skills and feed your curiosity in a rich learning environment that offers generous educational reimbursement for eligible courses and programs."[50]

What these have in common is that they emphasize the opening of doors to individual initiative, not a strategic training plan for company success. The offers make the companies sound like partners who will help individuals enhance their own self-driven employability (possibly somewhere else?) rather than stakeholders who will invest in and reskill workers who are facing layoffs.

Chipmaker Qualcomm inches closer to investing in workers and strategic training, advertising itself as a workforce developer, stating on its website, "We offer a learning organization," and "We care about our people and support them to learn, grow, advance and lead." Its efforts appear closely tied to career development but range from foundational skills such as communication to more technical skills in topic areas from machine learning and recurrent neural networks to managerial skills and leadership. It appears that this is not just for show: for example, Qualcomm reported that in 2019, its employees viewed 300,000 training "content items" and had access to 240,000 hours of instructor-led training and 900 on-site programs. Qualcomm also has offered tuition reimbursement for online learning through Coursera and Udacity.[51]

At the same time, however, firms that offer serious skills training can still lay off workers rather than retraining them to work in other divisions. Qualcomm does a lot of skills training, but it laid off about 270 workers in 2019, which was a follow-up to the 1,500 it laid off in 2018.[52] And these layoffs were on the heels of a much larger 15 percent reduction in Qualcomm's key mobile semiconductor business, including a major streamlining of its engineering staff. The head of the San Diego Regional Economic Development Corporation, Mark Cafferty, took an optimistic view to the media, commenting, "I think a lot of folks at Qualcomm, with a little bit of retraining or retooling, will be able to find their footing quite well in other parts of the innovation economy."[53] Implied here was the notion that these laid-off workers had *lost* their footing—a stressful experience for many in the work world—and they now needed skills training from . . . somewhere.

The flipside to the training-as-perk model, which is meant to entice workers to join a firm, is the training-as-layoff-gift model. In truth, this may not be common enough to be a "model," but it is striking that at least one manager thought it was normal enough to offer it, and it shows the peculiar attitude of some STEM employers toward worker training. In Erin Kelly and Phyllis Moen's study of a software firm in the Midwest (kept anonymous in their research), they found that the firm would go through periodic layoffs, jettisoning workers from particular divisions. When one middle manager, Zach, asked an executive how to handle the layoffs, the executive told Zach, "Well, the thing you can do is make sure your people are trained. So if or when they do lose their job, they have a better skill set to get another job *outside*" (emphasis added).[54]

In short, some firms that boast impressive training opportunities appear to do so as a perk, as something to offer individuals if they want it, and do not see training as a way to maintain scarce workers' continuing contributions to the firm and a means to provide job security. The threat of being let go may still hang over the heads of STEM workers, where they lose their footing and may suddenly have to find a new marketable skill set to learn in order to latch on somewhere else.

TRAINING AS PUBLIC RELATIONS AND BRAND BUILDING

Employers may also invest in training in what appears to be a public relations benefit, or a show of what some scholars call "corporate social responsibility."[55] In these efforts, the firms make sometimes huge contributions to training people who do not actually work for the company—and likely will never work for the company. In some ways, this is the *opposite* of what economists predict firms will do regarding training, which predicts firms will not want to train workers who might leave. For example, Microsoft announced a $25 million effort in 2020 to support training in digital skills among nonemployees. The plan would provide "$20 million in cash grants to help nonprofit organizations worldwide assist the people who need it most." In addition, Microsoft would give $5 million in cash grants "to community-based nonprofit organizations that are led by and serve communities of color in the United States."

Microsoft, it should be said, was worth more than $1 trillion in 2020, so this was not a massive commitment by any stretch, but it was still a significant amount of cash. So why did they do it? Though helping non-employees, the plan would use LinkedIn data (owned by Microsoft) to identify in-demand jobs, and training would culminate in Microsoft certifications that signal proficiency in a variety of Microsoft technologies.[56] The training initiative was a mix of brand burnishing, public relations, and market share reinforcement.

Notably, at the same time that Microsoft took this global training initiative, it was also announcing what business media described as its "usual" fiscal year-end layoffs, including from its STEM-worker-heavy cloud computing services division, as well as its sales and marketing team. Its MSN.com news division let go employees and contractors, replacing their human skills with AI.[57] Presumably, these newly unemployed editors could have used some digital skills training. Maybe they did get it, but apparently not from Microsoft.

Microsoft may have been following the lead of Google, though not in its scope. Google's education-related efforts are notable for their massive scale, and, like Microsoft, they similarly promote their own products while educating young people. In California, during the 2020 pandemic-related lockdown, when students were expected to have internet access for remote learning, Google donated 4,000 Chromebooks (Google-branded portable computers designed for internet usage) and funds to use 100,000 Wi-Fi hot spots for rural students as part of an effort to "bridge the digital divide," according to Google CEO Sundar Pichai.[58]

But this was just a tiny part of Google's strategy, which actually focused on "closing the world's education gap." The company was offering $1 billion ($770 million more than Microsoft) for training, but none of it was going to train Google's own workers. The funds would go to nonprofits to train kids and adults the world over (including the US) in both basic education and digital skills for the changing nature of work (STEMified jobs in particular).[59]

Google has also been involved in creating its own certificates, and its approach has some distinctive features. It is similar to Cisco, Oracle, and Microsoft in that Google's certificates carry the company's name. Google developed the certificates but for delivery partnered with Coursera, a for-profit online learning platform. Also similar was the IT focus: the certificates were in computer-related fields such as data analyst, UX designer, IT support specialist, and project manager. Google designed this training for jobs elsewhere, not at Google. But the efforts were different in that they were not focused on Google products. Learners could use the training for employment anywhere, for use with any products. Rather than reinforcing or increasing market share, it appeared instead to be an effort in branding or corporate social responsibility. Google's stated goal is to bring inexpensive STEM education and credentials to more people and more diverse people—people of color, those with different abilities, and those from lower incomes. Natalie Van Kleef Conley, a senior product manager with the division in charge of these efforts (called Grow with Google), shared with online education magazine *Inside Higher Ed* the official Google rationale for the effort: "We know that our best work will come when the work force truly reflects the world around us. As we develop these trainees for the work force of the future, it's really critical that people come from many different backgrounds and perspectives."[60]

Despite investing $1 billion in the "work force of the future," the deep-pocketed search and adtech giant still could lay off workers and not train them for redeployment in the firm. In March 2022, Google laid off 100 staff from its cloud computing division, including engineers and managers. They were told they had 60 days to find other positions at the firm, but Google provided no guidance on how to do that, nor did it provide training to enable transitions. Worse, some of the laid-off workers found out about the decision from news reports. The union at the firm, Alphabet Workers Union, got 1,400 signatures on a petition demanding that Google do more to help these workers. The petition stated, "Google has continued to maintain that workers are simply being offered an opportunity to transfer. This ignores the reality that many workers do not qualify for currently available roles and the complexity of the transfer process means that most workers are facing the termination of their livelihood in under two months."[61] A program manager at Google and also a member of the union, David Newgas, stated that "Google wants to keep its reputation for treating its workers well but doesn't want to pay for it."[62] Six months later, the company announced more reductions, and 1,400 workers signed a petition demanding 180 days to find a new position, arguing there were "barriers to transfer."[63]

THE HIGH-ROAD EMPLOYERS: HELPING EMPLOYEES RUN ON THE SKILLS TREADMILL

There are some employers who are doing more than training for onboarding and inculcating, offering training as a perk, and training outsiders for market share or public relations benefits. These employers appear to have engaged in STEM training as a business strategy and a way to solve skills gaps within the company. They can offer examples of how employers can be committed to training their workers so they can keep up on the STEM-skills treadmill—and even advance. One notable pattern, however, is that firms sometimes take the high road because they have no other choice—they have trouble hiring STEM grads. While this calls into question the moral meaning of "high road," it still has positive impacts on workers, including some of the most vulnerable.

First, Airbnb, the digital housing rental platform, created a "Data University" that imparted some skills that could be useful at multiple firms and some tailored to Airbnb specifically. Airbnb wanted its workers to be more data literate, and so rather than lay off current workers and hire from the outside, the firm created its own courses with varying levels of instruction, benefiting both technical workers and managers. As TechCrunch explained, referring to software languages and data visualization platforms, "Middle-tier classes on SQL and Superset have enabled some non-technical employees to take on roles as project managers, and more intensive courses on Python and machine learning have helped engineers brush up on necessary skills for projects."[64] Nevertheless, Airbnb laid off workers during the COVID-19 pandemic, and training these for redeployment elsewhere in the firm would be the true gold star for training workers, but the overall prepandemic approach—upskilling existing employees to fill skills needs rather than hiring from outside—is an example of a high-road approach to training.[65]

Another important part of the high-road story is that there is a whole ecosystem of specialized organizations that provide training and can partner with firms so they don't have to do it themselves like Airbnb did. For many years, federal and state governments, as well as other third parties such as labor unions and community colleges, have frequently contributed to skills training, though this has mostly targeted workers with less than a college degree.[66] But firms targeting workers with a college degree and above also use outside training providers.

We saw earlier that firms offering training as a perk might partner with Coursera and Udacity, online providers of higher education. University extension and continuing education schools are also big players. The best ones will know the local and national job markets, will have extensive experience in training, and can work with employers on just-in-time skill delivery.[67] In Silicon Valley, for example, the University of California, Santa Cruz (UCSC) is a major provider of training, growing rapidly after first establishing an outpost there in 1987. By the mid-1990s, UCSC Extension enrolled more than fifty thousand students, mostly adult learners who already had a college degree (or more), with software and hardware classes being the most popular. Employers reimbursed about 50 percent of tuitions.[68]

These kinds of partnerships can be used to get workers up to speed not only in basic STEM skills but also in cutting-edge technologies. Mary Walshok and Joel West's account of the role of University of California, San Diego (UCSD) in the development of the local wireless industry, which includes San Diego–based chipmaker Qualcomm, provides a picture of how this can work. Qualcomm had developed a new technology, "code-division multiple access" (CDMA), that enabled the cellular and data connections used on mobile phones. Its version of CDMA was so new that Qualcomm had trouble finding engineers to work on its new projects. Qualcomm approached UCSD Extension for a partnership and provided the firm's top-level research-and-development technical talent to work with the university and develop a curriculum to be taught both locally and online. Though Qualcomm wanted to upskill its own workers, the firm and UCSD intended these offerings for nonemployees as well because Qualcomm "needed new CDMA-specific training to support its ecosystem of suppliers and partners and to train its ever-increasing roster of engineers."[69] The company thrived as a result.[70]

For-profit training providers have also developed tailored programs to service high-road firms that wish to upskill their workers. For example, General Assembly is a training provider that specializes in software coding skills for people without STEM backgrounds. It started mainly as a training "bootcamp" (a short-term, highly intensive training program), aimed at anyone looking to develop software skills despite not having a STEM degree. But General Assembly pivoted to a business model wherein it contracted with firms taking the high road on training. This business model was so successful—because there were many firms willing to train their own employees—that a Switzerland-based staffing firm, Adecco, purchased General Assembly for $413 million in 2018.[71] In 2021, General Assembly claimed to have served more than twenty-five thousand employees at more than three hundred firms. Though some clients included tech firms (Microsoft, Google, and Adobe, which do not advertise their upskilling of incumbent employees, so it is unclear how common or significant these efforts are), General Assembly's niche appeared to be training in digital and coding skills in sectors outside tech as traditionally understood, such as retail (Walmart), finance (Citibank), insurance (Aetna), consulting (Booz Allen Hamilton), and media (Disney), where demand for STEM skills was growing.[72] None of these firms are sought-after destinations for STEM talent, and that is a theme for high-road firms on STEM-skills training: challenges recruiting STEM grads from the outside. In short, they took the high road on training because they were likely compelled to.

Other major efforts follow this pattern. Consider the case of the venerable telecommunications giant AT&T (originally American Telephone and Telegraph). Established in the 1870s, AT&T has gone through many changes in its long history, including a government-enforced breakup and then a private reconstitution. By the 2010s, the company was still a telecommunications firm, but it was in fierce competition with other telecommunications firms, such as Verizon, as well as tech firms such as Google and Amazon. New communications technologies led AT&T

to remake itself as a computer company, with communications moving through the cloud rather than through wires and switchboards. This change required a total rethinking of the skills needed to work at the company, which then required coding and data analysis, and led chairman and CEO Randall Stephenson to initiate a retraining of 280,000 workers.[73]

The AT&T effort was impressive but had some flaws. Though Stephenson offered a subsidy of $8,000 per year, he did not offer to pay for all the courses, nor did he give the workers time during work to train—it had to be done on their own time. Still, it was a major effort that helped workers stay at the firm. Stephenson explained succinctly to the *New York Times* the concept of the skills treadmill: "There is a need to retool yourself, and you should not expect to stop." William Blase, the head of personnel for AT&T, had a similar take: "There's going to be an expectation that your compensation will be tied to continuing to learn. We're at a crossroads as a business—and a country—where education has to keep up with technology." The leader of the union representing AT&T's workers, Communications Workers of America's Christopher Shelton, was on board with these efforts: "We realized a long time ago that you can't fight technology change and win." To deliver this training, AT&T partnered with online education provider Udacity along with the Georgia Institute of Technology. In some cases, AT&T provided tuition for online degrees, including master's degrees in such traditional STEM fields as computer science.[74] By 2019, about half of AT&T's workforce had participated, spending five to ten hours a week learning new skills.[75]

The energy company Royal Dutch Shell also trained workers in STEM skills rather than lay off employees and hire from the outside. The company was in a similar situation as AT&T, needing to remake itself as a tech company but unable to recruit STEM grads in the relevant fields. By the 2010s, Shell was making major moves into artificial intelligence (AI) and data science for new initiatives in alternative energy and also the management of their oil business. For the latter, AI could support the processing of seismic data and provide insights into underground rock formations. Shell's leaders believed that an old oil company (its history stretches back to the 1890s, almost as far back as AT&T's) had a branding problem and was not an exciting destination for talented AI and software workers, who mostly sought name-brand tech leaders such as Apple and Google. Younger workers in particular, an industry survey showed, associated jobs at oil companies with blue collar, dangerous, and physically demanding work, not interesting software development. So Shell partnered with online education provider Udacity to teach its incumbent workers, including some in their fifties, AI and data science skills. About two thousand of its eighty-two thousand workers around the world showed interest in learning skills in Python, neural networks, and other STEM subjects. Though voluntary, the firm paid for the training, which took four to six months to finish at a pace of about ten to fifteen hours per week. In a real boost for workers, they could train during work hours. The training culminated in a "nanodegree," or nondegree credential. As Gabe Dalporto, the CEO of Udacity (who clearly had an incentive to encourage such training) explained, "The worst case scenario is laying people off and then going out and hiring all new workers with the skills you need. . . . First of all, our universities can't turn out all the workers we'll need for the jobs of the future and it's expensive. The cost of reskilling is so much less."[76]

A third example of a high-road strategy to training in STEM skills does not involve partnerships with third parties. Amazon, the same firm that I described in chapter 3 as having a "bruising" workplace that leads many to leave, took a high-road strategy toward training for its skills needs. In 2019, the tech conglomerate created its own certificates, similar to other major tech firms, but instead of immediately making these available to anyone, Amazon chose to invest $700 million in the training of one hundred thousand of its own workers.

Like some of AT&T's moves, many of these training efforts were to bring non-STEM workers onto STEM-skills treadmills.[77] But one part of this effort was aimed specifically at workers already on STEM-skills treadmills. Amazon's Machine Learning University would help software developers learn new skills to keep up in this fast-growing field.[78] Amazon also plucked from academia an education researcher, Candace Thille, a specialist in using cognitive science and data to shape teaching strategies, to assume a position as "director of learning science and engineering."[79]

Though some observers argued that Amazon's efforts were made out of necessity in a tight labor market, it was still notable because many other firms were *not* making similar efforts to train their workers on such a massive scale, and Amazon thus bucked the trend of declining firm-provided training in the US.[80]

Why Most Employers of STEM Workers
Don't Want to Train Them

Why are these stories of employers training their workers in STEM skills exceptional and newsworthy? Why is it surprising when, during times when STEM workers were supposedly scarce, firms chose to train their workers in skills the firm needs?

Economist Gary Becker suggested one possible reason when he argued that it was not rational for employers to spend time and money to train their workers if those workers could leave and use those skills elsewhere. In this view, employers would be foolish to train if they would potentially be offering free workforce development services for other firms, including competitors. So when it came to what he called "general" skills—those most likely to be portable to other employers—Becker argued we should not expect to see much training. Employer investments in training made more sense, Becker argued, if they were specific to a particular employer, rooted in that employer's unique business practices—proprietary technologies or services. Competitors were less likely to use these "specific skills." If training focused only or at least mainly on these specific skills, Becker argued, employers were more likely to recoup their investments in a worker's skill sets. In this view, trained workers leaving represented money down the drain, so it was not rational to train in any skills that may be useful to other employers.[81]

But hiring from the outside is not free. As discussed in chapter 3, hiring from the outside for needed skills means the firm must pay recruitment costs (anywhere from $3,500 to $30,000, depending on salary level).[82] Moreover, research indicates that internal hires perform better than workers brought in from the outside. One study found that when firms invested in the technical training of workers, those workers were less likely to leave than workers who paid for their own education, suggesting that training could be an investment in a longtime human resource and a hedge against turnover.[83] Nevertheless, firms typically avoid training their own workers and buy needed skills from the outside.

Education scholar Jason Wingard has argued that there are several barriers to companies training their own workers. One is leadership goals: company leaders focus on short-term profits rather than the long-term growth that training facilitates. Another barrier is competing priorities, whereby a firm's leaders prefer that resources go into other strategic goals rather than training. But ultimately, Wingard's point is that there is often a cultural barrier to company-provided training, and it is the reason that short-term profits seem so enticing and other priorities more desirable.[84] Human resource expert Josh Bersin has argued that employer culture frames investing money in recruiting as rational but investing in training its own workers as not.[85] This might explain why Google and Microsoft might spend millions or hundreds of millions of dollars on public-relations training (that presumably will boost brand power and profits) while laying off their own workers.

From where did this culture come? As I discussed in chapter 1, short-term shareholder value maximization led investors to value that which made immediate profits above anything else. In this view, workers were expenses, and they were expendable. This led companies to adopt burn-and-churn management, and if you are going to burn and churn through workers, you are not likely to commit to training them. Economist William Lazonick has noted that firms could easily pay for training their employees if they chose not to buy back shares of their own stock, as stock buybacks serve no purpose except to increase stock prices and thus shareholder value.[86]

As I discussed in chapters 3 and 4, the burn-and-churn management approach created a self-reinforcing pattern of worker and employer mutual disloyalty. The more that employers bought skills on the open market and laid people off suddenly (even during good economic times), the more job-hopping among workers they encouraged. The workers' increasing tendency to job-hop then further decreased any remaining employer incentives for training workers (why train if they would leave?) and added more impetus for the buy decision over the build.[87] Even researchers studying how employers can solve their problems finding STEM workers sometimes *assume* these skills will have to be acquired through hiring rather than training existing workers in exactly the skills needed.[88]

This pattern of beliefs and behavior is especially strong in the US. Management scholar Peter Cappelli has described what happened when the German engineering giant Siemens brought its German-style apprentice training to Florida. Siemens found local firms hiring away those newly trained workers. According to Cappelli, "When Siemens complained to some of these companies that they were unfairly pirating its investment, the reply was, essentially, 'Welcome to America.'"[89]

A survey by McKinsey, the consulting firm, showed the differences between the US and Europe on preferences for training workers in

TABLE 5.1. Executives' responses (%) to question "How can your organization best resolve its potential skills gaps related to automation and/or digitization over the next five years?"

	Only by retraining	Mainly by retraining	Equal mix hiring and retraining	Mainly by hiring	Only by hiring
United States	4	27	35	30	5
Europe	0	45	49	7	0

Note: McKinsey panel survey of 1,549 European and US executives, private-sector organizations with greater than $100 million revenue who view the skills gap as a top-ten priority, % of respondents, November 2017.

STEM skills. When asked specifically how firms should resolve "potential skills gaps related to automation and/or digitization over the next five years," European executives showed great support for training and little for hiring alone: 45 percent supported "mainly by retraining," 49 percent supported "equal mix hiring and retraining," and only 7 percent said "mainly by hiring" (see table 5.1). But US executives were much more diverse in their responses, with a skew toward hiring instead of training. They were more than four times more likely than European executives to say "mainly by hiring" (30 percent compared with Europe's 7 percent) and were almost 20 percent less likely to select "mainly by retraining."[90]

Consulting firm survey results also fit with anecdotal evidence of a culturally embedded preference for hiring over training. For example, the chief technology and innovation officer for Accenture told the *Wall Street Journal*, "Executives have this idea that 'as my people become obsolete, I'll just hire new people.'" Andy Van Kleunen, head of the National Skills Coalition, agreed, stating, "Many countries we compete with see continual worker retraining as part of their economic strategy. The way we've traditionally treated education in this country is the government is responsible for your education until age 18, and after that it's more of a private matter."[91]

In short, many employers, especially in the US, take for granted that they should buy skills—hire new workers—when they have a skills gap. If they think about this decision at all, they appear to believe it is a waste of money if the worker can simply march off and sell those new skills to another employer. What is odd about this rationale is that hiring a new worker—which can cost thousands of dollars—also can be a waste of money if that new worker leaves. Moreover, new hires are unknown quantities, and they can be discovered to be difficult to deal with or not as skilled as they presented themselves.

Conclusion: How Should STEM Workers Keep Their Skills Up to Date?

STEM skills become obsolete, leading some workers to leave STEM altogether, thereby reducing the return on the national investment in STEM education and exacerbating any skills gaps that do exist. They leave in part because firms are decreasingly likely to offer training themselves, even while many business leaders demand more STEM grads and more STEM migrants. For those who wish to stay in STEM work, they will have to engage in training whether or not their employers direct them to specific skill upgrades or support their efforts. How should they do it?

STEM employees would be wise to be resourceful, similar to STEM contractors. If employers offer training as a recruitment perk, they should take advantage of it as much as they can. Studies also show that training can be part of the everyday tasks of the job in the sense that workers are always solving problems and thus learning. Mutual help and information exchange can be key sources of knowledge and skill development.[92] In software, simply working in a team can be a part of training if workers have communication skills and are managed to work collaboratively rather than competitively.[93]

Management scholars John J. Horton and Prasanna Tambe's insightful research on what happened to software contract workers when Adobe's Flash software went into rapid decline is instructive on how workers can respond to the rapid obsolescence in a skill. Software developers who took contract or "gig" jobs on an online platform researched and then learned new skills (60 percent saying these were "extremely important" responses). Being in the field, they had insights already about which skills had a lot of current and likely future demand, and the most common methods for learning the new skills were learning on the job (e.g., through "stretchwork," a strategy contractors use, as discussed in chapter 4) and visiting online forums such as Stack Overflow. But this wasn't an entirely lonely effort. Key to finding the right skills to learn was leveraging real-world and online social networks—communicating with other developers and reading content on online forums.

In describing their stretchwork strategies as they moved away from Flash, one explained, "Switching to new technology implies that you cannot directly go to expert level projects. It requires starting with easy level and enhance your learning as you work more on live projects." Another commented, "When working with a new technology, I start with simpler projects compared to what I would normally work in using a technology I have already been using for a long time. As I get more projects in with the new tech, I start applying for more complex jobs."[94]

The success of these developers should not blind us to how hard this can be, and why it may lead STEM workers to leave STEM altogether. For STEM workers in life sciences, energy, and chemicals, for example, access to labs and specialized equipment might be necessary. And in all cases, workers who have to train themselves on their own time are under more pressure if they have families or other priorities requiring attention.

Some poignant evidence for the strains of the STEM-skills treadmill was provided in an anonymous online post on Slashdot, a news and question-and-answer website focusing on tech. In response to the question "What are some hard truths IT must learn to accept?" a user calling himself "ErichTheRed," forty-two years old and a self-described "old fart when it comes to my IT job," had a response at the top of the heap, user-rated a 5 (top score) for "insightful." He explained, "My 'hard truth' about IT that surprisingly few people truly grasp is that you can't get comfortable being the expert at one particular thing and coast." He continued:

> Keeping up with all the knowledge needed to be the guy they keep on staff when all the routine work is offshore is *hard*. I have had to dedicate a lot of off-work time to it, because no company trains their staff anymore . . . one of the things I hate about IT not being recognized as a real profession. The reward for doing this is a very interesting job and, not surprisingly, a higher-pressure firehose to learn from. :-) Being a dad on top of this is tough also . . . it requires lots of time management, late night reading and watching videos at 2x speed to do this and be a functioning parent. So yeah . . . if you want to keep an IT job, especially as things get more and more abstract, broaden your skill set and learn as much as you can get your brain around.[95]

The personal account of "ErichTheRed" suggests that STEM work is especially challenging if employers are not offering training because the STEM-skills treadmills is unforgiving. As long as firms are driven by investors and a culture that makes training seem like a waste of company resources, however, we are likely to see many STEM graduates reject this life.

One possible high-road approach to training—a kinder, gentler approach that might ease some of this pressure—was suggested to me by a former executive at a Fortune 500 tech company. He saw a model for training of employees in what educators call Individualized Instruction Programs (or IEPs). School districts use these for students with special needs. In IEPs, educators and disability specialists evaluate students to determine their weaknesses and present level of performance. They then identify goals in skill development and also techniques for achieving those goals.[96] In an analogous way, human resources departments could use performance reviews (which are done anyway, as you'll recall from chapter 3) to understand current employees' strengths and weaknesses regarding specific skills. Since employers will know sooner than anyone which new skills will be needed, and especially which divisions or workers are most likely to be laid off, they are in an excellent position to help workers strategize their running on the STEM-skills treadmill—and maybe even allow them to advance to a newer, better-paying treadmill. Even if the employer does not organize the training, or even pay for it when taken with a third party, this kind of close guidance could be invaluable to current workers, such as those in highly technical, fast-changing STEM fields, and especially those with families or other time commitments, and where the wrong choice of training investment could force an exit from STEM work altogether.

CHAPTER 6

HOW STEM EMPLOYERS CONTRIBUTE TO THEIR OWN DIVERSITY PROBLEMS

In 2015, *Mother Jones* magazine shined a light on diversity among several wealthy, massively influential tech companies, including Facebook, Google, Microsoft, and Twitter. At none of them did women exceed 20 percent of the workforce in technical positions. Latinos made up only about 3 percent of these workers, and African Americans only about 1 percent.[1] Journalist Josh Harkinson observed that the entire African American workforces of Google, Facebook, and Twitter—758 people, or 1.8 percent of 41,000 total employees—could fit on a single Airbus A380 jumbo jet, with room to spare.[2]

These numbers have hardly changed. If policymakers, philanthropists, and individuals continue to invest huge amounts of money, time, and effort in STEM education, and employers keep complaining of shortages, we might reasonably expect every STEM grad to get a fair shot at STEM jobs. Silicon Valley's abysmal numbers in tech get the most attention given the massive valuation of these companies and their influence in American life, but tech outside "the Valley" and other sectors that hire STEM grads, including life sciences and energy, also have serious problems providing equal opportunities.

The response of many business leaders and policymakers is to look at these numbers and demand that the education system do better and supply more STEM grads. But there is a problem here: Why would students get degrees in fields in which they are likely to face discrimination, everyday hassles, and blocked opportunities? If you are going to invest a huge amount of time, energy, and money into a career, you will likely choose a path with better odds. Indeed, studies show that students pay attention to market signals in deciding their careers.[3]

Students are right to be skeptical of STEM employers. I make the case here that if we only focused on STEM education, we would likely never solve diversity problems in STEM workplaces because the women and members of minority groups who earn STEM degrees often choose not to enter STEM employment, often do not get hired, or often leave after being hired. My focus in this chapter is therefore on the role of employers, and understanding the reasons why women and minority STEM grads do not feel welcome in STEM employment, creating another factor that can lead them to leave for more fulfilling jobs outside STEM.

It is also likely the case that diversity problems are not just gender and race/ethnicity. Age is a neglected category of diversity in STEM, and there is evidence that older workers find STEM employers less interested in hiring and retaining them compared with those who are younger, and they may, like women and underrepresented minorities, feel unwelcome in STEM workplaces. Many of the diversity challenges in STEM flow from employers' hiring and management practices that are more inclusive and welcoming of workers who are male, young, and White (or Asian in some positions). Women, African Americans, Latinos, and older workers all may feel unwelcome and unvalued.

Another side of the diversity problem in STEM relates to foreign workers on temporary visas, especially the much-maligned H-1B visa. Critics in American politics and media sometimes characterize foreigners as "taking" American jobs (an absurd phrasing that ignores employers' power to select employees and implies that jobs are just waiting there, like fruit in bowls, available to be snatched away), and employers may use workers on H-1B visas to replace American STEM workers, as I discuss in this chapter. But these H-1B workers have their own claims to being treated badly as well, creating another diversity problem.

In other words, STEM jobs, especially in tech and computers, commonly feature exclusion and discrimination. For those who advocate greater investment in STEM education, these should be matters of concern and constitute a likely suspect in why so many STEM grads leave STEM work. Research shows that exclusion is a major part of toxic work culture, which is itself a major factor why employees leave jobs in any sector.[4]

Women and Minorities in STEM: How Bad Is the Diversity Problem?

Academic research and insightful journalistic accounts of diversity in STEM focus mostly on tech. Tech is especially important to assess on diversity because jobs in computers and software constitute about half of all STEM workers, shortages here are supposed to be the most acute and so efforts to solve diversity problems should be the most diligent, and many of these firms have the financial resources to solve diversity problems. Still, STEM is bigger than tech, and it is important to assess whether other STEM sectors have solved the problems. Numbers for comparison are harder to find, but what is available suggests some variation for women in STEM employment but less for African Americans and Latinos. Leadership opportunities look limited for everyone except White men in all STEM sectors.

WOMEN AND MINORITY STEM PERSISTENCE IN THREE SECTORS: TECH, BIOTECH, AND ENERGY

First, let's look more closely at tech, and Silicon Valley in particular. Despite this massive concentration of wealth and innovative people, diversity became worse there as the current tech titans emerged and became dominant.[5] A few years after the *Mother Jones* stories, the Center for Employment Equity at the University of Massachusetts–Amherst issued a report on diversity in Silicon Valley showing that employers continued to exclude women, African Americans, and Latinos in tech jobs. Diversity can vary by firms, even in the same region—a strong clue that management plays a significant role.[6]

This report aggregated numbers from a variety of firms, but other reports called out specific companies, showing that Uber was the standard bearer for exclusion of women and underrepresented minorities: tech employees were 48 percent Asian, 46 percent White (non-Latino), 2 percent Latino, and only 1 percent African American. Only 15 percent of technical employees at Uber were women.[7] Yet none of Uber's Silicon Valley peers looked impressive. Regarding hiring women, Facebook (17 percent female), Google (19 percent), and Airbnb (26 percent) had slightly better success employing women in tech jobs.[8] Outside Silicon Valley, the overall tech workforce average in 2017 was not too different from Uber's numbers on race/ethnicity: evenly split between White and

Asian (47 percent each), with only 6 percent Latino and 3 percent African American.[9] There has been upward movement at some companies, but the pace has been glacial.[10]

It is common for employers to point to faults in the education system for these low numbers, as I will show in this chapter. Employers can point to the low numbers of women receiving bachelor's degrees in computer science—about 19 percent of all such degrees in 2017, the most recent year for National Science Foundation (NSF) statistics.[11] That is a shockingly low number, especially given that women have composed the majority of bachelor's degree recipients for years.[12] Perhaps even more alarming is that the numbers were better years ago. Women received 21 percent of computer science degrees in 2006, and 27 percent in 1997.[13]

Yet low numbers of women and minority computer science graduates can also be framed as a failure of employers to entice more women into computer science, rather than the universities' failure to do so. Why would you get a degree for a sector that doesn't seem interested in hiring someone like you? The same is true with African American and Latino STEM graduates. For instance, some reports indicate that tech firms hire African Americans and Latinos at half the rate they earn computer science and computer engineering degrees.[14] Different studies have somewhat different numbers, but NSF data show that Latinos earn about 11 percent of computer science degrees, and African Americans about 9 percent—numbers far higher than their representation in the Silicon Valley and overall tech workforce.[15]

Diversity for women looks better in the life sciences, but only if we exclude leadership positions. The Biotechnology Innovation Organization, an advocacy group for biotech with a global reach but with membership mostly (almost 90 percent) in the US, surveyed its members regarding representation of women and minorities. Although the survey did not provide detailed information on STEM occupations, data from member companies showed that women made up nearly half the employees (about 45 percent) at the average company in the group—an impressive number, especially compared with Silicon Valley and tech. Women faced more and more barriers as they moved upward, however. Women constituted only 30 percent of executives, 18 percent of board members, and 16 percent of CEOs, numbers comparable to Silicon Valley and tech.[16] Despite the openness to women workers, the numbers for African Americans and Latinos in the surveyed biotech companies, however, were similar to those in Silicon Valley and tech throughout the hierarchy. African Americans constituted 4 percent of total employment, 3 percent of executives, and 1 percent of board members, while the numbers for Latinos were 5 percent, 3 percent, and 3 percent, respectively.[17]

The energy sector—specifically, the oil and gas industry—has devoted time and attention to diversity issues. For example, the World Petroleum Council has collaborated with Boston Consulting Group (BCG) to study gender inequality in the sector, and oil and gas executives cooperated with McKinsey for a study on diversity in their industry. BCG reported that for North America, the percentage of women overall in this sector—not just STEM—was only 23 percent in 2021. It also found the familiar story of the numbers of women decreasing at higher levels of the corporate ladder.[18]

The situation looked even worse according to McKinsey's oil and gas diversity report. In that assessment, women made up only 15 percent of this sector's workforce, which put it last in a list of nineteen sectors, even below software and "IT services and telecom." In addition, the McKinsey report noted that the oil and gas sector was last at hiring women in entry-level positions, and this sector also reduced their representation in leadership roles more severely than did other sectors.[19]

Why was the oil and gas industry studying its own diversity problems? McKinsey's report noted the urgency for this sector to diversify because young people showed unwillingness to work for this sector. Specifically, between 2009 and 2018 and among engineering and IT students, the oil and gas industry fell from the fourteenth most attractive sector to work for to the thirty-fifth.[20] This problem motivated Royal Dutch Shell's impressive efforts to train workers in STEM skills, as discussed in chapter 5.

WOMEN AND MINORITY STEM PERSISTENCE BY OCCUPATION

STEM employment is much bigger than the aforementioned three sectors, of course. The NSF's National Survey of College Graduates (NSCG) can give us a fuller and more rounded picture of what is going on regarding diversity in STEM, and where employers are succeeding or not in retaining women and minority STEM grads in STEM jobs. Employers are claiming shortages in the traditional STEM occupations, and government and philanthropic efforts have focused on creating more STEM

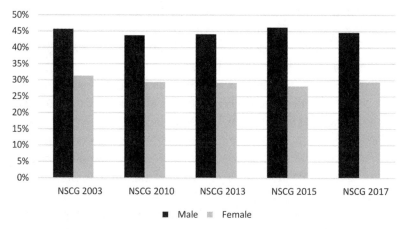

FIGURE 6.1 Persistence in STEM occupation by gender and National Survey of College Graduates (NSCG) survey year.

grads, so in this section I present data on persistence in STEM occupations by gender and ethnicity/race. I include a series of years to highlight whether there is improvement evident over time.[21]

Figure 6.1 shows how persistence of STEM grads in STEM employment varies by gender over several years. There are three big takeaways here. First, persistence is below 50 percent for both men and women, which may be surprising if we keep in mind the continual drumbeat of messages of the appeal of STEM jobs. Second, women STEM grads' persistence in STEM occupations is far lower than that of men. Third, it has hardly changed over time. In fifteen years of employers complaining about shortages, they have done nothing discernible to improve their attraction and retention of women STEM grads.

The story on race and ethnicity (figure 6.2) is a bit more complicated but also shows employers' failure to attract and retain African American and Latino STEM grads in STEM jobs. There are three takeaways here as well. First, we see again that overall persistence is low in STEM jobs, with only Asian Americans edging above 50 percent in some years. Second, White STEM grads consistently are more likely to persist in STEM occupations than are African Americans and Latinos, though the differences are about 5 percent rather than 15 percent, the approximate differential between men and women. Third, as with gender, the race/ethnicity numbers on persistence are, in a word, *persistent*. They persistently show inequality and failure of employers to equalize retention by race

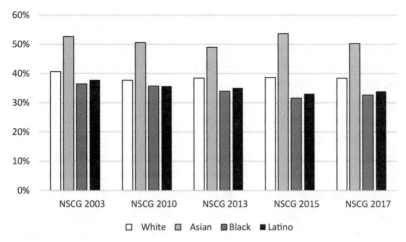

FIGURE 6.2 Persistence in STEM occupation by race and ethnicity, National Survey of College Graduates (NSCG) survey year.

and ethnicity despite their claims of scarcity. But before we get too sanguine about Asian Americans' high rates of staying in STEM, there is evidence that this is because of blocked opportunities, especially to the ranks of management.[22]

The broad STEM category obscures variation by field. Women's persistence in STEM occupations is boosted by their strong numbers in life sciences, where they compose nearly 50 percent of STEM workers. African Americans have concentrations in computer and math science (8 percent of the total) and Latinos in engineering (9 percent of the total).[23] Overall, however, the data consistently show that women and historically underrepresented minorities are earning STEM degrees yet avoiding traditional STEM occupations in order to use STEM expertise elsewhere or move out of STEM entirely. If we want to increase the return on our investments in STEM education, the employment conditions faced by these graduates are important targets for intervention. But what are employers doing that might lead minorities and especially women to leave?

Employers' Response: The Lack of Diversity in STEM Jobs Is Someone Else's Fault

What's behind these numbers? If there is a severe shortage of STEM workers, as tech employers claim, we might expect them to be bending over backward to do what they can to recruit and maintain a diverse workforce. Tech employers, for their part, have acknowledged that there are problems with gender and ethnic diversity, but they appear to have trouble acknowledging their own contributions to those problems.

Instead, these employers tend to avoid responsibility and blame others.[24] They typically locate the cause of their lack of diversity to be not in the culture and practices of their own firms but in the wider society, especially the schools. Facebook's former chief operating officer, Sheryl Sandberg, stated, "We are not going to fix the numbers for underrepresentation in technology or any industry until we fix our education system and until we fix the stereotypes about women and minorities in math and science." Sandberg thus saw the problems only on the supply side: "Girls are at 18% of computer science college majors. We can't go much above 18% in our coders if there's only 18% coming into the workplace, and at every level, more boys stay in than girls in every industry. In order to move numbers, we all understand that we have to increase the numbers going into the funnel." Sandberg called on the wider society to take responsibility: "How as a society do we get there? . . . I think we suffer from the tyranny of low expectations."[25] She wasn't referring to her apparently low expectations of what Facebook itself, a monopoly at one point worth half a trillion dollars, could do to help women at the firm.

As we saw in chapter 5, firms do sometimes make high-profile efforts to boost training, especially for underrepresented minorities and women, but these often appear designed to bring about some good publicity and encourage students to use their products. Sandberg herself announced a major effort in 2020 to support "Black and Diverse Communities," including efforts to boost tech diversity outside Facebook (millions of dollars to Black-owned small businesses, and a multitude of programs to train people from Black and Latino communities—who were not Facebook employees—in "digital skills"). Facebook did announce goals to employ more African American, Latino, and women workers but provided little detail on what changes the firm would make to achieve those employment goals.[26] Other tech firms, including Google and Microsoft, have also focused diversity efforts on the supply of workers going through the nation's schools rather than coming in their doors.[27]

Tech employers get most of the attention, but they are not alone in favoring a supply-side approach to diversity. High-profile reports and analyses, often published by the prestigious National Academy of Sciences, have also looked to the schools and the wider society to solve the perceived problems of STEM worker scarcity and diversity. Rather than focusing on employer practices and whether STEM grads of all backgrounds are thriving at work, however, they have called for schools to pump out more diverse STEM graduates.

For example, recall the influential report from 2005 that I discussed in chapter 1, provocatively titled *Rising Above the Gathering Storm: Energizing and Employing America for a Brighter Economic Future*. Despite the phrase "employing America" in the title, this report reinforced the frame that directs attention away from employers. It contained warnings and exhortations regarding America's investments in science and technology and STEM education. A joint project of the National Academy of Sciences, the National Academy of Engineering, and the Institute of Medicine, the authors, organized as the Committee on Prospering in the Global Economy of the 21st Century, consisted of leaders from a variety of sectors. These included higher education (Cornell, Harvard, Massachusetts Institute of Technology, Rensselaer Polytechnic, Rockefeller, Stanford, Texas A&M, University of Maryland, University of Virginia, and Yale), primary and secondary education (the Maryland State Superintendent of Schools), philanthropy (the education-focused O'Donnell Foundation), a national lab (Lawrence Berkeley National Laboratory), and industry (top executives from DuPont, Eli Lilly, ExxonMobil, Intel, Lockheed Martin, and Merck). *Rising Above the Gathering Storm* offered many strong recommendations for schools and colleges to increase and diversify the numbers of STEM students and majors. But it did not offer suggestions on what employers could do, proactively, as key partners in the retention of these workers.[28]

More recently, the market-oriented American Enterprise Institute came to similar conclusions about the proper targets of intervention in its otherwise insightful report on diversity in STEM. Though presenting a review of the literature and original interviews with women and minorities in STEM jobs that highlighted discriminatory experiences at work, the report's several recommendations for reform similarly focused on education and not employers, stating, "The underrepresentation of women and racial minorities among STEM professionals is a direct result of underrepresentation in the educational pipeline."[29]

There are indeed factors outside employers' control that affect diversity in STEM. For example, women's confidence and sense of self-efficacy, as well as their identities as engineers and sense of belonging, are related to persistence in STEM jobs.[30] Wider cultural beliefs about gender and ability can shape career preferences, and a pernicious linking of technology with masculinity in American culture can push women away from tech jobs.[31] Some women in STEM put responsibility for their lack of STEM jobs on themselves, referring to women's inferior skills or motivation. This is especially true of those in top levels of their organizations.[32] But rather than waiting for the wider society to somehow fix itself, or targeting women and minorities for attitude changes, other evidence strongly suggests that employers could constructively focus on what they can control: their own work environments.

The Unwelcoming Environment for Women and Underrepresented Minorities in STEM Jobs

There is evidence, both anecdotal and from social science research, that points to the kinds of workplace experiences that could lead women and underrepresented minorities to leave or be excluded from STEM employment. Here, I first consider personal and journalistic accounts and then present the evidence from social scientists revealing how widespread perceptions of unwelcoming environments are, as well as how they are experienced at particular stages of employment—recruitment, interviews, and everyday work.

THE VIEW FROM THE INSIDE: WHAT STEM WORKERS SAY ABOUT DIVERSITY

To understand why firms must change their practices to improve the outcomes of STEM education, it is crucial to incorporate the perspectives of women and minorities who have worked in STEM. Personal accounts—blogs, social media posts, essays, books, statements to reporters, and formal complaints of discrimination help us understand that simply graduating more diverse STEM students will not stop many women, African Americans, and Latinos from leaving.

For example, African American workers at Facebook—a major target of complaints—have described experiences that led them to feel excluded and unvalued. A former manager named Mark Luckie argued (in a Facebook post) that Facebook had a "Black people problem" and maintained that company practices made the few African Americans there feel marginalized. Luckie reported that Facebook executives did not consult the few African American workers at the firm for any insights on how to reach the African American market or cultivate their Facebook engagement—even though consultations with diverse employees are standard market outreach practice at many firms.[33] In fact, Luckie told of African American workers being *dissuaded* from sharing their thoughts at work in ways similar to other employees. In Luckie's view, this and other forms of everyday discrimination (e.g., being "accosted" by security; receiving discriminatory comments from managers) contributed to low morale among African Americans.[34]

An anonymous posting from current and former employees on the website Medium, an open platform for digital publishing, maintained in its title that "Facebook Empowers Racism Against Its Employees of Color." It stated that Black people at the company were "treated every day through the micro and macro aggressions as if we do not belong here."[35] Three African Americans even filed formal complaints against Facebook with the Equal Employment Opportunity Commission (EEOC), alleging bias against African Americans in hiring, evaluation, promotion, and pay. Though the complaint did not originate with STEM workers, it extended to the entire company:

> Donating millions of dollars to civil rights organizations does not wash away or justify the unfairness, inequality, and hostility that Black workers experience every day at Facebook—when they are turned down for jobs for which they are exceedingly qualified, when they are unfairly evaluated by mostly white peers and managers, when they are denied promotions by overwhelmingly white managers, when they are reprimanded or criticized for sharing their constructive views about diversity, when their lower pay reflects these systemic biases, and when they are assumed to not match the white-dominated "culture fit" that drives so many employment decisions at Facebook.[36]

Further evidence of the exclusionary impacts of an opaque goal of "culture fit" comes from Antonio García Martínez's book detailing his years working at Facebook. Martínez was a product manager at Facebook for two years, focusing on the advertising team.[37] In one revealing section—not about diversity specifically—Martínez described how tech firms celebrate their supposedly unique corporate cultures, but the imperative of preserving a firm's culture also affected hiring in ways that led to exclusion and discrimination. Specifically, he explained:

> Alignment with that culture is overwhelmingly important. Being handy with the C++ programming language isn't good enough—you also have to be one of us in thought and spirit.
>
> In reality, though, it usually worked like this:
>
> A female candidate who will buzzkill your weekly happy hour?
> "Cultural fit."
> A soft-spoken Indian or Chinese engineer, quietly competent but incapable of the hard-charging egotism that Americans almost universally wear like blue jeans?
> "Cultural fit."
> Self-taught kid from some crappy college you've never heard of, without that glib sheen of effortless superiority you get out of Harvard or Stanford?
> "Cultural fit."[38]

The use of a subjective "cultural (or culture) fit" standard is a common dynamic of exclusion, and not just in STEM,[39] but Facebook, supposedly facing a STEM worker shortage that required major lobbying for STEM migrants and education, seemed to use it especially egregiously. Rhett Lindsey, an African American who worked as a recruiter for Facebook for eleven months before he resigned in frustration, told the *Washington Post*, "There is no culture-fit check mark on an application form, but at Facebook it is like this invisible cloud that hangs over candidates of color."[40] An African American operations manager, Oscar Veneszee Jr., similarly explained, "When I was interviewing at Facebook, the thing I was told constantly was that I needed to be a culture fit, and when I tried to recruit people, I knew I needed to find people who were a culture fit. . . . But, unfortunately, not many people I knew could pass that challenge because the culture here does not reflect the culture of Black people."[41] Reproduction of company culture could therefore be a recipe for reproducing the demographic makeup of the firm, as Veneszee argued.[42]

Facebook is far from the only tech company that has been the site of racial controversy. Chanin Kelly-Rae, Amazon's global manager of diversity in the cloud computing division, quit her job in part because, as she told tech news site Recode, Amazon's human resources (HR) executives prevented her from seeing demographic data related to promotions to management jobs. African American women at Amazon also reported being asked to smile more, being asked for permission to touch their hair, and having White colleagues and managers steal credit for their work. Four African American women felt compelled to get mental health services, and others transferred, even took a demotion, to avoid toxic managers. Amazon also reportedly slotted African American workers into positions lower than their qualifications would indicate, including the placement of African Americans with PhDs into the same level as entry-level college grads from other backgrounds. At Amazon, interviewers excluded some diverse applicants based on a culture-fit criterion of "earns trust." Kelly-Rae commented, "What does it mean? It's a catchall. It means nothing so it can mean everything."[43]

Uber also has been the focus of critical appraisals on its diversity efforts. In chapter 3, I discussed the tragic story of Joseph Thomas, the software engineer at Uber whose torturous work experiences led him to take his own life. It is not a coincidence that Thomas was African American. According to the lawyer representing Thomas's widow, Uber maintained a "cutthroat environment . . . that had tones of racism in it, in that one big indicator of success is mentorship and leadership. But there is no real black leadership at Uber to help a young African-American employee. I don't think Uber cares about things like that."[44] At the time of Thomas's suicide, only 1 percent of Uber's tech employees were African American.[45]

Tech companies, no matter how profitable and wealthy, have also received unwanted attention for practices that exclude women, such as refusing to consider the needs of women who bear children or suffer from miscarriages or other pregnancy complications. At Amazon, a woman who endured the heartache of birthing a stillborn child was subsequently put on a special plan to improve her performance. That worker left, explaining "I had just experienced the most devastating event in my life," but Amazon told her she would be watched "to make sure my focus stayed on my job."[46] One worker told BuzzFeed that at Uber, "You pretty much have to behave like a man to succeed."[47] But not necessarily a good man. Blatant, boorish violations of sexual harassment law could be given a pass, even by employers supposedly desperate for STEM talent.

This was the experience of Susan Fowler, a computer engineer who worked for Uber and wrote a blog post that went viral in which she detailed the sexual harassment she experienced from one of her managers. Fowler had been on a team project that suited her skills. The manager in question allegedly told Fowler—via chat messages—that he had an open relationship with his girlfriend and was looking for female sex partners. When Fowler complained to HR, they told her that the manager was a "high performer" (as evidenced by performance reviews) and the company did not want to punish him. After all, he was a first-time offender, they explained. Fowler moved to another team, less suited to her skills. She later met more women at the company who also had experienced harassment, including from the same manager. They, too, said that HR told them to forgive him because this was his "first offense."[48]

Though some observers have described Uber as having an "asshole culture" (as described in chapter 3), others have pointed out that all of Silicon Valley has an "asshole problem" and is a "Brotopia"—meaning that these conditions can be found elsewhere.[49] Emi Nietfeld, formerly an engineer at Google, would likely agree, as she had a story remarkably similar to Fowler's. Nietfeld did not have a family of her own, explaining in the *New York Times* that she "structured my life around my job" at Google. This made it all the more painful when a manager repeatedly harassed her for about a year. When she finally complained, Google investigated for three months while still requiring Nietfeld to continue to work with him, eventually finding that the manager violated company rules. The investigative team told Nietfeld that the manager "received a consequence that was severe and that I would feel better if I could know what it was, but it sure seemed like nothing happened." She eventually left the firm. Google, supposedly trying to diversify its supposedly scarce STEM workers, made almost no effort to retain her, according to Nietfeld.[50]

Google's union has made exclusionary cultures an issue. First, an instigating incident to the union's formation was that the company paid million-dollar exit packages to executives accused of sexual harassment, including a massive $90 million payment to Andy Rubin, who was a force behind the creation of Android, Google's mobile phone software. Google offered the windfall despite a credible harassment claim against Rubin. When the story of the payment made it into the *New York Times*, Google employees were outraged, and they organized a walkout. More than twenty thousand workers participated around the world, including three thousand in New York City alone. It would not be long before they had a union. Following the firing of artificial intelligence (AI) expert Timnit Gebru after she criticized discriminatory AI models at the firm, the union expanded its concerns to include racism and other forms of exclusion at the tech giant. Similar efforts at other firms, including Kickstarter and some video game makers, have also pointed to gender and race discrimination issues at tech employers.[51]

SURVEY AND OTHER DATA REVEAL THE DIVERSITY PROBLEMS IN STEM EMPLOYMENT

The reports from women and underrepresented minorities discussed in the foregoing section are not selectively presented to make things look bad. Social science research mostly confirms the insider and journalistic accounts of how firms contribute to their own diversity problems. It also identifies some of the broader exclusionary patterns that can lead some workers to leave STEM jobs. Researchers most frequently focus on traditional binary gender, and I will highlight these studies of how women come to feel excluded, but it is easy to imagine how this work could translate to other dimensions of difference, including race, ethnicity, and the more nuanced concepts of gender found within the lesbian, gay, transgender, and queer/questioning (LGBTQ) community.

Though much of the work I describe in the sections that follow focuses on STEM without the non-STEM comparison, there are reasons to believe that discrimination is worse in STEM—despite the employer complaints of shortages. For example, the Pew Research Center found that 50 percent of women in STEM jobs say they have experienced gender discrimination, while only 41 percent of women in non-STEM jobs say the same. In computer jobs, 74 percent of women reported gender discrimination. The types of discrimination included earning less for the same job; treated as not competent; experiencing repeated, small slights at work; and feeling isolated at work. The numbers for race discrimination were also worse in STEM: 62 percent of African Americans in STEM jobs report race discrimination, but only 50 percent in non-STEM jobs.[52]

The Importance of Opportunities, Pay, and Work–Life Balance for Women in STEM Jobs

There is some social-science evidence that the exodus of women and minorities out of STEM is related to inequality on straightforward bread-and-butter issues. Economist Jennifer Hunt's study comparing women in engineering with women in non-STEM jobs found that women's higher exit rates from engineering were driven mostly by women un-happy with pay and promotion opportunities.[53] Psychologists Nadya A. Fouad and Romila Singh found similar issues when they conducted a survey of five thousand women engineering grads from thirty US univer-sities. They compared women who left STEM employment with women who persisted, finding that persisters were significantly more likely to perceive opportunities for advancement, to use opportunities to train for those promotions, and to use work-life balance benefits.[54] Perhaps most distressing for anyone wanting to maximize the STEM workforce, in this study there were strong correlations between intentions to leave one's firm with leaving engineering entirely.[55]

Researchers repeatedly find the importance of work-life balance for women in STEM. The issues also affect men but typically hit women much harder. Sociologists Mary Blair-Loy and Erin A. Cech have shown that women are almost twice as likely to leave full-time STEM employ-ment after having their first child as are men (43 percent of women leave, compared with 23 percent of men). Starting a family also is asso-ciated with staying full-time employed but outside STEM—12 percent of women of women with kids make the switch, and 71 percent of those say that the reasons were "family-related." Women who report being most devoted to their careers and employers are more likely to thrive in STEM jobs but tend to feel overloaded when they have children.[56]

How Recruitment Practices Can Limit Diversity

Much of the research into diversity in STEM employment has shown that the problems are not as easily remedied as simply equalizing pay, adding more training, improving perceptions of these factors, or adding a work-life balance program. Employers' culture—practices, beliefs, attitudes—also matters.[57] Toxic culture is both a powerful driver of exclusion and a difficult problem to fix because it can operate subtly yet be pervasive, unsettling, alienating, and impactful. These negative impacts may start even when firms are recruiting.

Sociologist Alison T. Wynn's study of technology firms' recruiting sessions at Stanford found that firms invited all students to attend yet signaled to women that they were less welcome and more marginal. Re-cruiters' presentations put women in background (nonspeaking) or sec-ondary roles while using men to discuss the company's technology. Pre-sentations also showed images of stereotypically masculine men (e.g.,

Don Draper, the womanizing lead character from the TV show *Mad Men*) and sexualized women (e.g., provocatively dressed women in the music video for the Korean global hit "Gangnam Style"). Students learned of supposedly fun work environments, but the fun catered to "brotopia" tastes—beer fridges and beer pong tables, foosball, scooters, and so on. The swag on offer also had brotopia themes, such as bottle openers, beer steins, and jokey T-shirts with sexualized, sophomoric messages such as "I'll show you my data if you show me yours." Geeky references to nerd culture especially popular with men (*Star Trek*, video games) were present in 40 percent of the sessions that Wynn studied.[58]

This early alienation may not be limited to the Valley's brotopia—the study of more than five thousand women engineering graduates across the US found that 11 percent never even took a job in engineering, with 24 percent of these early leavers reporting that they had lost interest in engineering (for some unstated reason), 18 percent left to start a company on their own, and another 17 percent disliked engineering culture. It is not clear whether feelings of exclusion were parts of these factors, but it is easy to imagine that would matter. Comments from these early leavers included, "I went to an interview, and there were no women other than secretaries in the firm," and "I'd have to go to the third floor to go to a women's bathroom."[59]

The interview process itself can also work to exclude women. As discussed in chapter 3, many STEM job interviews include segments where interviewees must solve technical problems in front of interviewers, typically on a dry-erase board. That might sound pretty stressful, and it is certainly stressful to many interviewees. A randomized control study compared computer science problem solvers in front of interviewers with other participants who solved the same problems but privately. The researchers measured stress and "cognitive load" levels, finding that both were higher in the dry-erase board situation, while performance was lower. Notably, the women in the study had consistently lower performances in the public setting—all women failed when others watched them, but all women succeeded in the private setting.[60]

Gergely Orosz, formerly an engineer at Uber, perceptively identified a way that Uber had made its culture an unwelcoming environment for women, and Orosz was able to identify a simple fix at the interview stage: include women interviewers and pay attention to how interviewees behaved toward them. As Orosz explained, "We started rejecting candidates just because they were unwilling to make eye contact with the female interviewer or acknowledge their presence." Orosz and members of his team found that some candidates simply refused in interviews to engage with women on a professional and technical level, and they took the unusual step of making this behavior disqualifying for STEM workers no matter their skill level. He wrote, "The shocking outcome of this change for me was this question: How many people did we hire in the past with all-male loops who were in the group of 'unwilling to acknowledge females or assume they are technical'?"[61]

The Unwelcoming Culture of Everyday STEM Employment

Exclusionary practices, beliefs, and attitudes are not just part of recruitment and interviewing. Once on the job, the unwelcoming culture and attitudes that Wynn and Orosz saw in recruiting may continue to be a regular part of work lives.

Sociologist Jennifer L. Glass and her colleagues showed this in their study comparing women in STEM jobs with professional women in non-STEM jobs. Women left STEM jobs at higher rates, and most surprisingly, women with advanced STEM degrees—those who had invested the most money, time, and effort toward their STEM education—actually were *more* likely to leave STEM careers. Most left in their first five years of employment, and analyses indicated it was not because of long hours, earnings, family leave policies, or moves into management at tech firms. After ruling out a variety of factors, Glass and her team concluded that the main factor pushing women out of STEM jobs was "the team organization of scientific work combined with the attitudes and expectations of coworkers and supervisors who hold more traditional beliefs about the competencies of women in these rapidly changing fields."[62] In other words, these women faced work cultures that defined them as less capable than men. Fouad and Singh's study of engineers across the country provides more insights: women and minorities who left engineering were more likely than those who stayed to report incivility in the workplace, being belittled, treated in condescending ways, and being undermined by supervisors.[63]

But we need to drill down more. Ethnographic and interview studies reveal that signals of exclusion or marginality could appear mild in isolation, but the cumulative impact could be severe. Researchers have highlighted how masculine cultures in engineering in both the US and UK affect styles of interacting, topics of conversation, humor, and social networks. Engineers working in oil fields, for instance, were shown to swear a lot, including using the adjective *fucking* with great frequency—a practice that made some women as well as both male and female workers from Middle Eastern backgrounds uneasy. Men's humor often was coarse and filled with sexual innuendo or graphic sexual references with similar effects. Powerful informal networks formed that were exclusively male.[64] A study of geoscientists in the oil and gas industry found that expectations of self-promotion (that is, statements and actions to call attention to one's own accomplishments and ideas) worked in favor of White men because they were more comfortable with these practices. Managers' broad discretion allowed bias to shape decisions: one male manager required a woman geoscientist to have her work approved by a male colleague before he would accept it, while doling out important responsibilities to male colleagues. Male managers provided explicit justifications when offering opportunities for women, highlighting their novelty and strangeness.[65]

Work cultures like these can make gender—and more specifically, how workers *perform* gender—a salient and fraught part of their workday. Researchers have found that some women in STEM jobs believe that behaving in stereotypically feminine ways leads male coworkers to view them as incompetent. To be perceived as competent, women needed to act like "one of the boys"—thus incorporating discriminatory stereotypes into their work lives.[66] Similarly, White and Asian women in STEM who identify as LGBTQ and present themselves as gender fluid can find a greater sense of belonging in STEM workplaces, enjoying perceptions of competence, and avoiding microaggressions that conventionally feminine women experienced (such as being ignored in meetings even if the meeting is about their projects, not being looked in the eye, and getting more questioning than men did about decisions they had made).[67]

At the same time, there is evidence that men in STEM might expect, and even ask, that women behave according to stereotypes that might cut against perceptions of their competence. An African American female engineer in the American Enterprise Institute study recounted, "No one really complained about my work. Everyone thought I did exceptional work, but comments got back to me like, 'Oh, Rick said you'd be nice if you smile more.' And I'm like, 'What does my smiling have to do with my work?' . . . I think I came in very naive and thinking, oh, I'm going to just work really hard like I did in school and I'll eventually rise up in the ranks but never saw that happening."[68] Not surprisingly, given these cross-pressures, another study of women in STEM found that moves to management could be welcomed in part because they allowed some escape from the stereotypically masculine-cultured world of IT.[69]

Sociologist Rebecca Franklin's interview study of college-level workers at a Silicon Valley company revealed how marginalized workers, especially African Americans, try to manage their workplace interactions to mitigate their feelings of exclusion. She found that these workers were painfully aware of how few African Americans worked in STEM-oriented firms in Silicon Valley compared with other sectors and regions. As one African American female project manager explained, "So, it's not about technical skill or ability, it's not about leadership quality, it's not about qualifications. It's about who you want, and who you don't want—and those people (Black people)—are not people that you want."[70] Somewhat analogous to some women performing gender in ways that allowed them to better integrate into STEM workplaces, Franklin showed how African American workers put energy into "relational labor," where they worked to find common ground with their non-Black coworkers on anything from following sports teams to having a nanny for their children. One African American male engineer who struggled to fit in with White colleagues' interests in country clubs, horses, bikes, golf, and boats, emphasized a shared interest in guns, but seeing his lack of advancement at the firm, chose to leave.[71] An African American male engineer in the American Enterprise Institute interview study of women and minority STEM workers similarly told of his efforts to connect with his White manager, even learning about hard rock bands such as Aerosmith and AC/DC.[72]

This extra amount of energy required to get through the day could make the worry about layoffs that all STEM workers experience even more devastating. An African American female electrical engineer in the American Enterprise Institute study said that although identifying as a "workaholic," she left engineering before an anticipated layoff could force her out, noting that her mental health had suffered at work. She explained poignantly, "Mentally, I had checked out. I didn't care because I was like, well, I don't feel like they care about me. . . . I knew that when that next round of layoffs came, that I probably was going to get laid off. And I didn't care because at that point I had been looking for other jobs for like a year before. . . . [My] boss came down and he was like, 'Carla, are you leaving?' And I'm like, 'Yes.' He's like, 'Why?' And I was like, 'I'm tired of fighting. I'm tired.'"[73]

Employers Claim STEM Shortages, but Older STEM Workers Feel Excluded

Older workers may also feel excluded from STEM jobs that are supposed to be facing shortages. A survey of leading STEM-oriented companies with a focus on tech showed that workers tend to be quite young, with median ages varying, depending on the firm, between twenty-nine (Facebook, LinkedIn, SpaceX) and thirty-eight (Hewlett Packard).[74] Tech companies, however, like employers in pharmaceuticals, biotech, energy, and other sectors, do not include age in their diversity statistics. This is the case even though some older workers complain about blocked opportunities and chilly work climates in STEM, especially IT.

Exclusion based on age is a major problem for anyone interested in growing the STEM workforce because older workers represent the greatest investment in STEM education and training. Moreover, age discrimination can affect women and minority workers as well as White and Asian men. My treatment of the topic is not as comprehensive as the exclusion of women and underrepresented minorities only because there is relatively little scholarly attention to age discrimination in STEM.

Journalists, however, have been quite willing to highlight age discrimination in STEM, especially for jobs related to software and computers.[75] They have shown that some STEM business leaders have openly discussed youth as a qualification for STEM work. For example, Mark Zuckerberg, then aged twenty-two, openly stated his agist stereotypes to an audience of 650 people at an event on start-ups at Stanford: "I want to stress the importance of being young and technical. . . . Young people are just smarter. Why are most chess masters under 30?" He then gave other reasons to avoid older workers: "Young people just have simpler lives. We may not own a car. We may not have a family." He summed up, "Simplicity in life allows you to focus on what's important."[76] Other titans of STEM speak this way and without shame. A cofounder of Sun Microsystems (once a major computer maker and a key developer of the Java programming language), Vinod Khosla, declared that "people under 35 are the people who make change happen; people over the age of 45 basically die in terms of new ideas."[77]

It is difficult to imagine CEOs or former CEOs speaking this way about any other category of people. Culture can be set at the top, and statements of open discrimination from some of the more powerful tech leaders can set standards and norms for how managers and workers in countless companies will behave.

A message of age exclusion seems to filter down to the rank and file in STEM. The *New York Times* profile of Amazon (discussed in chapter 3 and earlier in this chapter) found older workers filled with anxiety. For instance, "40-year-old men were convinced Amazon would replace them with 30-year-olds who could put in more hours, and 30-year-olds were sure that the company preferred to hire 20-somethings who would out-work them."[78] The *New Republic* reported on men in Silicon Valley getting cosmetic surgery—not to impress potential partners but to pass as younger at work.[79] A fifty-something worker at Google had a suggestion for making STEM work more welcoming to all ages, targeting the same brotopia culture that alienates some women ("bros" are male, White, and also young): "Team social events shouldn't require physical prowess or alcoholic excess—so forget paintball and bar crawls."[80] *USA Today* quoted Aileen Gemma Smith, forty-five years old and CEO of a tech start-up in New York City, who said, "Ageism is very real, especially in start-ups where being older is seen as a liability. . . . It assumes you won't work hard, [you'll avoid] long hours, and [you] have out-of-date skills. . . . I have certainly experienced investors in New York and Silicon Valley who looked down on myself . . . for not being 'young' enough to innovate."[81]

Quantitative data supports the media message of STEM as a younger person's game. In 2017, the job site Indeed surveyed tech workers in the US (methodology and response rates not reported, but respondents averaged almost sixteen years of work experience, so they were not entry level). It found that 43 percent worried about losing their job because of age, 18 percent said they worry about this "all the time," and 36 percent said they had experienced age discrimination.[82]

A 2017 survey of STEM workers by Modis, a staffing firm, was revealing in multiple ways. With respondents about evenly divided between men and women, the survey found that the greatest percentage of respondents reported age as the biggest challenge to diversity (39 percent), while gender was mentioned by 29 percent, ethnicity 23 percent, and religion 10 percent. Age mattered a lot in who had these perceptions, however, as younger workers (aged twenty-five or younger) were more likely to report gender as the biggest challenge (34 percent reported gender, while 25 percent reported age), while older workers were more likely to report age. Specifically, of respondents aged fifty-five through sixty-four,

59 percent believed age was the biggest diversity challenge.[83] Another study, conducted in the US and the UK in 2018 by Dice, a website that connects employers and STEM workers, similarly found that the older the STEM workers were, the more likely they were to be concerned about age being a barrier to getting a new job, with nearly 90 percent of workers aged fifty through fifty-five concerned about age discrimination.[84]

Older workers have taken legal action against major tech companies for age discrimination. Age-discrimination complaints to the California Department of Fair Employment and Housing have targeted Hewlett Packard (also known simply as HP), Cisco Systems, Apple, Google, Oracle, Genentech, Yahoo, Intel, LinkedIn, Facebook, Tesla, and Twitter. The *USA Today* report on a lawsuit against Google began with some snark directed at the company: "How does age factor into one's Googleyness? Plaintiffs Cheryl Fillekes and Robert Heath allege that it plays a significant role."[85]

A common age-discrimination complaint is that when tech firms initiate layoffs, they tend to target older workers. The lawsuit against Hewlett Packard alleged that the company deliberately "made it a priority to transform itself from an 'old' company into a 'younger' operation," through layoffs.[86] This age-related pattern in layoffs was the basis of a federal EEOC investigation of chip maker Intel, which laid off twelve thousand workers in 2016. Workers aged forty or older had double the chance of being laid off as those younger than forty, and those older than sixty seemed especially targeted—they had an eight times greater chance of being laid off than did those younger than thirty.[87] The EEOC has investigated similar practices at IBM, where 60 percent of layoffs were of workers older than forty. These workers were sometimes scored as high performers, sometimes replaced with younger workers, sometimes forced to train replacements before departing, and sometimes brought back as contract workers with lower pay and fewer benefits.[88]

For older workers, exclusion may be part of a conscious strategy. Economist William Lazonick has argued that STEM-oriented firms discriminated against older workers by deliberately structuring their retirement benefits to attract younger workers and to discourage workers from staying long—that is, they wanted "churn," with older out and younger in. They did so by exclusively using defined contribution (401[k]) plans rather than defined benefit (pension) plans that rewarded longer employment.[89]

These practices may be driven by cost concerns. Wages in STEM tend to go up with experience even if more experienced STEM workers must struggle to keep their skills current, and so older workers tend to make more money than younger workers. Employers using a burn-and-churn management strategy will find attractive targets in older workers because of the savings when they are forced out.[90] Not surprisingly, older engineers appear to have greater difficulty finding a new job if unemployed, and they spend more time unemployed. One study tracked this exclusion by age: for every year of age, unemployed engineers spent on average an additional three weeks without a job.[91]

The exclusion of older STEM workers makes it easier for the youth-oriented, brotopia culture to develop deep roots, alienating some older workers who do have STEM jobs, and not just women. One academic interview study of IT workers—one of the few to focus on age issues—affirmed that the gendered, masculine culture of tech was biased toward specifically *younger* men, linking youthfulness and technical ability and marginalizing older workers.[92] The youth culture of STEM may be especially salient to older workers if they had a manager who was younger than themselves.[93]

There are some indications of these patterns in job satisfaction surveys in the National Survey of College Graduates. It is a common pattern for older workers to express greater job satisfaction than younger workers (as a CBS News report on national job satisfaction poll put it, "Not happy with work? Wait until you're 50 or older"[94]). But this pattern does not seem to hold in all STEM jobs, and it looks especially different in computer jobs. For example, 48 percent of non-STEM workers in their fifties said they were "very satisfied" with their jobs, but only 41 percent of computer workers in their fifties felt the same way. On the younger end, where we expect lower satisfaction, 38 percent of non-STEM workers in their twenties said they were very satisfied, but 42 percent of workers in the youth-oriented computer occupations said so.[95] Though the differences are not great, younger STEM workers in computers are more likely to be satisfied than older workers, reversing the usual pattern.

To be sure, employers appear to target older workers for layoffs in every industry, not just tech or STEM, and the problem is growing.[96] But we should not expect STEM workers to look like everyone else on layoffs because STEM workers are supposedly in short supply. Employers desperate for STEM workers would presumably see the wisdom of sending signals that STEM provides both lucrative *and long* careers.

Foreign Workers and Diversity in STEM

Some final issues on the US return on investment in STEM education relate to STEM workers brought in from outside the United States. This issue is a little more complicated than employer discrimination against foreign STEM workers, though there is evidence that this occurs.[97] It regards foreign *temporary* workers, on what the federal government officially categorizes as "nonimmigrant visas," especially the H-1B visa. This visa has been the subject of considerable controversy since Congress created it in 1990. Supporters point out that when STEM-educated foreigners come here to work, or are educated here and then stay to work, they represent a boon to the STEM workforce. If educated abroad, the US might gain from their skills without paying for that education. If educated in US universities, Americans can gain as well, especially when they are the world's best and brightest who come for PhD STEM programs. The downside is that the structure of the visas allows too many employers to exploit H-1B workers, taking advantage of lax wage oversight and a provision that enables employers to sponsor the H-1B worker for a permanent residence visa (represented by an identity card known as a green card) and eventual citizenship in the US. Many workers covet the green card for access to high American wages and standards of living, and they thus will endure poor work conditions, overwork, and low pay in the hopes that the employer will choose them for green card sponsorship. Even worse, others may come to the US to learn how to do American jobs and then go back home, typically to India, to perform the job for lower pay, while American workers may be laid off. Researchers have shown these patterns in the visa and employment data for years, and whole businesses have grown to manage the use of the H-1B for job outsourcing.[98]

The pathways to green cards are not necessarily exploitative. Very highly skilled workers, including foreign STEM PhDs from American universities, use the H-1B as a bridge to a green card—and these workers are essential to drive the American innovation economy, with little indication of "crowding out" American citizens.[99] But the exploitation scenarios can significantly hurt the return on investment in STEM education.

Just as it was not likely a coincidence that the Uber engineer who died by suicide was an underrepresented minority, it is not likely a coincidence that Qin Chen, the Facebook worker who died by suicide, was on an H-1B temporary visa. Though not doing low-level work—Chen was doing "advertisement engineering," which was critical to Facebook's profits—it is likely that his status as a temporary foreign worker played into his decision to take his own life. As I described in chapter 3, Facebook covered up the incident as well as it could, but it is known that Chen had recently received a critical performance review, and (according to his colleague Yi Yin) felt especially vulnerable because of his visa status. Yin, who did his best to draw attention to the incident (Facebook fired him for his efforts), also pointed to H-1B workers' precarious status as a reason why other foreign workers stayed quiet. Yin explained, "Most Chinese workers are on H-1B visas, and don't want to make any trouble," adding, "I really wanted the Chinese engineers to stand up and speak for ourselves."[100] It is easy to imagine worried H-1B workers like Chen accepting low wages and poor conditions, not wanting to "make any trouble." The ripple effect is that American workers may fear being seen as too expensive in comparison and thus likely targets for the next layoff.[101]

In fact, many American citizens have been laid off and replaced by H-1B workers, though the typical pattern is that the job leaves the US with the foreign worker. Because the H-1B can enable US employers to outsource STEM jobs to other countries, the visa can make it easier for employers to lay off STEM workers in the US, thereby reducing returns on investments in STEM education. There are several high-profile cases of American workers being laid off, and employers have even forced them to perform the humiliating task of training their own replacements (they made severance packages contingent upon agreeing to do so). For example, Disney laid off about 250 tech workers in 2014 and forced them to train their H-1B replacements. Leo Perrero, one of the laid-off workers, said, "It was embarrassing to break it to my wife and children," adding that "to be cast aside like that was very demoralizing."[102] Tech workers at Southern California Edison faced a 500-person cut and were also compelled to train their replacements. One of those laid off, who feared losing her home, said, "They just want to get rid of us and clean house."[103]

The presumably kinder, gentler world of nonprofits is not immune from the practice. The University of California, San Francisco (UCSF), laid off forty-nine full-time IT workers and eliminated forty-eight contractor positions at the university's medical center, also compelling the laid-off workers to train their H-1B replacements. UCSF's H-1B scheme, which would save about $30 million over five years, led to unwanted media attention and a lawsuit. According to the *Los Angeles Times*, the jobs involved "managing and backing up most of the system's data; management and administration of its data networks; operations related to its telephones, email and video conferencing; and payroll and financial applications." These were not innovation economy jobs, but they were STEM jobs, and at least some of the workers mentioned in the article made $100,000 or more per year. Nine of the workers filed a discrimination complaint with the state; their ages ranged from forty-three to fifty-seven.[104]

Should STEM grads worry that they will be next? Scholars have debated what makes jobs more likely to be outsourced or automated, with no firm conclusions. Policy scholar Ron Hira, an expert on outsourcing and H-1B visas, cautions that the outsourcing trends and dynamics are shaped by many factors, including other countries targeting some business sectors for growth. This factor suggests that students in STEM fields (or any fields) should follow the news on their career of choice to see what its prospects are for outsourcing as they further their studies.[105] The rise of remote work in the 2020s, and the continually improving technologies that enable it, may soon make the visas unnecessary to outsource STEM jobs.[106]

Conclusion: What Should Firms Do to Improve Diversity—and Why Don't They Do It?

In early 2021, while the US was in the midst of the COVID-19 pandemic, National Public Radio interviewed Reshma Saujani, the CEO and founder of Girls Who Code, a nonprofit with the mission of increasing the supply of women with this in-demand STEM skill. Despite her supply-focused mission, Saujani knew, especially during the pandemic, that women's opportunities in STEM would not significantly increase without employers changing their practices. As Saujani explained it, "I don't think that companies are solving the talent gap in their company. So almost 40 percent of my Girls Who Code alumni said that their internship or their full-time offer had been reneged. . . . So, you know, I think that this next administration really has to shine the light on the private sector to say, 'What are you doing? What is your plan?'"[107]

The evidence in this chapter indicates that Saujani was exactly right to put the focus on the firms and how they have contributed to their own skills gaps and supply problems, pushing STEM grads away from STEM and reducing the payoff of the national investment in STEM education. The problems of diversity in STEM jobs do vary by field and how STEM is measured, but they seem especially bad for women and African Americans, and especially in IT and engineering jobs, which is exactly where STEM worker shortages are supposed to be the most pressing.

There is also evidence that age diversity is a problem, at least or especially in software and computer jobs. The exploitation of workers coming in from other countries on H-1B visas, while not a diversity problem in the traditional sense, is another employment practice that can drive away American STEM workers while unfairly burdening those who use these visas.

Like the leader of Girls Who Code, I have argued that employers are contributing to their own diversity problems. They engage in or tolerate practices that are driving women, underrepresented minorities, and older workers away while at the same time complaining that schools are failing to give them enough STEM grads. If they really care about access to the wide range of STEM talent, this behavior is irrational. There is evidence that from the moment they start recruiting new STEM workers, their own practices, policies, and cultures lead them to miss diverse talent and can drive away many potentially good workers. Especially in tech and engineering, employers maintain organizational cultures that are based on the assumption that workers are young and male, and typically White and American. If you are not one of these things—and especially if you are none of these things—you are likely to feel as though you do not belong. Extending that feeling over forty hours a week or more, for fifty weeks a year or more, is going to be a lousy way to live.

If employers really care about diversity, how can they take responsibility? Part of the solution is simple: hire workers from more diverse populations. I suggest this not only because it will get their numbers more in line with availability but also because having more workers of diverse backgrounds can lead more like them to want to come. There is research that shows that African Americans avoid STEM majors and working for tech firms precisely because these firms hire so few African Americans, and that they see the low numbers of Black employees at a firm or in an industry as a measure of racial climate. The fewer African Americans employed, the more hostile the firms were assumed to be toward African Americans.[108] The American Enterprise Institute's STEM diversity report also noted the burden of being the only woman or the only African American (or both), explaining, "Workers who do not feel welcome at work and cannot rely on the camaraderie and support of their colleagues are unlikely to stay."[109] A key strategy for firms would be to start hiring a more diverse workforce to attract a more diverse workforce—and for firms to widely publicize that their numbers are improving.[110]

That may be hard to do if workers keep leaving soon after they are hired. Besides hiring a critical mass of women and underrepresented minorities, how can firms retain the women and African American workers they do have? In Fouad and Singh's study of women engineers, those who stayed in the game were also "significantly more likely to report both supervisor and co-worker support, and that climate was supportive of their need to balance work and non-work roles."[111] The key here is targeting change not at women and underrepresented minorities but at the people with whom women and underrepresented minorities need to work every day. Managers can't constantly police the language and behavior of workers, but evaluation and monitoring of workplace cultures and practices for exclusionary impacts could significantly boost retention.

Sociologists Frank Dobbin and Alexandra Kalev, leading experts on what works to increase employee diversity, have identified strategies that can help: using formal mentors for women and minorities, hiring diversity managers, and assigning diversity task forces. In Fouad and Singh's research, employers' use of formal or informal mentors, and the amount of use of mentors, made no difference in women staying.[112] But Dobbin and Kalev show how mentors can be helpful if implemented properly. One way they can help is when mentors and also managers learn from these relationships about the obstacles that women and minorities face at work and how those barriers can be removed. Mentors can also learn of the abilities and strengths of women and minority workers, which might otherwise be unseen or ignored, so those workers can be moved up when appropriate. Mentor assignments should be formal, however, because informal mentorships tend to reproduce gender and race/ethnicity exclusions.

Dobbin and Kalev also argue that diversity managers and diversity task forces can help improve diversity—*if* they have real power (recall that Amazon's diversity officers felt powerless and marginalized by Amazon's HR leadership). They can direct attention to the structural and cultural factors that that I have discussed that can lead women and minorities to leave, and if they have power, inform managers that they will be evaluated on the dimension of diversity. Managers may thus think twice about hiring or promoting yet another young White male and may regularly evaluate themselves for possible bias. Put simply, when those making the decisions are worried about their own bias, they are more likely to be unbiased. One can see how this new focus on diversity might lead to changes like that described by Gergely Orosz at Uber, where having women sit in on interviews allowed interviewers to see how workers and prospective hires treated women in a professional setting.

Another reason that diversity managers and task forces have an impact is that these centers of authority have incentives (beyond solving perceived skill shortage problems) to make sure that strategies to make workplaces more welcome are actually implemented appropriately. If there is oversight over the ideas, then there is more likely to be follow-through, which avoids the problem of great ideas that are quickly forgotten. At the same time, Dobbin and Kalev note that diversity "training" is typically *not* effective in changing hiring and promotion patterns.[113]

Regarding age discrimination, analogous actions can work as well. Simply hiring (or not laying off) older workers can create a welcoming critical mass and signal openness to age diversity. Ensuring that supervisors and other workers are aware of the cultural issues around age discrimination and that diversity officers and task forces include age discrimination in their missions can both contribute to a more inclusive environment that can relieve employers' perceived skill shortages.

But older workers are different from women and minorities in a crucial way that makes them more vulnerable: they tend to earn more. They earn more because they typically have more experience, and in most jobs that require skills, experience is linked with higher salaries. For this reason, employers' desires to cut costs make older workers vulnerable to layoffs and to replacement by cheaper, typically younger workers and, as we saw, by cheaper H-1B temporary workers.

The desire to cut costs by eliminating older workers points to business factors contributing to diversity problems in STEM employment. Corporations must answer to their shareholders, and if shareholders care most about stock prices over the short term, they won't care much about diversity. Employers may then pay lip service to the idea that diversity is important for their public relations but put the blame for workforce diversity problems on schools and the wider society, effectively offloading the issue while displaying concern.

There is indeed evidence that shareholders not only do not reward diversity but even punish corporations that take action that improves it. For instance, one study showed that firms that increased the number of women on their boards of directors saw their stock prices decline, and the decline was worse for firms that did more for diversity in their organizations.[114] Another study highlighted how hedge funds tended to avoid investing in firms that engage in "corporate social responsibility" because these activities indicated the firms had goals other than maximizing shareholder value over the short term.[115] The problems extend to start-up investment as well. Historian Margaret O'Mara notes that venture capital is "the tech ecosystem's least diverse domain," with White and Asian men constituting 78 percent of those who make start-up investment decisions, and they control 93 percent of all dollars invested. These findings, added to a clubby, insider-driven venture capital culture, provide clues to why exclusion in STEM remains chronic.[116]

As long as investors push employers to be laser-focused on generating profits and increasing stock prices in the short term, and as long as executives believe that the way to achieve these objectives is to cut costs at the expense of their own supposedly scarce workers, diversity will suffer, and the return on investment in STEM education will suffer. STEM grads will flee to other occupations, and we can hardly blame them.

CHAPTER 7

STEM EDUCATION FOR WHAT?

Investors, Employers, and the Purpose of STEM Work

Federal, state, and local governments, joined by employers, philanthropic foundations, and educators, push for more and more education in science, education, technology, and math (STEM). Students and their families are responding, and STEM majors are growing. Money, time, and energy flow into the effort to produce more and more STEM grads, over and above other (non-STEM) education. There appears to be a consensus that STEM education is an unmitigated good for society. But good for what? What are all these STEM graduates supposed to do? For what purpose should they deploy their STEM skills?

A quick recap: As we have seen, the three primary rationales driving the STEM education juggernaut in the US emphasize three different goals. First, STEM education is the answer to private-sector employers' regular complaints about a shortage of STEM workers. Second, STEM education is the answer to policymakers' desire for a more competitive, stronger America. Third, STEM education is the answer to opening up middle-class lifestyles for a more diverse range of the American population, as well as making more diverse talent available for employers.

As I have argued in the previous chapters, a problem with all these rationales is that they do not take into account how US employers treat our STEM grads—the products, so to speak, of our STEM education investment. I do not mean to suggest we should only care about STEM grads. We invest in the education of all workers, not just STEM. But we invest especially in STEM. STEM grads are supposed to be special, and especially scarce, and this why we should expect to see them treated especially well to keep them in the STEM game. The statistics showing that half or more of STEM grads move to non-STEM jobs should be alarming to anyone who believes we need more STEM education to produce more STEM workers.

These three rationales share another blind spot, one that is the topic of this concluding chapter: none of them say anything about the *purpose* of STEM jobs. The shortage rationale supports STEM education to fill job openings for STEM workers for any purpose. The competitiveness rationale supports STEM education to innovate but says nothing about what the innovations should be. The diversity rationale implies that STEM jobs should pay at least a middle-class wage but is silent on what kind of work these wages would compensate.

Less prominent but most important to me in writing this book is a fourth rationale: STEM education is needed to produce innovations to solve a great number of urgent and severe crises sweeping the planet, including climate change, plastic pollution, pandemics, and the destruction of biodiversity. This rationale *does* speak directly to what STEM grads might do with their STEM skills and knowledge. It is about innovation, but specifically innovation to save the planet from its current path of human-caused destruction. Though the competitiveness rationale may include innovations for national security (such as military defenses), it is silent about the nature of innovations for economic growth and economic competitiveness. For example, economist Enrico Moretti, who has argued for more investment in STEM education to produce more STEM workers, has stated, "In the end, it does not matter whether American workers make something physical, like more efficient lithium batteries for electric cars, or something immaterial, like a better search engine. What really matters is that American workers produce goods or services that are innovative and unique and not easily reproduced. This is the only way to generate jobs that pay well in the face of stiff global competition."[1]

Many workers, however, have value systems that lead them to reject some ways of producing goods or services that are "innovative" and "not easily reproduced." The purpose and meaning of work, and the nature of STEM employers' business models, can play a role in the exit of STEM grads from STEM if those business models do not align with STEM grads' values.

For example, although many STEM grads will be comfortable working for the defense industry for its role in national security and challenging technical problems, others may feel uncomfortable, especially when war, with its accompanying loss of life, starts. There are many jobs that have purposes and meanings that might make STEM grads feel uncomfortable and cause them to leave those jobs and possibly STEM, thereby diminishing the return on the STEM education investment. We observed this situation in chapters 5 and 6 with the struggles of the oil and gas industry in attracting STEM grads. But pollution-causing oil and gas are not the only morally troubling STEM employment sectors.

Here, in this last chapter, I examine this final factor that can lead STEM grads to leave STEM jobs: the purpose of the job. I do not mean to criticize workers who are excited about STEM work for the puzzles, the technical challenges, and the thrill of solving them, regardless of industry or business model. My point is only that not everyone is motivated by these more purely intellectual thrills, just as not everyone can tolerate, or get a positive adrenaline rush, from burn-and-churn management, the possibility of layoffs at any time, working as a contractor, the need to self-train just to keep skills current, and the challenge of staying or advancing in workplaces dominated by a brotopia culture. If there are forces directing STEM grads to jobs that don't improve the world and may even make it worse, and dissatisfaction with this environment can cause many to leave STEM, it is a problem for the return on investment of the STEM education enterprise.

I will argue here that job purpose *is* a problem for at least some STEM grads, and it goes beyond companies that pollute. Some of the most valuable companies in America are major employers of STEM workers, and some have business practices that have driven workers away. These practices, and these companies, are problematic, but the companies are caught in larger economic and cultural forces that lead investors to prefer precisely these kinds of companies. Improving the return on investment in STEM education requires understanding why investors support some businesses and not others, and how this situation can be changed to better serve STEM grads—and the planet.

STEM Education for . . . Morally Stressful STEM Jobs?

There are a lot of ways that people can find purpose and meaning in their lives, and work does not need to be a source of these for everyone or anyone. One can find purpose by being a parent, by volunteering in their community, by adopting abandoned pets, or by simply engaging in a social life.[2] But for many of us, work must have purpose, and moral meaning, because it is something we spend many hours a day doing, and perhaps more than half our waking hours, five or more days a week. It is reasonable for people to want a job that provides meaning and purpose, and STEM grads are no exception.

Jobs can provide a sense of purpose and meaning even if they have nothing to do with the world-saving/world-destroying dynamic I have in mind here. For example, researchers have shown that one's job tasks can be an expression of one's "authentic self"—for example, when they involve use of skills with which one might strongly identify. This might be especially likely if one is really good at those skilled tasks. A job also can provide a sense of purpose and meaning if one really likes one's co-workers. In that sense, a job can provide a sense of meaning through belonging and flourishing through enjoyable human interaction.[3] In this chapter, I am interested in jobs that provide a sense of *moral* purpose and the alignment of a job with a personal value system that emphasizes contribution to the greater good.

Research shows that when jobs lack meaning in this way, people may leave them or not take them in the first place.[4] Some scholars call it "moral stress," while others refer to "moral injury," but the result is the same: a feeling of conflict between one's work with one's personal values and beliefs about what is right.[5] Many moral challenges can occur on the personal level, such as colleagues backstabbing each other or a worker being aware that embezzlement is going on.[6] A study of why workers leave their jobs, using 1.3 million reviews on the employer review site Glassdoor, identified "toxic culture" as the primary driver pushing them to the exits, and one of the worst aspects of this toxic culture was "unethical" workplaces. Words that came up in reviews included "ethics," "integrity," "unethical," "shady," and "mislead," along with discussions of failure to comply with government regulations.[7] But workers can leave jobs because of larger problems with the business.

INNOVATION IS GOOD, BUT WHAT IF IT CREATES POLLUTION, ADDICTION, AND CANCER? OR JUST SELLS ADS?

I have had friends leave jobs because they were uncomfortable with the business model of the firm. It's a common problem and certainly not limited to STEM. For example, one left a job because its business was lending money to low-income people and charging exorbitant fees and interest rates. But when we promote investments in STEM education for the innovations that the application of STEM knowledge and skills can create, we would be wise to keep in mind that some innovations cause harms or do little to improve life, and this can affect STEM grads' choices about jobs.

I have already discussed the struggles of the oil and gas industry in attracting STEM talent for their new era of using data science and artificial intelligence (AI), forcing them to train their incumbent workforce (employers training their own workers is a good thing, in my view). Though there are no academic studies of exactly why STEM workers avoid oil and gas firms, and those firms seem to believe the cause is the blue-collar image of the industry (as discussed in chapter 5), the moral stress of producing pollution and destructive effects on the climate may be part of it. STEM grads may also be uncomfortable with fossil fuel companies' efforts to confuse the public about the causes of climate change.[8] This might be why some oil and gas firms have tried to burnish their image with increasing their talk about "climate," "low-carbon," and "transition," as well as pledges and opaque spending related to clean energy.[9]

Other companies that have business models that could cause moral stress to STEM workers are in pharmaceuticals. Some of these companies are justifiably celebrated for partnering with academia and the government to develop vaccines for COVID-19. But there are others in the pharmaceutical space that have different business models. Some firms buy the rights to drugs and then raise the prices to shocking and morally troubling levels. For example, a company called Questcor bought the rights to a drug used to treat childhood epilepsy and then increased the price per vial of that medication from $40 to $23,000. Following a $5.6 billion acquisition by another firm called Mallinckrodt, what was formerly Questcor ended up paying a $100 million settlement to the Federal Trade Commission for illegally acquiring the rights to a competitor drug in an effort to maintain its price gouging.[10] Other problematic practices can include drug marketing. Purdue Pharma, which developed the opioid painkiller OxyContin, aggressively marketed the drug. This marketing effort likely contributed to mass addictions and the deaths of about half a million people—but billions of dollars in profits for the company and the Sackler family who owned it. After a series of lawsuits filed by state and local governments, Native American tribes, hospitals, and individuals, the company declared bankruptcy and was dissolved in accordance with the terms of a criminal case settlement that required the Sacklers to turn over $4.5 billion to fund addiction treatment and prevention programs in exchange for receiving personal protection against civil claims.[11]

STEM workers innovating chemicals can have their own moral stresses. Chemicals can improve life in countless ways, but they can also cause great harm. Syngenta, a company that develops fertilizers and herbicides, uses a chemical called atrazine that scientists have shown causes birth defects in the male reproductive organs of amphibians and humans. Atrazine has made its way into human drinking water. That might trouble STEM workers at Syngenta, but also morally stressing is that the firm made major efforts to discredit scientists who found the relationship between atrazine and birth defects.[12] Then there is Monsanto, the company that makes a weedkiller called Roundup that has an ingredient, glyphosate, that research has linked to cancer. Bayer bought Monsanto—but now has to pay $10 billion in a legal settlement over the cancer that Roundup apparently caused.[13]

Then there are the tech companies. As I've said at multiple points in this book, about half of all STEM workers work with computers and software, and so retaining them will go a long way toward improving the return on investment in STEM education. Business models based on information technology (IT) might seem less life-threatening than fossil fuels, pharmaceuticals, and chemicals, but there are moral stresses that come with working in these jobs as well, including at some of the biggest and most valuable companies. Most basically, they center around the fact that the purpose of a lot of tech business models, their way of generating profit, is simply to sell stuff and not improve life. A quotation that multiple media picked up in the early 2010s captured the meaninglessness (and by implication, the moral stress) of STEM jobs provided by many of the world's most profitable tech companies: "The best minds of my generation are thinking about how to make people click ads." An article in *Bloomberg Businessweek* attributed that quote to Jeff Hammerbacher, then a research scientist at Facebook. Hammerbacher added his own judgment to this state of affairs: "That sucks."[14] Other news outlets quickly used his quote, both in the US and abroad.[15]

Hammerbacher struck a nerve because, I believe, he highlighted how business models based on software in general and selling stuff in particular were attracting both investors and STEM grads in great numbers.[16] The business of selling ads has created a premium for STEM software skills that can help target ads. Firms were hiring workers skilled in AI and data science so they could make predictions about the purchasing behavior of individuals, in tracking people using apps and internet browsers ("surveillance capitalism"[17]), in making the transfer of money more efficient (a big part of fintech and use for blockchain), and in other areas. The demand for such skills has attracted top STEM talent, including PhDs. But the demand for these skills goes well beyond the household-name tech giants like Google, as there are many firms using such technologies as part of their business models. For example, the magazine *Fast Company* lovingly profiled Stitch Fix, an online clothing retailer, that hired STEM PhDs. The firm did not hire PhDs for their sartorial sense but because of their computational and programming skills, including one who had his training in astrophysics. Stitch Fix invited users to input their fit, style, and cost preferences, and then the company would present to users clothes that match those preferences. The PhDs designed the software that made this matching possible.[18]

At the time of this writing, investors are also pouring billions of dollars into newer versions of AI that can write text and create images ("generative AI") even without clear business models.[19] Facebook has pivoted to the "metaverse" (hence the name change to Meta), which would continue the pattern of moneymaking through software and selling stuff.[20]

The demand for these kinds of skills allowed a former physicist named Jake Klamka to create an education company, called Insight, that has helped advanced STEM graduates in fields without direct commercial applicability seize these existing and growing opportunities in the innovation economy. Over seven weeks, Insight's fellows programs have equipped scientists with skills in AI, data science, data engineering, blockchain engineering, "devops" engineering (linking software development and other IT operations), and health-data science. Insight claimed to have placed fellows at more than seven hundred companies, including not only tech giants such as Amazon, Facebook, PayPal, and Salesforce but also firms far from Silicon Valley (Vanguard, Anheuser-Busch, Macy's).[21]

In short, tech employer demand for STEM skills is greatest in tracking, profiling, and selling. This may sound quite benign compared with dangerous chemicals and other pollutants, but as I explain later in this chapter, tech business models may be the most morally stressful of all.

ARE STEM WORKERS SATISFIED WITH THE PURPOSE AND MEANING OF THEIR JOBS?

The PhDs being recruited to do this kind of tech work are just the tip of a growing iceberg, with many more master's-level and bachelor's-level

STEM grads below them. Are they finding happiness and meaning that leads them to continue working in these jobs?

Academic researchers have not yet explored this question in detail, but some evidence does suggest that job purpose matters to STEM workers, and some of them experience moral stress or injury from working at tech companies. For some of these workers, this moral stress or injury relates to specific, discrete decisions that tech firms have made, but for others, it relates to the business model of the firm itself—that is, how it makes money.

First, there is survey evidence of variation in beliefs about the contributions of particular companies. In a survey of leading tech companies by Payscale, a firm that collects data on salaries so that employers and employees alike know what the wage norms are, among the questions was one on job meaning: "Does your work make the world a better place?" The survey found great variation in responses to this question. SpaceX, a company devoted to making rockets for travel outside the Earth's atmosphere, came out on top, with 92 percent saying "Very much so" or "Yes" in answer to this question. However, several companies had fewer than 50 percent of employees agreeing, including Amazon, HP, IBM, Samsung, and Oracle. Adobe came in at the bottom (only 24 percent said that working at Adobe made the world better). Unfortunately, the survey does not include any biotech or pharmaceutical companies, which might beat out SpaceX on the question of job meaning (especially if they do not make opioids or sell overpriced drugs).

Survey evidence is one way to look at how STEM workers feel about the meaning of their jobs, but it can miss a lot, too. Some STEM workers may easily adapt to the demands of consumer-oriented data science and be attracted to the intellectual challenge of, for example, building AI that can guess the clothing tastes of people thousands of miles away. But certainly not all. Reactions may range quite a bit. Marcel Haas, an astrophysicist turned data scientist, wrote poignantly in a blog about regretting his decision, stating that he was no longer motivated to work and missed having motivation. He admitted that it was "hard to get satisfaction out of my current job," explaining, "I miss passion and being proud of what I do" even though "the internet says I have 'the sexiest job of the 21st century.'" A commenter on Haas's post, Steve Herrin, felt similarly about this career move, explaining, "Thank you for writing this. I left neutrino physics to do the same thing in 2013 and this resonated with my own experience. I wish I had advice to offer. I try to tell myself the increased financial security and stability are better for me, but the alienation from my work takes its toll on my soul."[22] At the far end of the negative reaction spectrum is Wendy Liu, a former intern at Google, who left STEM work and wrote a memoir and political manifesto called *Abolish Silicon Valley*.[23] She argued that technology needs to be reclaimed for the public good, profits be damned.

The survey numbers hide this range of reactions and the level of moral stress. For example, two companies that Payscale showed as having high percentages of workers saying their work makes the world a better place are also at the center of controversy for their negative impacts on the world: Facebook (78 percent agreeing working at Facebook makes the world better) and Google (72 percent agreeing). Three-quarters of employees rallying around the purpose of their jobs sounds like a victory for tech's moral contributions, but a closer look suggests a high degree of moral stress and injury at these companies.

Let's start with Google. The search and advertising giant has long attracted not just STEM-skilled but also idealistic workers, and the founders themselves showed a moral side when they made "Don't Be Evil" Google's corporate motto at its founding in 2000. The company used the phrase in its corporate code of conduct, and it was even a Wi-Fi password on Google corporate shuttles. But sometime around late April or early May 2018, Google removed the language from its code of conduct.[24]

The change appeared to be more than cosmetic, as things were changing at the company. Employees had begun to have second thoughts and concerns about Google leadership's choices, which, by the 2010s, were getting into areas far away from internet search and ad sales, the original business. When some decided to form a union, they had some issues that one does not normally see among union activists, at least for blue-collar jobs: the ethics of the business model and strategies of the company. These concerns clearly reflected on the moral meaning of their work.

For example, the leaders of the unionization effort called out the company from moving away from its "Don't Be Evil" motto and listed several Google projects or strategies that they rejected, referring to Alphabet, the less-known parent company that officially owns Google:

Our bosses have collaborated with repressive governments around the world. They have developed artificial intelligence technology for use by the Department of Defense and profited from ads by a hate group. . . .

Organized workers at the company forced executives to drop Project Maven, the company's artificial-intelligence program with the Pentagon, and Project Dragonfly, its plan to launch a censored search engine in China. . . . We want Alphabet to be a company where workers have a meaningful say in decisions that affect us and the societies we live in. . . . But right now, a few wealthy executives define what the company produces and how its workers are treated. This isn't the company we want to work for. We care deeply about what we build and what it's used for. We are responsible for the technology we bring into the world. And we recognize that its implications reach far beyond the walls of Alphabet.[25]

Other employees left Google for reasons related to morality and purpose. Bruce Hahne, a fifteen-year veteran of the company, explained his decision to leave: "Google's current business practices and ethics are incompatible with me continuing to work for the company." Hahne mentioned "persecution" of LGBTQ employees, Google Cloud's contracts with fossil fuel companies, and military contracts that got Google into the "business of killing." Another employee left because he said the company demoted him after he started a human rights program.[26]

Whereas these complaints did not reach Google's ad-focused business model, they clearly reflected moral stress, and other complaints did get to fundamental ways that the firm makes money, at least on YouTube, Google's video streaming site. For example, some Google workers began to complain that YouTube was selling ads on anti-LGBTQ videos, but "demonetizing" videos (i.e., not compensating creators) that were supportive of the LGBTQ community.[27] About one hundred Google employees wrote a letter helping to convince San Francisco Pride to remove Google as a sponsor for the annual parade because Google was so slow to respond to their concerns.[28]

The complaints about YouTube got to the very business model of this Google division, which is similar to that of Facebook—a site that is itself free and distributes free products but makes money through the ability of the software to monetize user data through the selling of ads.[29] Facebook, despite a strikingly high percentage of employees who said they found moral purpose in their work in the Payscale survey, has also seen worker revolts over the firm's business model.

To get the most money for ads, both Facebook and YouTube seek to drive user engagement—that is, the number of times per day users go on the platforms, and the length of time of each session—with their free services in order to sell more narrowly targeted ads. To target the ads, the model calls for aggressively gathering as much data as possible on each user to both drive the user engagement (by giving each user more and more of what the AI will predict that they like) and microtarget the ads. Users see these ads when they log into Facebook or watch videos on YouTube (they also are served microtargeted ads when they perform searches on Google or Amazon). The companies auction off advertising opportunities through automated means designed to give the ad opportunity to the company that values each user's characteristics the most.

The problem is what appears to work best to drive people's engagement. As one critic put it, "The models that maximize engagement also favor controversy, misinformation, and extremism: put simply, people just like outrageous stuff."[30] Facebook and Google and a massive ecosystem of lesser-known companies involved in adtech turbocharge user engagement and data collection by cranking up the "outrageous stuff" that enrages users. These companies end up spreading lies and exacerbating conflict and hate.[31]

According to Joseph Bak-Coleman and his colleagues who researched the process, "Algorithms designed to recommend information and products in line with supposed individual preferences can create runaway feedback wherein both the user's information preferences and subsequent exposure to content become more extreme over time. Such path dependencies may have transformative effects, changing the preferences and values of the users themselves and leading to radicalization." Their study argued for increased public control of tech companies because of the toxic effects of this business model in health and policing, as well as its tendency to move young users to age-inappropriate content.[32]

Facebook seemingly has been involved in every important topic where distortions, lies, and conspiracy theories could drive user engagement. In early 2021, for example, when the federal government was rolling out lifesaving COVID-19 vaccines, the most frequently viewed articles on Facebook about the vaccines linked the vaccines—not the virus—to death.[33]

Though algorithmic feedback has implicated Facebook as a factor in death and violence, Facebook's leadership has shown little concern for the harm it was causing, apparently refusing to dial down its outrage machine because the outrage sells ads. Workers' performance reviews and thus salaries were dependent on *not* doing anything about the carnage the company seemed to be causing.[34]

But some workers did find the moral injuries of working at the company to be intolerable. In 2020, BuzzFeed reported on "key people" leaving Facebook and "torching" it in their departure notes. One who left was part of a "Violence and Incitement" division (meaning they were supposed to control violence and incitement, not produce more of it), and stated that although they were proud of their work, their efforts were futile: "With so many internal forces propping up the production of hateful and violent content, the task of stopping hate and violence on Facebook starts to feel even more sisyphean than it already is. . . . It also makes it *embarrassing to work here.*"[35]

That worker feared revealing their name, but others have been bolder. Max Wang, a software engineer, left Facebook and shared a video in which he explained his reasons for leaving, stressing his moral injuries. "I think Facebook is hurting people at scale," he said, adding that "we are failing" and "what's worse, we have enshrined that failure in our policies." Another engineer posted on an internal message board that he was taking time off work "to refocus, but I can't shake the feeling that the company leadership has betrayed the trust my colleagues and I have placed in them."[36]

The tendency for President Trump to make racist, name-calling, and otherwise inflammatory comments on Facebook created more dissension, as the company executives let it go, even when rival social media platform Twitter started to put warning labels on such statements saying they incited violence. The situation became more heated following a decision to let a Trump post remain on Facebook. The post in question attacked Black Lives Matter protestors, and Trump appeared to call for his followers to use violence to stop them when he wrote, "When the looting starts, the shooting starts." Jason Toff, a Facebook director of product management, said on Twitter that he was "not proud of how we're showing up." Internal polls showed workers' plummeting support for Facebook leadership and the idea that Facebook was making the world a better place.[37] One employee commented to BuzzFeed news about Facebook's involvement in political misinformation, "Personally this makes me so angry and ashamed of this company."[38] There was more employee criticism when insurrectionists openly planned on Facebook their January 6, 2021, attack of the US Capitol.[39]

In perhaps the most damning instance of a Facebook employee expressing regrets about the meaning of their work, former Facebook data scientist Sophie Zhang—who had just been fired—authored a 6,600-word memo, apparently sent to her colleagues, in which she blasted Facebook's pernicious effects on world politics. Her moral injuries and stress were palpable. As a key employee on the Facebook Site Integrity team, she reported that "I have personally made decisions that affected national presidents without oversight, and taken action to enforce against so many prominent politicians globally that I've lost count." She saw governments using fake accounts to push public opinion in various ways to help or hurt candidates and outcomes in a great variety of countries, including India, Ukraine, Spain, Brazil, Bolivia, Ecuador, Honduras, Azerbaijan—and, of course, the United States. She explained, "There was so much violating behavior worldwide that it was left to my personal assessment of which cases to further investigate, to file tasks, and escalate for prioritization afterwards." Facebook's policy was to prioritize issues that were public relations problems for Facebook, and not to protect democracy and people. In the latter cases, Zhang stated, "we simply didn't care enough to stop" the antidemocratic manipulations and harassments. "I have blood on my hands," Zhang agonized.[40]

Though Google and Facebook have been prominent sites of moral stress and injury, other tech companies have made business decisions that have alienated their workers or made their jobs feel meaningless or worse. The spur to the formation of a union at Kickstarter, the online crowdfunding platform for creative projects, was a business decision to cancel support for a particular project. The project, a satirical, anti-racism comic book, gained attention because it was called *Always Punch Nazis*. This offended the right-wing media gadfly Breitbart News, which argued that the project violated Kickstarter's terms of service (these stated that funded projects must not encourage violence). Kickstarter leadership agreed, but employees fought back. At an all-hands meeting, according to *Slate*, "One engineer stood up and said he couldn't continue to work at a place that would give in to people trying to have a 'both sides' debate about Nazis."[41]

A company does not have to do something as dramatic as support Nazis, aid political repression, or spread life-endangering misinformation to lead workers to feel that a job is meaningless or causes them to feel moral stress. Some business models for firms hiring STEM graduates may simply encourage vanity, lower people's self-esteem, or get people addicted to video games.[42] What is important to understand is why so many employers of STEM workers do not make the world better and why so few of those employers seem to be using STEM grads to help solve urgent national or global problems. The answer requires us to understand the people who have power over employers: the investors.

How Investors Lead STEM Grads Away from Morally Meaningful Work

Tech employers have appeared most frequently in this book as case studies and examples. It made sense because they include the most valuable companies in America, they employ a lot of computer and software experts, and these kinds of jobs make up half of all STEM jobs. Despite the huge roles that pharmaceuticals and biotech (e.g., Pfizer), oil and gas (e.g., ExxonMobil), and engineering (e.g., GE), play in our lives, tech companies typically far outpace them in market capitalization—that is, in the total value of shares of that company. Investors flock to these kinds of companies. The reason is because, as I discussed in chapter 1, many people in the investment world—fund managers, consultants, business journalists, executives, and scholars—appear to have converged on a set of ideas related to shareholder maximization. Put simply, this approach says that the more a company can generate short-term profits without employees or tangible assets, the more attractive it is for investment. This mindset has led to the treatment of STEM grads as expendable despite their supposed scarcity, and it also has led investors to tech companies and away from other business models. Somewhat similar dynamics direct venture capitalists to invest in start-ups that look like these tech companies.

The problem is that many of the key technologies we will need to improve and even save the planet will require manufactured, tangible products. Better energy sources (think fusion reactors), better batteries, better plastics, better energy transmitters, better ways to capture carbon in the atmosphere, better food sources for a growing population—all of these will require something more than software.

Consider the companies that typically lead the rankings of most valuable companies. While the order will jump around a bit depending on the day, five tech companies tended to dominate the 2010s and early 2020s: Alphabet (Google's official parent company), Amazon, Apple, Facebook, and Microsoft. As described previously, these companies make most of their money from nontangible products, and the manufactured products they do have are made abroad. Even Apple's fastest-growing revenue generator, however, is not tangible: "services," which includes media streaming, cloud computing, and financial products.[43] None of these companies are really about selling products that make the world better in direct ways, such as clean energy or new drugs, and in fact critics have complained that they are now or have been monopolies that abuse their market power and snuff out innovation by crushing competitors.[44]

There are exceptions to the rule of intangible products made with few employees in the US attracting private investment. Some companies or sectors can become hot for a time, seemingly defying these patterns. Plant-based substitutes of animal products, such as Impossible Foods, became popular among some investors in the 2020s, and they have physical products made in the US, and also hold great promise in addressing climate change.[45] Tesla, another darling among investors in the early 2020s, manufactures cars and batteries in the US.

Tesla's story is illuminating in that it likely would not exist if it relied on private investors alone, and if it did not receive late-stage, significant government aid. It is thus an exception that proves the rule. Government funding was crucial for other tech giants as well—an unambiguous fact that is oddly invisible to many, including some of the beneficiaries of the government's key support.[46] The internet itself is a government creation, as anyone can see if they google "ARPANET," and Google's origins lie in the NSF's Digital Library Initiative.[47] But Tesla could not rely only on private investors even well after its start in 2003. Tesla was near bankruptcy in 2009 when the Obama administration's Department of Energy loaned the company $465 million. In 2011, the California Alternative Energy and Advanced Transportation Financing Authority provided tax breaks and incentives worth $31 million. On top of that, California's Zero Emission Vehicle Program provided California Tesla buyers a tax break of $7,500 for each vehicle purchased.[48] After that came some irrational exuberance among investors that baffled Wall Street analysts, who pointed out that Tesla appeared to be massively overvalued relative to its earnings, and certainly overvalued compared with other car manufacturers.[49] So there are certainly exceptions to the patterns I describe here, but they are rare cases with unique circumstances and relied on government help to a greater degree than most tech firms have.

Why Venture Capitalists Also Support Software over World–Saving Innovations

It is not just Wall Street investors who love firms that make profits without tangible assets or workers, however. Early-stage companies, which have no shares available on Wall Street, also encounter an investing environment that discourages innovations that are tangible and that depend on manufacturing, especially in the US. This is because venture capitalists (VCs), who provide the funding source of many innovation-oriented start-ups, have multiple reasons for avoiding firms that make products that can provide immediate moral meaning and purpose to STEM workers.

First, it is a buyer's market—there are far more innovators than there are investor dollars, and so VCs have a lot of choices. One study found that only about 7 percent of firms that had innovated (defined as having filed a patent) were able to secure VC investment.[50] Another found that only "one-sixth of 1 percent of new start-ups each year get venture backing."[51] Thousands of companies, many very worthy, can find no funding at all.

Second, if we look at those innovators grasping for investment dollars, we see that software companies are especially prevalent for the simple reason that it is much easier to innovate if you only have to write code or think up some other computer service, rather than invent something physical that will need to be manufactured. You can get started without any outside funding at all. You might not be able to prove there is a market for your innovation, but you can prove that your innovation works technically. You also do not have to worry about government regulatory approval, as is the case with medical treatments. Software companies can more easily predominate the range of start-up investment targets.[52]

Third, early-stage company investments are almost by definition risky because they are unproven, even for software—and most fail. About 60 percent of investment dollars go to projects that lose money. Only a few investments hit it big, such that about 70 percent of returns come from 8 percent of invested dollars.[53]

But there is more to the story of why so many STEM job opportunities in start-ups are geared toward some software niche. The VC aversion to funding innovations that are physical things that must be manufactured has been around for a while, and before software became so dominant among start-ups. For example, engineers in the US invented the now-ubiquitous flat panel electronic display that is a part of every laptop computer and television, but what became a $114 billion industry developed overseas in the 1980s owing to a lack of US-based investors.[54] Similar patterns continue today because of a factor that is not legislated anywhere: VCs want quick returns. They might have longer horizons than stock market investors, but they typically raise funds for ten-year periods, while expecting commercial viability in half that time or less. Uncertainty about an innovation's future must be resolved quickly in this set of expectations and beliefs.[55]

Management scholars Josh Lerner and Ramana Nanda point out that software companies are able to resolve that uncertainty with quick market feedback because the product itself is readily available.[56] It's a different situation for tangible inventions. As the economists Jonathan Gruber and Simon Johnson explain:

> The structure of venture funds is not well designed to provide financing for capital-intensive, long-run projects of the type that are often required for major technological advances. Such projects face a problem of going from the idea to demonstration of product viability that is known as the *valley of death*: a range where there are large investments required and the time period can be long before the investor knows for sure that there is a product that can be brought to market. . . . Sectors such as information technology in general and software in particular require relatively low levels of initial capital investment and short sales cycles that exhibit general commercial viability quickly. The venture model is perfectly suited for such opportunities.[57]

Thus, the "valley of death"—when the firm has started, is burning through cash at a rapid pace, but does not yet generate any revenue—is a major problem for start-ups outside software because they need to spend far more money to get going.

Given this context for funding and investing, it is not surprising that world-saving clean energy funding has languished at about 1.5 percent of the total venture capital funding.[58] A 2017 study by the Brookings Institution on the broader category of "cleantech" (defined as "technologies and services across a number of industries that minimize natural resource use or pollution, including advanced green materials, air, bioenergy, conventional fuels, energy efficiency, energy storage, geothermal, hydro and marine power, nuclear, recycling and waste, smart grid, solar, transportation, water and wastewater, and wind") found a pattern of decline from already low numbers. Cleantech investing grew rapidly from less than $1 billion in 2004 to a high of nearly $8 billion in 2011. But then—even as the world continued to experience ever hotter temperatures because of fossil fuel emissions—a decline started. For example, between 2011 and 2016, overall investment in cleantech declined about 30 percent, to $5 billion, the number of deals fell from 649 to 455, and the average deal size was smaller. Cleantech's share of overall VC investment dollars fell from about 17 percent in 2011 to 8 percent in 2016, while software grew from 32 percent to 48 percent, and pharmaceutical/biotech grew only slightly, from 10 to 11 percent.[59] A study of investments in the 2015–20 period found that three of the sectors with the most deals were all areas with, typically, no tangible products and thus no factories: fintech, AI, and digital health.[60]

Even worse for these world-saving investments is not just that they are riskier than software investment but also that the software investments provide big returns to VCs. Software investments had annualized gross returns of about 24 percent per year between December 1991 and September 2019. In contrast, cleantech yielded about 2 percent.[61]

So why not just have longer time horizons for investing? Lerner and Nanda have called the "uniformity of rules" dictating the short-termism of investors "puzzling" given that some innovations, such as new, safer, cleaner battery materials, require long gestation periods and extended periods of uncertainty. This "norm" (their word) of short fund lives was around in the twentieth century in many areas, not just technology, and "with the passage of time, such arrangements have then been taken as gospel by limited and general partners alike."[62]

The life sciences sector would seem to violate these basic cultural norms of investing that have a hold on American investors and greatly shape what work opportunities are like for many STEM grads. Biotech and pharmaceutical employment can have tremendous meaning for STEM workers because it can contribute to longer and more enjoyable human lives. Biotech and pharmaceutical companies, while not in the same league as the Big Five tech companies in terms of value, are important parts of the innovation economy, especially in the Silicon Valley, San Diego, and Boston regions.[63] But the life sciences are another exceptional case, and the situation here is not optimal for the life sciences, nor is it a model for other sectors.

There are three primary reasons the life sciences sector is different.

First, pharmaceuticals are exceptional in that they have very high profit margins, somewhere between 15 and 20 percent at the largest companies, whereas nondrug companies have profit margins typically around 4 to 9 percent.[64] One analyst predicted that Pfizer would earn profits of 60 to 80 percent on its COVID vaccine.[65] Healthcare investments from VCs yielded about 13 percent returns per year between 1991 and 2019, which lagged behind software (24 percent) but significantly exceeded cleantech's relatively paltry 2 percent return.[66] Moreover, new drugs can typically take advantage of existing factories and therefore do not require the massive start-up costs of innovations in areas such as batteries and clean energy. And indeed, new cell and gene therapies that *do* require new factories, which can cost about $200 million, struggle to find funders.[67]

Second, the long road of clinical trials on the way to a finished product, required by the US government to ensure that new therapies are safe, means that companies exist for many years without actually having anything to sell.[68] Many of these productless companies are listed on the NASDAQ stock market. As economist William Lazonick and his colleagues have argued, these firms "can raise funds through primary and secondary stock issues because of the willingness of stock-market traders, including hedge fund managers, to speculate on publicly traded biomedical shares, buying and selling them on 'news' such as that generated by clinical trials, but without any concern whether a commercial drug is ever actually produced." Yet while this strategy can supply needed funding to keep a company going (through stock issues), these investors are impatient and can quickly disappear—not the ideal situation for any longer-term innovations.[69]

The third, and perhaps the most significant and exceptional trait of the life sciences sector, is that the US government foots the bill for a tremendous amount of the basic science research that goes into new drugs and therapies. For instance, federal support of research in the life sciences in 2017 totaled about $34 billion. This was more than the *combined* funding of the other STEM fields ($33 billion, including computer sciences/math; physical sciences; other sciences; environmental sciences; and engineering). The next highest field was engineering, at about $13 billion.[70]

For examples of government commitment to—and subsidy of—biomedical innovation, look no further than the COVID-19 vaccines. Though labeled in the press as "the Moderna vaccine" and "the Pfizer vaccine," these labels obscured the massive public financing for both. Moderna would not have a vaccine if it were not for years of federally funded research at the University of Pennsylvania, the National Institutes of Health, the Defense Department, and a number of academic labs; then the federal government, through Operation Warp Speed, pumped in another $2.5 billion, as well as other technological aid and clinical trial support, for Moderna's efforts. Pfizer's vaccine was done in a partnership with a German firm, BioNTech, that developed the key technology with the help of what amounted to nearly half a billion dollars from the German government.[71]

In short, employers of STEM workers find themselves in a financial environment that creates incentives for business models that generate revenue without tangible assets and ideally without tangible products. This environment opens up opportunities for software innovations and closes off opportunities for the kinds of products that can save the planet. There are exceptions of firms that get hot and the biotech and pharmaceutical sectors, but these are exceptions, and they have relied on government help at crucial stages. The result is that without government action (as discussed in the following section), students interested in STEM subjects and innovation will find far more opportunities in software, especially software that helps companies sell stuff, than in saving the planet.

How to Deploy STEM Education with Less Moral Stress and More Positive Impact

Both government and private investors can have a positive influence in providing funding for innovations that can not only help save the planet but also create jobs that STEM grads will want to take because they find the work less morally stressful and more meaningful. I describe these influences in the following two subsections.

THE POSITIVE INFLUENCE OF GOVERNMENT FUNDING AND INCENTIVES

If the market is failing to provide optimal outcomes, more government funding for research and development in areas that can solve our manifold global crises could help not only solve the problems that desperately need solving but also provide a lot of rewarding and meaningful employment opportunities for STEM grads. There are some promising moves now bearing fruit. The 2005 National Academies report, *Rising Above the Gathering Storm*, which I have discussed critically at several earlier points in this book, contained the important recommendation to build on successes in defense research and private-sector partnerships in the Defense Advanced Research Projects Agency (DARPA) and create a new private-sector partnership for energy, the Advanced Research Projects Agency–Energy (ARPA-E). Congress listened and finalized this recommendation in 2007 in the America COMPETES Act. By 2009, ARPA-E had $400 million to spend. A 2020 analysis of the program's outcomes for cleantech start-ups showed some success, though the valley of death remained a problem.[72]

The Biden administration and Congress have been major forces in boosting investments in clean energy with a focus on making the transition from internal combustion engines to electric vehicles (EVs). Several pieces of legislation—the Bipartisan Infrastructure Law, Creating Helpful Incentives to Produce Semiconductors (CHIPS) and Science Act, and the Inflation Reduction Act—used a combination of grants, loans, and tax incentives to encourage investment in US-based EV battery production and other clean energy technologies. The Biden administration has also engaged the Defense Production Act, procurement, federal land use, and other measures to direct more government and private money toward planet-saving technologies.[73] Early indications are that the private sector is responding to the incentives, including energy companies that had previously worked against transitions to a clean energy future. With this new legislation, they see these moves as good business.[74]

THE POSITIVE INFLUENCE OF PRIVATE INVESTORS

However, we do not have to rely solely on the government for support of science crisis–solving opportunities for STEM workers. Other sources of support are available, such as corporate funding. Big companies in the life sciences have a track record of funding start-ups in that sector, for example.[75] There is less of this investment in the cleantech arena, though a few corporations have stepped up. A group of utility companies from around the world have created Energy Impact Partners, which has invested to help later-stage companies get through the valley of death.[76]

There are other possibilities—including, ironically, the support of billionaires who made their fortunes in tech. For example, Bill Gates, the founder of Microsoft, has shown great interest in global crises and even authored a book on the science needed to address climate change.[77] In 2015, he helped found Breakthrough Energy, an effort to support new technological development for clean energy. According to its website, "Breakthrough Energy's groundbreaking initiatives fund, develop, commercialize, and scale the technologies we need to build a net-zero economy and avoid a climate disaster."[78] Gates is also a major investor in Impossible Foods, the plant-based food company, along with Google Ventures—the investment wing of another company that made billions of dollars without tangible products.[79]

Though Amazon founder Jeff Bezos is known for his private space flight company, Blue Origin, he also used his billions of dollars in private wealth to create in 2020 the Bezos Earth Fund, which he described as an effort to "fund scientists, activists, NGOs—any effort that offers a real possibility to help preserve and protect the natural world." He put $10 billion into the fund (he was worth almost $200 billion at the time). In addition, and more squarely in the venture capital space, Amazon created a "Climate Pledge" fund with $2 billion for firms developing sustainable technologies to reduce carbon emissions and preserve nature.[80]

John Doerr, a Silicon Valley billionaire venture capitalist, also has made climate action a major goal and has invested in cleantech. Doerr made his fortune from investments in Google and Amazon, among others, and seems to care about the environment even though Google's YouTube platform has algorithms that spread misinformation about climate change.[81] Like Gates, he authored a book about the climate crisis, offering an action plan of how to move forward.[82] Doerr's firm, Kleiner Perkins, is a leader in investing in emerging technologies that can mitigate climate change, such as batteries, electric vehicles, and systems for accounting for carbon emissions. Doerr also donated $1.1 billion to Stanford University to create the Stanford Doerr School of Sustainability.[83]

Massive investments in software companies, which then create gigantic amounts of personal wealth for a very lucky few billionaires or companies, allow those billionaires or their companies to fund planet-saving initiatives that other investors shun. This is a roundabout way toward creating more meaningful jobs for STEM grads, but it is better than ever more money going for software and adtech.

Relatedly, the shareholder value maximization culture that has apparently led to so many destructive businesses and management practices could be a force for good—*if* investors see their value maximization as including inhabiting a livable planet.[84] There are some moves in this direction. Some investors have begun taking into account the risks and costs of loss of biodiversity, for example. As reported in *Vox*, in 2022, the World Economic Forum has ranked failure to act on climate change, extreme weather, and biodiversity loss as the top three most severe risks to the global economy in the next ten years. Banks, insurers, and large investors, have (according to *Vox*) "started pushing companies to disclose risks linked to the natural environment—known as *nature-related risks*—that might make their investments lose value over time."[85] Shareholder votes supporting action from corporations to mitigate carbon emissions increased from 25 percent support in 2017 to 59 percent support in 2021.[86] Even Carl Icahn, whom the *Wall Street Journal* called a "relentless Wall Street billionaire" and compared to a "ruthless corporate raider," used his shareholder influence to force McDonald's restaurants to have pigs treated more humanely at its supplier farms.[87]

It is an odd situation wherein some business and investing leaders may be more powerful than political leaders in protecting the planet—creating meaningful STEM jobs in the process—even though it is the job of political leaders to protect the commons. Some Republican members of Congress and their staff have even resorted to lobbying businesses to join them in the fight to preserve the carbon-based economy.[88] For now, at least, the momentum is moving the other way, toward planet-saving STEM-based efforts.

Choosing the High Road—or Legislating the High Road

There may be another approach to spur the creation of more morally meaningful STEM job opportunities. Perhaps we can stop or limit the number of opportunities that cause moral stress and injury. Perhaps in doing so, we can also discourage the burn-and-churn management, aversion to training, and lack of responsibility for diversity problems in STEM as well—all also related to the same financial environment that discourages morally meaningful STEM work.

I have emphasized at various points in this book the role of choice and decision-making by employers. There is a growing body of work on the decisions that firms make regarding the treatment of their workers. The common theme in this research is that, even in a financial environment that encourages practices harmful to workers, *employers do not have to do what they do*. Social scientists refer to this as "agency," but it essentially refers to the ability to make choices.[89]

Employers can *choose* to develop fair and efficient recruitment mechanisms. They can choose to pay their workers generously rather than the least amount possible. They can choose to manage them with care, professionalism, and respect. They can choose to make their employment secure and not precarious. They can choose to train existing workers for openings in the organization where new skills are needed. And they can choose to make their organizations more inclusive and welcoming to women, African Americans, Latinos, older workers, and workers from other countries. As management scholar Zeynep Ton has argued, employers can choose to take a "good jobs strategy," in which they provide jobs with good pay, benefits, and stability, and also manage in ways that employees "can perform well and find meaning and dignity in their work."[90]

The good news is that companies that make these choices perform well and can be among the most profitable companies in their sectors. The good-jobs strategy is therefore not just about values and morality, though those are in play here, but about being a well-run, profitable business. Ton's work focused on employers of low-skilled workers, but her arguments translate to employers of STEM workers as well. Indeed, it should be easy and uncontroversial to use a good-jobs strategy if there really is a scarcity of STEM skills and STEM workers really are greatly valued. Similarly, management scholar Thomas Kochan exhorts employers to use "high performance organizational models" and avoid low-road strategies that treat workers as costs rather than assets.[91] At a minimum, these choices can improve the lives of STEM workers—and all workers—no matter where they work or whether their jobs are really related to innovation.

Choosing the high road can encompass more than the treatment of workers. These simple ideas of choosing good paths can be extended to the business models of firms and the funding strategies of investors, including the government, in ways that make STEM jobs morally meaningful for STEM workers and can make real progress toward solving the various crises facing humanity. Google's motto of "Don't Be Evil," later modified to "Do the Right Thing," seems flippant and insincere in retrospect, but it was a start on the high road.

In short, even if investors want to put their money into planet-destroying business models, entrepreneurs do not have to create those opportunities. I once met a Silicon Valley business leader who told me of a friend's idea for an app that would encourage users to display their clothing choices for the day for other users to rank, praise, or criticize. They both agreed it would simply encourage superficial, narcissistic, and self-centered behavior that the world already had plenty of. They decided that this business model was not a good way to make money, even if investors might like it. More thinking like this might lead to shifts toward more morally meaningful businesses, and thus more STEM job opportunities, for STEM workers who want them.

The other way to make job opportunities more meaningful and less morally stressful to STEM grads is to use the law to close off options that are especially pernicious. In short, we can legislate high-road business models by prohibiting some of the low-road business models. We can enforce existing laws and regulations on pollution and product safety, but we will likely need to pass new laws that make some pernicious business models illegal, taxed, or regulated so that they are unprofitable.

Congress has made other profitable business models illegal after their harms became apparent. For example, after the Great Recession, Congress passed the Dodd-Frank Act, which limited what banks could do when it became apparent that banks' activities caused or worsened the Great Recession. Similarly, some academics and activists have seen the dangers in some tech business models and have called for legislative limitations.

One report by a group of legal scholars laid out what they called "a ledger of harms" committed by Google and Facebook. The list was extensive:

- "Spreading misinformation during a pandemic"
- "Invading user and business privacy"
- "Destroying local and independent journalism" (by controlling digital ad revenue)
- "Propagating fake news, disinformation, and polarization"
- "Facilitating discrimination" (because user profiles can have race, gender, age, or sexuality information)
- "Enabling unaccountable political censorship" (since they alone control what is on their platforms)
- "Imposing a start-up and small business tax" (firms must advertise on Facebook and Google to reach consumers)

- "Reducing innovation" (the firms acquire or undermine competitors)
- "Harming mental health" (they design their products to "promote addiction and unhealthy use" as well as feeding users increasingly radical content)
- "Harming physical health" (by allowing advertisers to target people who have disorders with ads that will make their disorders worse or will not help)[92]

It is exceedingly difficult in the US to restrict content on Facebook or Google (and its subsidiary, YouTube) because laws regarding government attempts to restrict speech have specified that attempts at restriction, with few exceptions, need to be neutral regarding the content of the speech. But American law makes a distinction between speech and expressive behavior (e.g., a sit-in protest), on the one hand, and simple behavior (e.g., speeding), on the other hand. There is nothing controversial about restricting *behavior* that is not expressive, and certain business models—including selling online microtargeted ads—are certainly fair game for restriction.[93]

For example, the federal or state governments can make it illegal to target ads based on data unique to specific individuals. Such an action would instantly destroy the incentives to collect data without the user's knowledge, and thus also at least some of the incentive to turbocharge extreme content—lies and conspiracy theories. Moreover, there may be no downside because banning this business model might not hurt the companies that want to buy these microtargeted ads very much. The rush to microtargeted ads is based on a *belief* that they work best, but some experts argue it is far from clear that this microtargeted advertising is superior to traditional advertising.[94]

Another legal approach to close off bad business models would be to make digital platforms legally liable for the lies that they spread. Here the legal strategy would be to reform existing law, specifically Section 230 of the Communications Decency Act. Congress passed this law in 1996, in the early days of the internet before any ad-based social media or internet search business models had become dominant. Courts have interpreted Section 230 to shield internet platforms from any legal challenges arising from content posted by third parties. This basically allows Facebook and YouTube to say, "We don't have legal responsibility or liability for the lies and conspiracy theories that our users post onto our platforms and that we, using algorithmic techniques designed to max-imize user engagement, push in front of as many eyeballs as possible." Therefore, some critics of these adtech business models have argued that to limit social harms, "platforms must be required to take urgent remedial action against controllable social harms, data collection that corrodes broader social values, and unregulated anonymity" and call for "adjustments to platforms' current blanket immunity from responsibil-ity under Section 230 of the Communications Decency Act."[95]

Encouraging firms to choose the high road on their treatment of workers and in their business models could help keep STEM grads in STEM jobs. Cutting off low-road business models could also help keep STEM grads in STEM jobs and thus improve the return on investment in STEM education by driving investor dollars to more useful compa-nies, creating more job opportunities at these companies, and making it less likely that STEM grads will say their job sucks, is embarrassing, or (in the worst case I've discussed) makes them feel as though they have blood on their hands.

• • •

Countless times since I started this project, I have had people question why I was writing about what I was writing about. "College-educated STEM workers have it great!" I was told. "Everyone wants these jobs." "This is not a sympathetic population you are researching and writing about." I have begged to differ and that is why I pressed on.

Certainly many STEM workers, including those in the traditional STEM occupational titles, love their jobs and are flourishing in them. That's great. But I believe the stakes are too high, and the efforts in STEM education too great, to not cast a critical eye toward how American so-ciety and especially American employers and investors treat scientists, engineers, and those in related occupations. As the authors of one study wrote, after reviewing wage disparities between STEM workers and oth-ers who were more highly paid, "If a society values science and tech nological progress, why aren't scientists compensated accordingly?"[96]

Why not indeed. As a former major in philosophy and sociology, I confess I have felt a bit odd at times in arguing for better treatment of graduates in subjects that were only marginal parts of my own univer-sity education. We invest a lot in the education of all Americans, and we should encourage respectful, fair treatment of all graduates, as well as doing what we can to maximize morally meaningful job opportunities for them. But what motivated this book was that we invest even more in the education of those studying STEM subjects—public and private funds, time, and effort—and we pin so many hopes on them. To solve STEM worker shortages (if they exist), boost American competitiveness, bring more diverse people into the middle class, and unleash the full power of scientists and engineers to dream up world-saving technologies to solve our multitude of global crises, we will have to do more than focus on school and university STEM education. We can do better to value what our educational institutions produce, and improving the treatment of STEM grads is a great place to start.

ACKNOWLEDGMENTS

This project was a long time in the making. It has required talking to and getting crucial support from a lot of smart and generous people.

My interests in this topic started with my interests in immigration. As director of the Center for Comparative Immigration Studies (CCIS), and with support from the Japan Foundation's Center for Global Partnership, CCIS organized a conference comparing the US (which takes in the most immigrants of any nation) and Japan (which takes in very few). I was surprised to learn from Philip Martin and Lindsay Lowell, both participants at the conference, that most science, technology, engineering, and math (STEM) graduates don't work in STEM, and the shortage narrative was badly flawed. My interests in STEM grew when the German Marshall Fund invited me to participate in its 2011 Brussels Forum. One panel there impressed on me the importance of technological innovation for economic growth, the importance of scientists and engineers in creating this innovation, and getting the policy right. Senator Mark Warner (D-VA) and Richard Fisher, then head of the Federal Reserve Bank of Dallas, vividly made these arguments. I thank all these individuals for unintentionally starting me on this project.

Much of the research for this project was supported by generous grants from the Alfred P. Sloan Foundation and the National Science Foundation (NSF). Daniel Goroff at Sloan and Nirmala Kannankutty at NSF were absolutely crucial early supporters of the ideas that eventually led to this project, with special focuses on worker training (Sloan) and movement in and out of STEM (Sloan and NSF). Others at NSF patiently answered many questions about the limits and possibilities of their data, especially John Finamore and also Lynn Milan and Steven

Proudfoot. Goroff also played a crucial role in getting me in contact with other scholars who expanded my knowledge and helped make related articles and this book possible. Both Goroff and Kannankutty were important sounding boards and inspirations.

With support from the Sloan Foundation and the Yankelovich Center for Social Science Research, I was able to organize two conferences related to the issues in this book. I thank both organizations for support and for all who attended and otherwise contributed to those conferences. I also thank, for providing opportunities for me to share some of the ideas contained in this book as well as for providing insightful audience feedback, the following organizations: Harvard Inequality Seminar, Kennedy School of Government; National Academies of Science, Engineering, and Medicine; National Science Foundation; Non-Degree Credential Research Network at George Washington University; Scandinavian Consortium for Organizational Research at Stanford University; University of California Center–Sacramento; and University of Arizona Department of Sociology. I am grateful to the Rockefeller Foundation's Bellagio Center for providing me with an inspiring environment and wonderful colleagues to aid the writing of this book.

Elizabeth Branch Dyson, editor at the University of Chicago Press, was a key supporter for the project, and I cannot express enough gratitude for all that she did. Her ideas and insights both inspired and improved this book in countless ways. Cutting text is often painful for authors, but she was able to show me how I can say more with less. Mollie McFee, also at University of Chicago Press, answered my endless questions regarding the process of getting the book to the finish line. Lori Meek Schuldt provided exceptional copyediting services and was a source of support during the process.

When you work a long time on a new project and talk to a lot of people, you realize it is impossible to thank them based on the contributions, and so in alphabetical order, I list everyone I can think of (and regret and apologize for leaving off some other others for whom I did not keep adequate records): Stephen Barley, Phil Blair, Mary Blair-Loy, Stephen Blyth, Diane Burton, Craig Callender, Peter Cappelli, Sean Carroll, Erin Cech, Neil Charness, Gerald Davis, Frank Dobbin, Doug Downey, John Evans, Rebecca Franklin, Richard Freeman, Paul Frymer, Neil Gong, Peter Gourevitch, Michael Handel, Ron Hira, Edward Hunter, Tomás Jiménez, Michael Kamal, Mel Katz, Erin Kelly, Lane Kenworthy, Anne Kim, Eric Klinenberg, David Land, Jennifer Lee, Kevin Lewis, Elaine

Liong, Peter Marsden, Aidan McKay, Steven Morgan, Rand Mulford, Daniel Navon, Mike Nicholson, Jason Owen-Smith, Juan Pablo Pardo-Guerra, Joe Pawlowski, Joel Podolny, Brian Powell, Ron Pyke, Michael Roach, Ain Roost, Jake Rosenfeld, Hal Salzman, Shawn Schaffer, Steve Sheiner, Audrey Singer, Mitchell Stevens, April Sutton, Prasanna Tambe, Emily Tang, Michael Teitelbaum, Eduardo Velasquez, Hugo Villar, Lisa Wade, Mary Walshok, Kim Weeden, Nathan Wilmers, Susan Yonezawa, and Steve Zimmers.

For research assistance, I thank Emma Greeson, David Keyes, Jack Jin Gary Lee, Yana Morgulis, Natalie Novick, Anh Pham, and Karina Shklyan.

On a personal level, I thank my wife, Minh, for several years of listening patiently when I talked excitedly about STEM, STEM education, and the STEM workforce, as well as for her expertise in data analysis. I thank our dog, Doug, for the serotonin boost I experienced every time he came into the room where I was working. Lastly, I thank my newborn daughters, Ava and Zoe, for being—just being. I dedicate this book, and especially any progress at all it can make toward my favored rationale for STEM education—saving the planet—to them.

NOTES

CHAPTER 1

1. Gerald F. Davis, *The Vanishing American Corporation: Navigating the Hazards of a New Economy* (Oakland, CA: Berrett-Koehler, 2016), 147.

2. Jennifer Cheeseman Day and Anthony Martinez, "STEM Majors Earned More Than Other STEM Workers," United States Census Bureau, June 2, 2021, https://www.census.gov/library/stories/2021/06/does-majoring-in-stem-lead-to-stem-job-after-graduation.html; Philip Martin, "High-Skilled Migrants: S&E Workers in the United States," *American Behavioral Scientist* 56, no. 8 (August 2012): 1058–79.

3. B. Lindsay Lowell and Hal Salzman, "Into the Eye of the Storm: Assessing the Evidence on Science and Engineering Education, Quality, and Workforce Demand," Urban Institute Research Report, October 29, 2007, https://doi.org/10.7282/T3X068P1. See also B. Lindsay Lowell, Hal Salzman, and Hamutal Bernstein, with Everett Henderson, "Steady as She Goes? Three Generations of Students through the Science and Engineering Pipeline," paper presented at the Annual Meeting of the Association for Public Policy Analysis and Management, Washington, DC, November 7, 2009, https://doi.org/doi:10.7282/T31R6S4K.

4. The greatest number of programs and federal dollars have focused on undergraduate learners. Boris Granovskiy, *Science, Technology, Engineering, and Mathematics (STEM) Education: An Overview* (Washington, DC: Congressional Research Service, June 12, 2018), 5.

5. On the lack of openings in higher education for STEM PhDs, see Paula Stephan, *How Economics Shapes Science* (Cambridge, MA: Harvard University Press, 2012).

6. Glassdoor, the employer review website, ranked STEM jobs, almost all in computers, tech, and IT, in nine of the top ten best jobs in America. See Glassdoor, "50 Best Jobs in America for 2022," https://www.glassdoor.com/List/Best-Jobs-in-America-LST_KQ0,20.htm. The ranking criteria included number of openings.

7. Corey Moss-Pech has explored the domination of STEM and other "practical arts" majors in *How College Students Get Jobs: Majors Matter, but Not How You Think* (Chicago: University of Chicago Press, forthcoming).

8. American Academy of Arts and Sciences, "Humanities Indicators: STEM Fields

Growing among Four-Year College Degree Recipients," *American Academy of Arts and Sciences Summer 2017 Bulletin*, https://www.amacad.org/news/humanities-indicators -stem-fields-growing-among-four-year-college-degree-recipients; Jill Barshay, "The Number of College Graduates in the Humanities Drops for the Eighth Consecutive Year," Proof Points, *Hechinger Report*, November 22, 2021, https://hechingerreport .org/proof-points-the-number-of-college-graduates-in-the-humanities-drops-for-the -eighth-consecutive-year/; Robert B. Townsend and Norman Bradburn, "The State of the Humanities circa 2022," *Daedalus* 151 (2022): 11–18. Data from the National Center for Education Statistics show that between 1990 and 2018, the percentages of students majoring in STEM subjects such as computer and information sciences, engineering, and biological and biomedical sciences have all increased, while majors in the humanities (English literature, philosophy) and business have lost a share of the total. Author's calculations from National Center for Education Statistics, *Digest of Education Statistics*, "Table 322.10: Bachelor's Degrees Conferred by Postsecondary Institutions, by Field of Study; Selected Years, 1970–71 through 2017–18," November 2019, https:// nces.ed.gov/programs/digest/d19/tables/dt19_322.10.asp.

9. John D. Skrentny and Kevin Lewis, "Beyond the 'STEM Pipeline': Expertise, Careers, and Lifelong Learning," *Minerva* 60 (2022): 1–28.

10. Harold Salzman and Lindsay Lowell, "Making the Grade," *Nature* 453 (2008): 28–30.

11. The National Academies of Sciences, Engineering, and Medicine have put major effort here and in 2022 had published twenty-nine book-length reports on STEM education since 2001. National Academies of Sciences, Engineering, and Medicine, "STEM Education Collection," accessed December 6, https://nap.nationalacademies .org/collection/39/stem-education. Also see Robert W. Conn, Michael M. Crow, Cynthia M. Friend, and Marcia McNutt, "The Next 75 Years of US Science and Innovation Policy: An Introduction," *Issues in Science and Technology*, July 12, 2021, https://issues .org/the-next-75-years-of-us-science-and-innovation-policy-an-introduction/.

12. See, for example, Audra J. Wolfe, *Competing with the Soviets: Science, Technology, and the State in Cold War America* (Baltimore: Johns Hopkins University Press, 2013) and John D. Skrentny and Natalie Novick, "From Science to Alchemy: The Progressives' Deployment of Expertise and the Contemporary Faith in Science to Grow the Economy and Create Jobs," in *The Progressives' Century: Political Reform, Constitutional Government, and the Modern American State*, ed. Stephen Skowronek, Stephen Engel, and Bruce Ackerman (New Haven, CT: Yale University Press, 2016), 405–27.

13. Eleanor Chute, "STEM Education Is Branching Out," *Pittsburgh Post-Gazette*, February 10, 2009, https://www.post-gazette.com/news/education/2009/02/10/STEM -education-is-branching-out/stories/200902100165; Jerome Christenson, "Ramaley Coined STEM Term Now Used Nationwide," *Winona (MN) Daily News*, November 13, 2011, http://www.winonadailynews.com/news/local/article_457afe3e-0db3-11e1-abe0 -001cc4c03286.html.

14. US Government Accountability Office (GAO), *Science, Technology, Engineering and Mathematics Education: Strategic Planning Needed to Better Manage Overlapping Programs across Multiple Agencies*, Report to Congressional Requesters, report no. GAO-12-108, January 2012, https://www.gao.gov/assets/590/587839.pdf. GAO recommended

consolidation, and the Office of Science and Technology Policy worked to eliminate redundancies. A couple of years later, the list of 209 had been pared down to 158 STEM-related education programs, still spread across the same thirteen agencies. US Government Accountability Office, *Science, Technology, Engineering, and Mathematics Education: Assessing the Relationship between Education and the Workforce*, Report to Congressional Requesters, report no. GAO-14-374, May 2014, 7–8, https://www.gao.gov /assets/670/663079.pdf. Also see US Government Accountability Office, *Government Efficiency and Effectiveness: Inconsistent Definitions and Information Limit the Usefulness of Federal Program Inventories*, Report to Congressional Committees, report no. GAO-15-83, October 2014, https://www.gao.gov/assets/670/666735.pdf.

15. Liana Loewus, "When Did Science Education Become STEM?," *Science* (blog), *Education Week*, April 2, 2015, https://www.edweek.org/teaching-learning/when-did -science-education-become-stem/2015/04.

16. America Creating Opportunities to Meaningfully Promote Excellence in Technology, Education, and Science Act of 2007, Pub. L. No. 110–69, 121 Stat. 572 (2007).

17. Barack Obama, "Remarks on Education Reform," September 16, 2010, https:// www.govinfo.gov/content/pkg/PPP-2010-book2/pdf/PPP-2010-book2-doc-pg1337.pdf; President's Council of Advisors on Science and Technology, *Prepare and Inspire: K-12 Education in Science, Technology, Engineering and Math (STEM) for America's Future*, September 2010, v, https://nsf.gov/attachments/117803/public/2a--Prepare_and_Inspire- -PCAST.pdf; Barack Obama, "Proclamation 9052—National Entrepreneurship Month, 2013," October 31, 2013, https://www.govinfo.gov/content/pkg/DCPD-201300743/pdf /DCPD-201300743.pdf.

18. President's Council of Advisors on Science and Technology, *Engage to Excel: Producing One Million Additional College Graduates with Degrees in Science, Technology, Engineering, and Mathematics*, Executive Office of the President, Report to the President, February 2012, https://files.eric.ed.gov/fulltext/ED541511.pdf.

19. White House, "President Donald J. Trump Is Working to Ensure All Americans Have Access to STEM Education," Fact Sheet, December 4, 2018, https://trump whitehouse.archives.gov/briefings-statements/president-donald-j-trump-is-working -to-ensure-all-americans-have-access-to-stem-education/.

20. Jessica Campisi, "Trump vs. Obama: Presidential Strides in STEM Education," *Education Dive*, January 9, 2019, https://www.k12dive.com/news/trump-vs-obama -presidential-strides-in-stem-education/543663/. Trump's Department of Education later boasted that it vastly exceeded Trump's request, having distributed $540 million for research and discretionary grants for STEM education. US Department of Education, "US Department of Education Advances Trump Administration's STEM Investment Priorities. Funding Will Prepare Students for Success in High-Demand Career Fields," press release, November 8, 2019, https://www.ed.gov/news/press-releases/us -department-education-advances-trump-administrations-stem-investment-priorities (content no longer available); Committee on STEM Education of the National Science & Technology Council, *Charting a Course for Success: America's Strategy for STEM Education*, December 2018, Executive Office of the President, https://www.energy.gov/sites /default/files/2019/05/f62/STEM-Education-Strategic-Plan-2018.pdf; Jeffrey Mervis, "Trump Emphasizes Workforce Training in New Vision for STEM Education," *Science*,

December 3, 2018, https://www.sciencemag.org/news/2018/12/trump-emphasizes-work force-training-new-vision-stem-education.

21. White House, "The Biden-Harris Administration FY 2023 Budget Makes Historic Investments in Science and Technology," press release, April 5, 2022, https://www.whitehouse.gov/ostp/news-updates/2022/04/05/the-biden-harris-administration -fy-2023-budget-makes-historic-investments-in-science-and-technology/.

22. Courtney C. Carmichael, "A State-by-State Policy Analysis of STEM Education for K-12 Public Schools" (PhD diss., Seton Hall University, 2017).

23. Susan G. Magliaro and Jeremy V. Ernst, *Inventory of Statewide STEM Education Networks*, Center for Research in SEAD Education, Virginia Tech, December 5, 2018, https://serc.carleton.edu/StemEdCenters/statewide-STEM.

24. Inside Philanthropy, "Funders: STEM Education," accessed October 20, 2020, https://www.insidephilanthropy.com/science-education-grants.

25. Michael S. Teitelbaum, *Falling Behind? Boom, Bust & the Global Race for Scientific Talent* (Princeton, NJ: Princeton University Press, 2014), 25–69.

26. For reviews of the debate about the need for and benefits of increasing the numbers of STEM-skilled migrants, see Martin, "High-Skilled Migrants"; Teitelbaum, *Falling Behind?*; William Kerr, *The Gift of Global Talent: How Migration Shapes Business, Economy & Society* (Stanford, CA: Stanford University Press, 2018).

27. Josh Constine, "Zuckerberg and a Team of Tech All-Stars Launch Political Advocacy Group FWD.us," TechCrunch+, April 11, 2013, https://techcrunch.com/2013/04 /11/fwd-us/.

28. FWD.us, "Retaining US International Student Graduates Could Help the US Win the Global Talent Race," February 3, 2022, https://www.fwd.us/news/us-international -students/.

29. The quote is from an appearance by Schmidt at MIT's Computer Science and Artificial Intelligence Lab. Liam Tung, "Ex-Google Chief Schmidt: My 20-Year Fight Against H-1B Caps Has Just Been 'Trumped,'" ZDNET, May 4, 2017, https://www.zdnet .com/article/ex-google-chief-schmidt-my-20-year-fight-against-h-1b-caps-has-just-been -trumped/.

30. The November 15, 2007, letter from Jack Krumholtz, Microsoft's Managing Director of Federal Government Affairs and Associate General Counsel to Michael Chertoff was made available by Bloomberg investigative journalist Rachel Rosenthal in her article "The STEM Graduate System Is Broken: Here's How to Fix It," *Bloomberg Opinion*, March 10, 2021, https://www.bloomberg.com/graphics/2021-opinion-optional -practical-training-problems-stem-graduates-deserve-better-jobs-opportunities/.

31. *Competitiveness and Innovation on the Committee's 50th Anniversary with Bill Gates, Chairman of Microsoft: Hearing before the Committee on Science and Technology*, 110th Cong. (2008), https://www.govinfo.gov/content/pkg/CHRG-110hhrg41066/pdf /CHRG-110hhrg41066.pdf.

32. Business Roundtable, "CEOs Say Skills Gap Threatens US Economic Future," news release, n.d., https://www.businessroundtable.org/archive/media/news-releases /ceos-say-skills-gap-threatens-us-economic-future. The survey was reportedly conducted from September 9 to November 6, 2014.

33. President's Council of Advisors on Science and Technology, *Engage to Excel*, 2.

34. Jacqueline Varas, "The Native-Born STEM Shortage," *American Action Forum*, April 5, 2016, https://www.americanactionforum.org/research/native-born-stem-shortage/.

35. Selene Angier, "Employers Need Skilled STEM Graduates: Here's Why International Students Can Meet the Demand," *US News Global Education*, March 30, 2022, https://www.usnewsglobaleducation.com/employers-need-skilled-stem-graduates-heres-why-international-students-can-meet-the-demand/.

36. STEM unemployment rates are not lowest in the US. Lawyers—a non-STEM occupation—had an unemployment rate of only 0.7 percent, while healthcare jobs (which some scholars consider to be STEM and some do not), had unemployment ranging from 1.2 percent (registered nurses) to 0.5 percent (physicians and surgeons) to 0.4 percent (dentists). John F. Sargent Jr., *U.S. Science and Engineering Workforce: Recent, Current, and Projected Employment, Wages, and Unemployment*, Congressional Research Service Report (Washington, DC: Congressional Research Service, November 2, 2017), 9.

37. A balanced assessment can be found in Yi Xue and Richard C. Larson, "STEM Crisis or STEM Surplus? Yes and Yes," *Monthly Labor Review*, US Bureau of Labor Statistics, May 2015, https://doi.org/10.21916/mlr.2015.14.

38. The Congressional Research Service traces the federal interest in STEM education all the way back to 1798, arguing that that year's law established the Federal Marine Hospital Service, which evolved into the US Public Health Service and later the Department of Health and Human Services. Granovskiy, *STEM Education: An Overview*, 21.

39. David Kaiser, "The Physics of Spin: Sputnik Politics and American Physicist in the 1950s," *Social Research* 73 (2006): 1225–52, at 1231.

40. National Defense Education Act of 1958, Pub. L. No. 85-864, 72 Stat. 1580 (1958), Title I, Sec. 101.

41. Skrentny and Novick, "From Science to Alchemy."

42. National Academy of Sciences, "History: Founding and Early Work," accessed December 7, 2022, https://www.nasonline.org/about-nas/history/archives/founding-and-early-work.html.

43. National Academy of Sciences, National Academy of Engineering, and Institute of Medicine, *Rising Above the Gathering Storm: Energizing and Employing America for a Brighter Economic Future* (Washington, DC: National Academies Press, 2005).

44. According the report's sequel (with the even more alarming subtitle, *Rapidly Approaching Category 5*), the original report was a major influence on getting the act passed. National Academy of Sciences, National Academy of Engineering, and Institute of Medicine, *Rising Above the Gathering Storm, Revisited: Rapidly Approaching Category 5* (Washington, DC: National Academies Press, 2010), x.

45. Here the report mentioned both college grads and skilled workers in trades. Office of Science and Technology Policy, *Progress Report on the Implementation of the Federal STEM Education Strategic Plan*, December 2021, 1, https://www.whitehouse.gov/wp-content/uploads/2022/01/2021-CoSTEM-Progress-Report-OSTP.pdf.

46. National Academy of Sciences, National Academy of Engineering, and Institute of Medicine, *Rising Above the Gathering Storm*, 166–67.

47. National Academies of Sciences, Engineering, and Medicine, *Call to Action for*

Science Education: Building Opportunity for the Future (Washington, DC: National Academies Press, 2021), 16.

48. Granovskiy, *STEM Education: An Overview*, 15.

49. American Innovation and Competitiveness Act, Pub. L. No. 114-329, 130 Stat. 2969 (2017), https://www.congress.gov/bill/114th-congress/senate-bill/3084/text.

50. See Space Center Houston, "Girls STEM Academy, Presented by Phillips 66," accessed December 7, 2022, https://spacecenter.org/education-programs/outreach/girls-stem-academy/; STEM Like a Girl, "Our Mission," accessed December 7, 2022, https://stemlikeagirl.org/our-mission/; Girls Who Code, "We're on a Mission to Close the Gender Gap in Tech," accessed December 7, 2022, https://girlswhocode.com/about-us; Black Girls CODE, "The Future Looks Like Me: Our Story," accessed December 7, 2022, https://wearebgc.org/about-us/.

51. Quotation regarding Howard Hughes Medical Institute from Chloe Tenn, "HHMI Kickstarts $2 Billion Initiative to Boost Diversity in STEM," *Scientist*, November 23, 2021, https://www.the-scientist.com/news-opinion/hhmi-kickstarts-2-billion-initiative-to-boost-diversity-in-stem-69458. On the other organizations, see Alfred P. Sloan Foundation, "Call for Letters of Inquiry: Creating Equitable Pathways to STEM Graduate Education," accessed December 7, 2022, https://sloan.org/programs/higher-education/diversity-equity-inclusion/equitable-pathways-loi; William and Flora Hewlett Foundation, "Bates College: For Launching the Institute for Racially Just, Inclusive, and Open STEM Education," accessed December 7, 2022, https://hewlett.org/grants/bates-college-for-launching-the-institute-for-racially-just-inclusive-and-open-stem-education/; Carnegie Math Pathways, "Our Mission," accessed December 7, 2022, https://www.carnegiemathpathways.org/about/who-we-are/.

52. See, for example, Cassidy Puckett, *Redefining Geek: Bias and the Five Hidden Habits of Tech-Savvy Teens* (Chicago: University of Chicago Press, 2022).

53. This is the first sentence of the abstract of Yu Xie, Michael Fang, and Kimberlee Shauman, "STEM Education," *Annual Review of Sociology* 41 (2015): 331–57.

54. See Eric Larson et al., *Net-Zero America: Potential Pathways, Infrastructure, and Impacts*, Final Report, Princeton University, October 29, 2021.

55. Smithsonian Science Education Center, "The STEM Imperative," accessed December 7, 2022, https://ssec.si.edu/stem-imperative.

56. National Academy of Sciences, National Academy of Engineering, and Institute of Medicine, *Rising Above the Gathering Storm*, 166.

57. Skrentny and Lewis, "Beyond the 'STEM Pipeline,'" 21.

58. For these and other approaches to alleviating worker shortages, see Burt S. Barnow, John Trutko, and Robert Lerman, *Skill Mismatches and Worker Shortages: The Problem and Appropriate Responses*, Report Submitted to the Office of the Assistant Secretary for Policy, US Department of Labor, February 25, 1998; Bridget Anderson and Martin Ruhs, "Migrant Workers: Who Needs Them? A Framework for the Analysis of Staff Shortages, Immigration and Public Policy," in *Who Needs Migrant Workers? Labour Shortages, Immigration, and Public Policy*, ed. Martin Ruhs and Bridget Anderson (New York: Oxford University Press, 2010), 15–52.

59. On the rise and persistence of shareholder value maximization, I've relied on

the following: Frank Dobbin and Jiwook Jung, "The Misapplication of Mr. Michael Jensen: How Agency Theory Brought Down the Economy and Why It Might Again," *Research in the Sociology of Organizations* 30 (2010): 29–64; Mark S. Mizruchi and Howard Kimmeldorf, "The Historical Context of Shareholder Capitalism," *Political Power and Social Theory* 17 (2005): 213–21; William Lazonick and Mary O'Sullivan, "Maximizing Shareholder Value: A New Ideology in Corporate Governance," *Economy and Society* 29 (2000): 13–35; Davis, *Vanishing American Corporation*; Peter A. Gourevitch and James Shinn, *Political Power and Corporate Control: The New Global Politics of Corporate Governance* (Princeton, NJ: Princeton University Press, 2007).

60. Lazonick and O'Sullivan, "Maximizing Shareholder Value."

61. An excellent review of these concepts focuses on low-wage work but applies to employers of STEM workers as well. Paul Osterman, "In Search of the High Road: Meaning and Evidence," *ILR Review* 71 (2018): 3–34.

CHAPTER 2

1. On the organizational uniformity of universities, see David John Frank and John W. Meyer, *The University and the Global Knowledge Society* (Princeton, NJ: Princeton University Press, 2020).

2. John D. Skrentny and Natalie Novick, "Research Universities and the Global Battle for the Brains," in *Education in a New Society: Renewing the Sociology of Education*, ed. Jal Mehta and Scott Davies (Chicago: University of Chicago Press, 2018), 271–96.

3. Elizabeth Redden, "Is Econ STEM?," *Inside Higher Ed*, February 19, 2018, https://www.insidehighered.com/admissions/article/2018/02/19/economics-departments-reclassify-their-programs-stem-attract-and-help.

4. The NYU STEM extension list can be found at https://www.nyu.edu/content/dam/nyu/globalServices/documents/forms/students/inboundtonyc/NYU_STEM_Programs.pdf. See also Rosenthal, "STEM Graduate System Is Broken."

5. I thank Lisa Wade for this clarifying phrase.

6. Moss-Pech, *How College Students Get Jobs*.

7. See Abigail Okrent and Amy Burke, "STEM Pathways: Degree Attainment, Training, and Occupations," in *The STEM Labor Force of Today: Scientists, Engineers, and Skilled Technical Workers*, National Science Board, August 31, 2021, https://ncses.nsf.gov/pubs/nsb20212/stem-pathways-degree-attainment-training-and-occupations.

8. President's Council of Advisors on Science and Technology, *Engage to Excel*, 3.

9. Office of Science and Technology Policy, *Progress Report*.

10. President's Council of Advisors on Science and Technology, *Engage to Excel*, 68.

11. Some of this is spelled out in Granovskiy, *STEM Education: An Overview*.

12. See Table LBR-4 in Abigail Okrent and Amy Burke, "STEM Labor Market Conditions and the Economy," in *The STEM Labor Force of Today: Scientists, Engineers, and Skilled Technical Workers*, National Science Board, August 31, 2021, https://ncses.nsf.gov/pubs/nsb20212/stem-labor-market-conditions-and-the-economy.

13. See Table LBR-A in Abigail Okrent and Amy Burke, "US STEM Workforce: Definition, Size, and Growth; Growth of the STEM Workforce," in *The STEM Labor Force of*

Today: Scientists, Engineers, and Skilled Technical Workers, National Science Board, August 31, 2021, https://ncses.nsf.gov/pubs/nsb20212/u-s-stem-workforce-definition-size-and-growth#growth-of-the-stem-workforce.

14. Enrico Moretti, *The New Geography of Jobs* (Boston: Houghton Mifflin Harcourt, 2012), 49–52.

15. Will Markow, Jonathan Coutinho, and Andrew Bundy, *Beyond Tech: The Rising Demand for IT Skills in Non-Tech Industries* (Boston: Burning Glass Technologies, September 2019), https://academy.oracle.com/pages/Burning_Glass_Report_Beyond_Tech.pdf.

16. These companies, among others, were listed on General Assembly's website, accessed February 24, 2021, https://generalassemb.ly/corporate-digital-training#section-industries.

17. Nate Swanner, "These Companies are Hiring the Most Software Developers Right Now," Dice, October 14, 2019, https://insights.dice.com/2019/10/14/compaies-hiring-software-developers-engineers/; Glassdoor Team, "Top Companies Hiring Software Engineers," *Glassdoor* (blog), accessed April 11, 2019, https://www.glassdoor.com/blog/top-companies-hiring-software-engineers/.

18. These data can be found at National Science Foundation, National Survey of College Graduates (NSCG WMPD), 2017, November 7, 2019, https://www.nsf.gov/statistics/2020/nsf20300/. I thank Karina Shklyan for the data analysis.

19. Lowell et al., "Steady as She Goes?," 31. Also see Lowell and Salzman, "Into the Eye of the Storm," 31.

20. Hal Salzman and Beryl Lieff Benderly, "STEM Performance and Supply: Assessing the Evidence for Education Policy," *Journal of Science Education and Technology* 28 (2019): 9–25.

21. Cheeseman Day and Martinez, "STEM Majors Earned More."

22. Lowell et al., "Steady as She Goes?," 30.

23. These numbers in Carnevale, Smith, and Melton's data are dragged down by the category of "math/life/physical scientists," who work in their field at a rate of only 35 percent after graduation and 24 percent after ten years. But the percentages for those with degrees in computers were not as high as we might expect given the hype around these jobs—64 percent after graduation and 72 percent ten years later. See Anthony P. Carnevale, Nicole Smith, and Michelle Melton, *STEM: Science, Technology, Engineering, Mathematics* (Washington, DC: Georgetown University Center on Education and the Workforce, 2011), 44.

24. These numbers are almost unchanged in comparing 2003, 2010, 2013, and 2015. Skrentny and Lewis, "Beyond the 'STEM Pipeline.'"

25. Salzman and Benderly, "STEM Performance and Supply"; Teitelbaum, *Falling Behind?*

26. Okrent and Burke, "STEM Labor Market Conditions and the Economy."

27. Hal Salzman, Daniel Kuehn, and B. Lindsay Lowell, *Guestworkers in the High-Skill US Labor Market*, EPI Briefing Paper no. 359 (Washington, DC: Economic Policy Institute, 2013).

28. Carnevale, Smith, and Melton, *STEM*; Lowell et al., "Steady as She Goes?"; Teitelbaum, *Falling Behind?*; David J. Deming and Kadeem Noray, "Earnings Dynamics,

Changing Job Skills, and STEM Careers," *Quarterly Journal of Economics* 135 (2020): 1965–2005.

29. Skrentny and Lewis, "Beyond the 'STEM Pipeline,'" 14.

30. Carnevale, Smith, and Melton, *STEM*, 48. Their data show a salary difference of $78,550 and $110,090 for STEM grads in these jobs.

31. For historical accounts of the American Medical Association's activities limiting the supply of physicians, see Paul Starr, *The Social Transformation of American Medicine: The Rise of a Sovereign Profession and the Making of a Vast Industry* (New York: Basic Books, 2008); Owen Whooley, *Knowledge in the Time of Cholera: The Struggle over American Medicine in the Nineteenth Century* (Chicago: University of Chicago Press, 2013). I describe how the American Medical Association restricted physician supply by attacking medical schools at historically Black universities in John D. Skrentny, *After Civil Rights: Racial Realism in the New American Workplace* (Princeton, NJ: Princeton University Press, 2014), 41–42. On informal processes affecting physician supply, see Tania M. Jenkins, *Doctors' Orders: The Making of Status Hierarchies in an Elite Profession* (New York: Columbia University Press, 2020). For the argument that the AMA, and not market forces, drives up physician salaries, see Shikha Dalmia, "The Evil-Mongering of the American Medical Association," *Forbes*, August 26, 2009, https://www.forbes.com/2009/08/25/american-medical-association-opinions-columnists-shikha-dalmia.html?sh=3fb1164442f2.

32. I considered these positions to be part of the "STEM pipeline" in Skrentny and Lewis, "Beyond the 'STEM Pipeline.'"

33. See Lowell and Salzman, "Into the Eye of the Storm."

34. Teitelbaum, *Falling Behind?*, 129–40; Ron Hira, "Is There Really a STEM Workforce Shortage?," *Issues in Science and Technology* 37 (2022): 31–35. With STEM, as with most fields, aggregation masks variation. Yu Xie and Alexandra A. Killewald, *Is American Science in Decline?* (Cambridge, MA: Harvard University Press, 2012), 61.

35. Carnevale, Smith and Melton, *STEM*, 48–50.

36. Teitelbaum, *Falling Behind?*, 152.

37. Cary Funk and Kim Parker, *Women and Men in STEM Often at Odds over Workplace Equity*, Pew Research Center, January 9, 2018, 46, https://www.pewresearch.org/social-trends/wp-content/uploads/sites/3/2018/01/PS_2018.01.09_STEM_FINAL.pdf.

38. "Big Tech Salaries Revealed: How Much Engineers, Developers, and Product Managers Make at Companies Including Apple, Amazon, Facebook, Google, Microsoft, Intel, Uber, IBM, and Salesforce," *Business Insider*, April 28, 2022, https://www.businessinsider.com/tech-engineer-developer-salary-google-amazon-microsoft-ibm-apple-intel-2021-6.

39. Cade Metz, "A.I. Researchers Are Making More Than $1 Million, Even at a Nonprofit," *New York Times*, April 19, 2018, https://www.nytimes.com/2018/04/19/technology/artificial-intelligence-salaries-openai.html.

40. Cade Metz, "Tech Giants Are Paying Huge Salaries for Scarce A.I. Talent," *New York Times*, October 22, 2017, https://www.nytimes.com/2017/10/22/technology/artificial-intelligence-experts-salaries.html.

41. Leonard Lynn, Hal Salzman, and Daniel Kuehn, "Dynamics of Engineering Labor Markets: Petroleum Engineering Demand and Responsive Supply," in *U.S.*

Engineering in a Global Economy, ed. Richard B. Freeman and Hal Salzman (Chicago: University of Chicago Press, 2018), 243–62.

42. Teitelbaum, *Falling Behind?*, 140–43; Fredrik Andersson, Matthew Freedman, John Haltiwanger, Julia Lane, and Kathryn Shaw, "Reaching for the Stars: Who Pays for Talent in Innovative Industries," *Economic Journal* 119 (2009): F308–F332.

43. See, for example, Zeynep Ton, *The Good Jobs Strategy: How the Smartest Companies Invest in Employees to Lower Costs and Boost Profits* (Boston: Houghton Mifflin Harcourt, 2014); Susan Helper and Ryan Noonan, *Taking the High Road: New Data Show Higher Wages May Increase Productivity, Among Other Benefits*, US Department of Commerce, Economics and Statistics Administration Issue Brief no. 04-15, August 4, 2015.

44. Jake Rosenfeld, *You're Paid What You're Worth: And Other Myths of the Modern Economy* (Cambridge, MA: Harvard University Press, 2020), 6–16.

45. High wages for managers are common throughout the economy. Even during periods of corporate downsizing, managerial wages have increased. Adam Goldstein, "Revenge of the Managers: Labor Cost-Cutting and the Paradoxical Resurgence of Managerialism in the Shareholder Value Era, 1984 to 2001," *American Sociological Review* 77 (2012): 268–94.

46. Sargent, *Science and Engineering Workforce*, 6, 17.

47. See, for instance, the private pay survey firm Glassdoor's data at Glassdoor, "Stem Salaries," accessed January 16, 2023, https://www.glassdoor.com/Salary/Stem-Salaries-E490845.htm. Recent data from the Bureau of Labor Statistics continue to show managers on top: US Bureau of Labor Statistics, "Occupational Employment and Wage Statistics: Highest and Lowest Paying STEM Occupations, May 2021," modified March 31, 2022, https://www.bls.gov/oes/2021/may/stem4.htm.

48. Josh Constine, "Damning Evidence Emerges in Google-Apple 'No Poach' Antitrust Lawsuit," TechCrunch+, January 19, 2012, https://techcrunch.com/2012/01/19/damning-evidence-emerges-in-google-apple-no-poach-antitrust-lawsuit/; Alex Wilhelm and Sarah Buhr, "Apple, Google, Other Silicon Valley Tech Giants Ordered to Pay $415M in No-Poaching Suit," TechCrunch+, September 3, 2015, https://techcrunch.com/2015/09/03/apple-google-other-silicon-valley-tech-giants-ordered-to-pay-415m-in-no-poaching-suit/.

49. Natarajan Balasubramanian, Jin Woo Chang, Mariko Sakakibara, Jagadeesh Sivadasan, and Evan Starr, "Locked In? The Enforceability of Covenants Not to Compete and the Careers of High-Tech Workers" (Working Paper Number CES-17-09, Center for Economic Studies, US Census Bureau, Washington, DC, January 2017), https://www.census.gov/library/working-papers/2017/adrm/ces-wp-17-09.html; Nathan Wilmers, "Solidarity Within and Across Workplaces: How Cross-Workplace Coordination Affects Earnings Inequality," *RSF: The Russell Sage Foundation Journal of the Social Sciences* 5 (2019): 190–215.

50. US Department of the Treasury, *The State of Labor Market Competition*, March 7, 2022, i–ii, https://home.treasury.gov/system/files/136/State-of-Labor-Market-Competition-2022.pdf.

51. A lack of opportunities to move up is itself a reason people change jobs. One study found that 55 percent of those who wanted to leave their job said that being "dissatisfied" or "very dissatisfied" with career advancement opportunities was a reason.

Matt Ferguson, Lorin Hitt, and Prasanna Tambe, *The Talent Equation: Big Data Lessons for Navigating the Skills Gap and Building a Competitive Workforce* (New York: McGraw-Hill, 2013), 187–88.

52. Michael J. Handel, "Theories of Lean Management: An Empirical Evaluation," *Social Science Research* 44 (2014): 86–102.

53. Lotte Bailyn and John T. Lynch, "Engineering as a Life-Long Career: Its Meaning, Its Satisfactions, Its Difficulties," *Journal of Occupational Behavior* 4 (1983): 263–83, at 281.

54. Bailyn and Lynch, "Engineering as a Life-Long Career," 264.

55. Jack Downey, "Careers in Software: Is There Life after Programming?," *SIGMIS-CPR '10 Proceedings of the 2010 Special Interest Group on Management Information System's 48th Annual Conference on Computer Personnel Research on Computer Personnel Research*, Vancouver, BC, 1–7, at 5.

56. Hal Salzman and Leonard Lynn, "Engineering and Engineering Skills: What's Really Needed for Global Competitiveness," paper presented at the annual Fall Research Conference of the Association for Public Policy Analysis and Management, Boston, November 4, 2010, 9n10.

57. Danielle Li, Kelly Shue, and Alan Benson, "Promotions and the Peter Principle," *VoxEU*, Centre for Economic Policy Research, April 24, 2019, https://voxeu.org/article/promotions-and-peter-principle. This article makes the connection to job ladders at "technical organisations," though the research focuses on sales workers at 131 firms. For the academic version, see Alan Benson, Danielle Li, and Kelly Shue, "Promotions and the Peter Principle," *Quarterly Journal of Economics* 134 (2019): 2085–134. The other possibility is to include more non-STEM skills in STEM training. When Salzman and Lynn interviewed engineering managers, those managers complained of a lack of communication, interpersonal, and managerial skills in their workers, rather than a shortage of technical skills—despite the ubiquitous complaints from business of the severe lack of STEM skills among American workers. Leonard Lynn and Hal Salzman, "What Makes a Good Engineer? U.S., German and Japanese Perspectives," paper presented at the European Applied Business Research Conference, Rothenburg, Germany, June 2002. A major effort to rectify the situation was the Alfred P. Sloan Foundation's creation of a "Professional Science Master's Degree." Sloan worked with industry to create a program to give STEM students skills in business and communications. Alfred P. Sloan Foundation, "Professional Science Master's Degree," accessed December 16, 2022, https://sloan.org/programs/completed-programs/professional-science-masters-degree.

58. Tom Ziller, "The Argument for Paying Your General Manager Lots of Money," *SB Nation* (blog), Vox Media, May 30, 2013, https://www.sbnation.com/nba/2013/5/30/4379182/nba-general-managers-coaches-payscale-masai-ujiri.

59. L. Garicano and E. Rossi-Hansberg, "Organization and Inequality in a Knowledge Economy," *Quarterly Journal of Economics* 121 (2006): 1383–435; David H. Autor and Michael J. Handel, "Putting Tasks to the Test: Human Capital, Job Tasks, and Wages," *Journal of Labor Economics* 31 (2013): S59–S96.

60. See the insightful discussion in Rosenfeld, *You're Paid What You're Worth*, 6–16.

61. Sargent, *Science and Engineering Workforce*, 17.

CHAPTER 3

1. Bryce Covert, "How Kickstarter Employees Formed a Union," *Wired*, May 27, 2020, https://www.wired.com/story/how-kickstarter-employees-formed-union/; Hugh Langley and Isobel Asher Hamilton, "The US Labor Board Accused Google of Illegally Spying on Employee Activists, Firing Them, and Blocking Workers from Organizing," *Business Insider*, December 3, 2020, https://www.businessinsider.com/us-labor-board -says-google-illegally-spied-on-fired-employees-2020-12; Parul Koul and Chewy Shaw, "We Built Google: This Is Not the Company We Want to Work For," *New York Times*, January 4, 2021, https://www.nytimes.com/2021/01/04/opinion/google-union.html; Cecilia D'Anastasio, "A Big Union Wants to Make Videogame Workers' Lives More Sane," *Wired*, January 7, 2020, https://www.wired.com/story/big-union-make-videogame -workers-lives-sane/.

2. Tech firms might not be representative of other employers of STEM workers because they have shorter product cycles than other sectors in the innovation economy and thus may have different work cultures. The development of new drugs, for example, can take many years, and even after a finished product takes shape, there are many safety and regulatory hurdles required for government approval before new drugs or devices hit the market. The process of discovery and preclinical and clinical trials may take ten years or more. This, as we will see, is very different from the fast pace that characterizes firms that make their money from software, computers, and the internet. I thank Michael Roach for shaping my thinking on the differences between different sectors in the innovation economy (Michael Roach, email message to author, March 8, 2020). Chris Young, a tech blogger, has also insightfully noted several differences between biotech and tech start-ups: Chris Young, "Why Biotech Startups are Not the Same as Tech Startups," *Techli* (blog), November 14, 2011, https:// techli.com/biotech-startups-not-tech-startups/12915/. For more on the average time for a new drug and differences between STEM sectors, see Homer A. Neal, Tobin L. Smith, and Jennifer B. McCormick, *Beyond Sputnik: U.S. Science Policy in the 21st Century* (Ann Arbor: University of Michigan Press, 2008), 139; and Gary P. Pisano, *Science Business: The Promise, the Reality, and the Future of Biotech* (Boston: Harvard Business School Press, 2006).

3. Daisuke Wakabayashi, "Google's Plan for the Future of Work: Privacy Robots and Balloon Walls," *New York Times*, April 30, 2021, https://www.nytimes.com/2021/04/30 /technology/google-back-to-office-workers.html.

4. As I write these words, a battle is being played out where employers (not just employers of STEM workers) are trying to get workers back into the office. Whether or not this effort succeeds will not matter for the arguments in this chapter because the topics I discuss and the stress that many STEM workers feel are likely to remain unchanged whether the work is done in the office or at home.

5. I rely here on the discussion of job satisfaction surveys in Arne L. Kalleberg, *Good Jobs, Bad Jobs: The Rise of Polarized Employment Systems in the United States, 1970s to 2000s* (New York: Russell Sage Foundation, 2011), 164–65. On how comparisons can affect assessments, also see Guillermina Jasso, "Methods for the Theoretical

and Empirical Analysis of Comparison Processes," *Sociological Methodology* 20 (1990): 369–419. On the value of these self-assessments, also see Arne L. Kalleberg, "Work Values and Job Rewards: A Theory of Job Satisfaction," *American Sociological Review* 42 (1977): 124–43; Francis Green, *Demanding Work: The Paradox of Job Quality in the Affluent Economy* (Princeton, NJ: Princeton University Press, 2006); Andrew E. Clark, "What Makes a Good Job? Job Quality and Job Satisfaction," *IZA World of Labor*, December 2015, https://wol.iza.org/uploads/articles/215/pdfs/what-makes-good-job-job-quality -and-job-satisfaction.pdf.

6. Kalleberg, *Good Jobs, Bad Jobs*, 243n10; Theodore Caplow, "Decades of Public Opinion: Comparing NORC and Middletown Data," *Public Opinion* 5 (1982): 30–31.

7. There is indeed some evidence of job satisfaction declining since the 1970s, especially by managers, who enjoyed more stability before that decade. Kalleberg, *Good Jobs, Bad Jobs*, 176.

8. Kalleberg, *Good Jobs, Bad Jobs*, 170.

9. Randy Hodson, "Gender Differences in Job Satisfaction: Why Aren't Women Workers More Dissatisfied?," *Sociological Quarterly* 30 (1989): 385–99.

10. For this analysis, I used the 2017 National Survey of College Graduates. I thank Karina Shklyan for this data analysis.

11. Peter Cappelli, "Your Approach to Hiring Is All Wrong," *Harvard Business Review*, May–June 2019, https://hbr.org/2019/05/recruiting#your-approach-to-hiring-is -all-wrong.

12. There is evidence that employers are wasting money with their focus on external hiring. If firms did look into it, they would find that internal hires have better performance for the first two years and are less likely to leave or be fired. This is true even though external hires are paid almost 20 percent more and have higher levels of education and experience (Cappelli, "Your Approach to Hiring Is All Wrong"). See also Mathew Bidwell, "Paying More to Get Less: Specific Skills, Matching, and the Effects of External Hiring versus Internal Promotion," *Administrative Science Quarterly* 56 (2011): 369–407; Jonathan Rothwell, *Still Searching: Job Vacancies and STEM Skills*, Metropolitan Policy Program at Brookings (Brookings Institution, Washington, DC, July 2014); Josh Bersin, *Rethinking the Build vs. Buy Approach to Talent: How Savvy Employers are Building Tech Skills from Within*, Report commissioned by General Assembly and produced by Whiteboard Advisors, October 2020.

13. These five regions account for 90 percent of American innovation, according to a report from the Brookings Institution. Robert D. Atkinson, Mark Muro, and Jacob Whiton, *The Case for Growth Centers: How to Spread Tech Innovation across America* (Washington, DC: Brookings Institution, December 9, 2019).

14. This is a major point in Ilana Gershon, *Down and Out in the New Economy: How People Find (or Don't Find) Work Today* (Chicago: University of Chicago Press, 2017), especially chapters 4 and 5.

15. This is apparent from articles describing what career coaches do. See, for example, Marlo Lyons, "Do You Need a Career Coach?," *Harvard Business Review*, February 9, 2022, https://hbr.org/2022/02/do-you-need-a-career-coach.

16. Gershon, *Down and Out*, 172–73.

17. Gershon, *Down and Out*, 108.

18. Peter Cappelli, *Why Good People Can't Get Jobs: The Skills Gap and What Companies Can Do about It* (Philadelphia: Wharton Digital Press, 2012), 61.

19. National Academy of Engineering, *The Importance of Engineering Talent to the Prosperity and Security of the Nation: Summary of a Forum* (Washington, DC: National Academies Press, 2014), 12.

20. Peter Cappelli, "Why Is It So Hard to Find Information Technology Workers?," *Organizational Dynamics* 30 (2001): 87–99, at 95. Also see Avron Barr and Shirley Tessler, *How Will the Software Talent Shortage End?*, Stanford Computer Industry Project Software Industry Study, November 4, 1997, http://www.aldo.com/papers/how1197.pdf. Though both of these studies are quite old in an industry that moves quickly, Gershon's corroboration of the basic arguments suggests their continuing relevance.

21. Cappelli, *Why Good People Can't Get Jobs*, 20.

22. Gershon, *Down and Out*, 76.

23. Ifeoma Ajunwa, "The Paradox of Automation as Anti-Bias Intervention," *Cardozo Law Review* 41 (2020): 1671–744; Cappelli, *Why Good People Can't Get Jobs*, 62–68; David B. Bills, Valentina Di Stasio, and Klarita Gërxhani, "The Demand Side of Hiring: Employers in the Labor Market," *Annual Review of Sociology* 43 (2017): 291–310.

24. Mahnaz Behroozi, Shivani Shirolkar, Titus Barik, and Chris Parnin, "Does Stress Impact Technical Interview Performance?," *ESEC/FSE 2020: Proceedings of the 28th ACM Joint Meeting on European Software Engineering Conference and Symposium on the Foundations of Software Engineering* (New York: Association for Computing Machinery, November 2020), 481–92.

25. For an insightful analysis, see Cappelli, "Your Approach to Hiring Is All Wrong."

26. Louis Hyman, *Temp: The Real Story of What Happened to Your Salary, Benefits, and Job Security* (New York: Penguin Books, 2018).

27. Gershon, *Down and Out*, 191–92.

28. Gershon, *Down and Out*, 188, 192–93, 202; William Finlay and James E. Coverdill, *Headhunters: Matchmaking in the Labor Market* (Ithaca, NY: Cornell University Press, 2002); James E. Coverdill and William Finlay, *High Tech and High Touch: Headhunting, Technology, and Economic Transformation* (Ithaca, NY: ILR Press, 2017).

29. Gershon, *Down and Out*, 191–97 and elsewhere; Rich Bellis, "Former Recruiters Reveal the Industry's Dark Secrets That Cost You Job Offers," Fast Company, July 20, 2017, https://www.fastcompany.com/40441093/former-recruiters-reveal-the-industrys-dark-secrets-that-cost-you-job-offers.

30. Analysis of 2017 National Survey of College Graduates performed by Karina Shklyan.

31. American Institute of Stress, "Workplace Stress," accessed January 2, 2023, https://www.stress.org/workplace-stress. The survey is from the career research firm Zippia: Caitlin Mazur, "40+ Worrisome Workplace Stress Statistics [2022]: Facts, Causes, and Trends," Zippia, September 18, 2022, https://www.zippia.com/advice/work place-stress-statistics/.

32. National Institute for Occupational Safety and Health (NIOSH), *Stress . . . at Work*, DHHS (NIOSH) Publication No. 99–101 (Cincinnati, OH: NIOSH, 1999), https://www.cdc.gov/niosh/docs/99-101/pdfs/99-101.pdf?id=10.26616/NIOSHPUB99101.

33. Ferguson, Hitt, and Tambe, *Talent Equation*, 184–86.

34. Donald Sull, Charles Sull, and Ben Zweig, "Toxic Culture Is Driving the Great Resignation," *MIT Sloan Management Review*, January 11, 2022, https://sloanreview.mit .edu/article/toxic-culture-is-driving-the-great-resignation/.

35. Donald Sull, Charles Sull, William Cipolli, and Caio Brighenti, "Why Every Leader Needs to Worry about Toxic Culture," *MIT Sloan Management Review*, March 16, 2022, https://sloanreview.mit.edu/article/why-every-leader-needs-to-worry-about-toxic -culture/.

36. Sull, Sull, and Zweig, "Toxic Culture Driving Resignation."

37. Peter Kuhn and Fernando Lozano, "The Expanding Workweek? Understanding Trends in Long Work Hours Among US Men, 1979–2004" (NBER Working Paper No. 11895, National Bureau of Economic Research, Cambridge, MA, revised January 2008), https://www.nber.org/papers/w11895. Also see J. Rodrigo Fuentes and Edward E. Leamer, "Effort: The Unrecognized Contributor to US Income Inequality" (NBER Working Paper No. 26421, National Bureau of Economic Research, Cambridge, MA, November 2019), https://www.nber.org/papers/w26421.

38. Jeffrey Pfeffer, *Dying for a Paycheck: How Modern Management Harms Employee Health and Company Performance—and What We Can Do about It* (New York: Harper Business, 2018), 129–30.

39. Nicholas Bloom, "Hybrid Is the Future of Work," Stanford Institute for Economic Policy Research Policy Brief, June 2021, https://siepr.stanford.edu/publications /policy-brief/hybrid-future-work.

40. Management scholar Jeffrey Pfeffer's important work on the harms of modern management only anecdotally mentions STEM jobs, saying that the tech sector, "with its Red Bull-fueled all-nighters, is another place where overwork reigns." He describes the operation of a mobile medical facility in Silicon Valley to serve tech companies because tech workers are too busy to visit a doctor's office despite generous health insurance. Pfeffer, *Dying for a Paycheck*, 121.

41. Sull, Sull, and Zweig, "Toxic Culture Driving Resignation."

42. Erin L. Kelly and Phyllis Moen, *Overload: How Good Jobs Went Bad and What We Can Do about It* (Princeton, NJ: Princeton University Press, 2020), 17.

43. Kelly and Moen, *Overload*, chapter 2.

44. Kelly and Moen, *Overload*, 53–57.

45. Lindsay J. DePalma, "The Passion Paradigm: Professional Adherence to and Consequences to and Consequences of the Ideology of 'Do What You Love,'" *Sociological Forum* 36 (2021): 134–58; Aliya Hamid Rao and Megan Tobias Neely, "What's Love Got to Do With It? Passion and Inequality in White-Collar Work," *Sociology Compass* 13, no. 12 (December 2019): e12744, https://doi.org/10.1111/soc4.12744.

46. Erin Cech, *The Trouble with Passion: How Searching for Fulfillment at Work Fosters Inequality* (Berkeley: University of California Press, 2021), 206–8.

47. Gershon, *Down and Out*, 214.

48. Gershon, *Down and Out*, 217.

49. Dan Lyons, *Lab Rats: How Silicon Valley Made Work Miserable for the Rest of Us* (New York: Hachette, 2018), 46.

50. Ofer Sharone, "Engineering Overwork: Bell-Curve Management at a High-Tech

Firm," in *Fighting for Time: Shifting Boundaries of Work and Social Life*, ed. Cynthia Fuchs Epstein and Arne L. Kalleberg (New York: Russell Sage Foundation, 2004), 191–218.

51. Max Nisen, "Why GE Had to Kill Its Annual Performance Reviews after More Than Three Decades," *Quartz*, August 13, 2015, https://qz.com/428813/ge-performance -review-strategy-shift/.

52. David Rock, Josh Davis, and Beth Jones, "Kill Your Performance Ratings," *Strategy + Business*, no. 76, August 8, 2014, https://www.strategy-business.com/article/00275 ?gko=c442b.

53. Leslie Kwoh, "'Rank and Yank' Retains Vocal Fans," *Wall Street Journal*, updated January 31, 2012, https://www.wsj.com/articles/SB10001424052970203363504577 186970064375222.

54. Sharone, "Engineering Overwork," 205–6.

55. See, for example, Susan M. Stewart, Melissa L. Gruys, and Maria Storm, "Forced Distribution Performance Evaluation Systems: Advantages, Disadvantages and Keys to Implementation," *Journal of Management and Organization* 16 (2010): 168–79; Johannes Berger, Christine Harbring, and Dirk Sliwka, "Performance Appraisals and the Impact of Forced Distribution—An Experimental Investigation," *Management Science* 59 (2013): 54–68; Sue H. Moon, Steven E. Scullen, and Gary P. Latham, "Precarious Curve Ahead: The Effects of Forced Distribution Rating Systems on Job Performance," *Human Resources Management Review* 26 (2016): 166–79.

56. Rock, Davis, and Jones, "Kill Your Performance Ratings."

57. Rock, Davis, and Jones, "Kill Your Performance Ratings"; Nisen, "GE Performance Reviews"; David Burkus, "How Adobe Scrapped Its Performance Review System and Why It Worked," *Forbes*, June 1, 2016, https://www.forbes.com/sites/davidburkus /2016/06/01/how-adobe-scrapped-its-performance-review-system-and-why-it-worked /#b1379a355e8f; Lillian Cunningham, "In a Big Move, Accenture Will Get Rid of Annual Performance Reviews and Rankings," *Washington Post*, July 21, 2015, https://www .washingtonpost.com/news/on-leadership/wp/2015/07/21/in-big-move-accenture-will -get-rid-of-annual-performance-reviews-and-rankings/; Leonardo Baldassarre and Brian Finken, "GE's Real-Time Performance Development," *Harvard Business Review*, August 12, 2015, https://hbr.org/2015/08/ges-real-time-performance-development.

58. Pfeffer, *Dying for a Paycheck*, 127–28.

59. Dan Lyons, "In Silicon Valley, Working 9 to 5 Is for Losers," *New York Times*, August 31, 2017, https://www.nytimes.com/2017/08/31/opinion/sunday/silicon-valley-work -life-balance-.html.

60. Jeffrey Bezos to shareholders, [1997], http://media.corporate-ir.net/media_files /irol/97/97664/reports/Shareholderletter97.pdf.

61. Amazon, "Leadership Principles," accessed December 17, 2022, https://www .amazon.jobs/en/principles.

62. Jodi Kantor and David Streitfeld, "Inside Amazon: Wrestling Big Ideas in a Bruising Workplace," *New York Times*, August 15, 2015, https://www.nytimes.com/2015 /08/16/technology/inside-amazon-wrestling-big-ideas-in-a-bruising-workplace.html.

63. Kantor and David Streitfeld, "Inside Amazon."

64. Susan Adams, "How People Who Work for Amazon Really Feel," *Forbes*, Au-

gust 18, 2015, https://www.forbes.com/sites/susanadams/2015/08/18/how-people-who
-work-for-amazon-really-feel/#49b294d33059.

65. Pfeffer, *Dying for a Paycheck*, 9.

66. Marco della Cava, "An Uber Engineer Killed Himself: His Widow Says the Work-place Is to Blame," *USA Today*, updated April 28, 2017, https://www.usatoday.com/story
/tech/news/2017/04/27/is-uber-culture-to-blame-for-an-employees-suicide/100938330/.

67. Della Cava, "Uber Engineer Killed Himself." Also see Carolyn Said, "Suicide of an Uber Engineer: Widow Blames Job Stress," *San Francisco Chronicle*, April 25, 2017, https://www.sfchronicle.com/business/article/Suicide-of-an-Uber-engineer-widow
-blames-job-11095807.php.

68. Mike Isaac, "Inside Uber's Aggressive, Unrestrained Workplace Culture," *New York Times*, February 22, 2017, https://www.nytimes.com/2017/02/22/technology/uber
-workplace-culture.html.

69. Caroline Donovan and Priya Anand, "How Uber's Hard-Charging Corporate Culture Left Employees Drained," BuzzFeed News, July 17, 2017, https://www.buzzfeed
news.com/article/carolineodonovan/how-ubers-hard-charging-corporate-culture-left
-employees.

70. Oliver Staley, "Uber Has Replaced Travis Kalanick's Values with Eight New 'Cultural Norms,'" *Quartz*, November 7, 2017, https://qz.com/work/1123038/uber-has
-replaced-travis-kalanicks-values-with-eight-new-cultural-norms/.

71. Donovan and Anand, "Uber's Hard-Charging Corporate Culture."

72. Donovan and Anand, "Uber's Hard-Charging Corporate Culture."

73. Donovan and Anand, "Uber's Hard-Charging Corporate Culture."

74. Salvador Rodriguez, "Facebook Employee Says He Was Fired for Speaking Out about His Colleague's Suicide," CNBC.com, October 15, 2019, https://www.cnbc.com
/2019/10/15/facebook-employee-i-was-fired-for-talking-about-colleagues-suicide.html.

75. Charlie Wood, "A Chinese Engineer Says He Was Fired from Facebook after Dis-cussing a Colleague's Death, and It's Caused Outrage in China," *Business Insider*, Oc-tober 11, 2019, https://www.businessinsider.com/firing-of-chinese-facebook-engineer
-prompts-anger-in-china-2019-10.

76. Gideon Kunda, *Engineering Culture: Control and Commitment in a High-Tech Cor-poration*, rev. ed. (Philadelphia: Temple University Press, 2006).

77. Antonio García Martínez, "How Mark Zuckerberg Led Facebook's War to Crush Google Plus," *Vanity Fair*, June 3, 2016, https://www.vanityfair.com/news/2016/06/how
-mark-zuckerberg-led-facebooks-war-to-crush-google-plus; Antonio García Martínez, *Chaos Monkeys: Obscene Fortune and Random Failure in Silicon Valley* (New York: HarperCollins, 2016).

78. Salvador Rodriguez, "Inside Facebook's 'Cult-Like' Workplace, Where Dissent Is Discouraged and Employees Pretend to be Happy All the Time," CNBC.com, Jan-uary 8, 2019, https://www.cnbc.com/2019/01/08/facebook-culture-cult-performance
-review-process-blamed.html.

79. Rodriguez, "Inside Facebook's 'Cult-Like' Workplace."

80. Shalini Ramachandran and Joe Flint, "At Netflix, Radical Transparency and Blunt Firings Unsettle the Ranks," *Wall Street Journal*, October 25, 2018, https://www

.wsj.com/articles/at-netflix-radical-transparency-and-blunt-firings-unsettle-the-ranks -1540497174. As the journalist Dan Lyons pointed out, in a withering critique of the Netflix approach and the executives at other firms who have emulated it or spoken admiringly of it (such as Facebook's chief operating officer, Sheryl Sandberg), the sports team analogy is inapt because sports teams succeed when the players feel like they are part of family, a notion that was antithetical to Netflix's approach. Lyons, in reflecting on Netflix's "We're a team, not a family" credo, rephrased it as, "We're cruel assholes who treat our workers poorly." D. Lyons, *Lab Rats*, 111–12.

CHAPTER 4

1. Society for Human Resource Management, "What Is the Difference Between a Furlough, a Layoff and a Reduction in Force?," accessed January 3, 2023, https:// www.shrm.org/resourcesandtools/tools-and-samples/hr-qa/pages/furloughlayoff reductioninforce.aspx.

2. Robert N. Charette, "What Ever Happened to STEM Job Security?," *IEEE Spectrum*, September 5, 2013, https://spectrum.ieee.org/the-changing-pattern-of-stem -worker-employment.

3. TheLayoff.com, "News, Personal Experiences, Rumors and Speculations about Layoffs at Your Company," accessed December 17, 2022, https://www.thelayoff.com/.

4. Kalleberg, *Good Jobs, Bad Jobs*, 22–24.

5. Peter Cappelli, introduction to *Employment Relationships: New Models of White-Collar Work*, ed. Peter Cappelli (New York: Cambridge University Press, 2008), 1–30, at 7.

6. Cappelli, introduction to *Employment Relationships*, 9.

7. Raghuram G. Rajan and Julie Wulf, "The Flattening Firm: Evidence from Panel Data on the Changing Nature of Corporate Hierarchies," *Review of Economics and Statistics* 88 (2006): 759–73, at 772.

8. Pew Research Center, *The State of American Jobs*, October 6, 2016, 45, https:// www.pewsocialtrends.org/wp-content/uploads/sites/3/2016/10/ST_2016.10.06_Future -of-Work_FINAL4.pdf.

9. See Cappelli, introduction to *Employment Relationships*, 6–8, for a discussion.

10. Ed Crooks and Lindsay Fortado, "Activist Investor Trian Wins Seat on GE Board," *Financial Times*, October 9, 2017, https://www.ft.com/content/956eef3e-acf6-11 e7-aab9-abaa44b1e130; Alwyn Scott, "GE's New CEO Preparing Job Cuts in Bid to Reduce Costs: Source," Reuters, August 31, 2017, https://www.reuters.com/article/us-ge -jobs/ges-new-ceo-preparing-job-cuts-in-bid-to-reduce-costs-source-idUSKCN1BB1CD; Steve Blank, "Why GE's Jeff Immelt Lost His Job: Disruption and Activist Investors," *Harvard Business Review*, October 30, 2017, https://hbr.org/2017/10/why-ges-jeff-immelt -lost-his-job-disruption-and-activist-investors.

11. Davis, *Vanishing American Corporation*, 66.

12. Pfeffer, *Dying for a Paycheck*, 74–76.

13. Pfeffer, *Dying for a Paycheck*, 72.

14. Sull, Sull, and Zweig, "Toxic Culture Driving Resignation."

15. Mark Minevich, "The Rise of Strategic Global Outsourcing and Implications on American Talent," Fast Company, January 26, 2022, https://www.fastcompany.com

/90715511/the-rise-of-strategic-global-outsourcing-and-implications-on-american
-talent; Ron Hira, *Outsourcing America: What's Behind Our National Crisis and How We
Can Reclaim American Jobs* (New York: American Management Association, 2005).

16. Davis, *Vanishing American Corporation*, 72–75.

17. "Around 60 Percent of Pharmaceutical Manufacturing Is Outsourced," *European
Pharmaceutical Review*, October 8, 2018, https://www.europeanpharmaceuticalreview
.com/news/77293/pharmaceutical-manufacturing-outsourced/.

18. Rick Mullin, "Bringing Drug Production Back to the US," *Chemical & Engineering News*, June 29, 2020, https://cen.acs.org/business/outsourcing/Bringing-drug
-production-back-US/98/i25.

19. Cappelli, introduction to *Employment Relationships*, 14.

20. Rick Wartzman, *The End of Loyalty: The Rise and Fall of Good Jobs in America*
(New York: PublicAffairs, 2017).

21. Analysis of 2017 National Survey of College Graduates performed by Karina
Shklyan.

22. Hal Salzman, *The Impact of High-Skill Guestworker Programs and the STEM Workforce*, statement for the Senate Hearing on the Impact of High-Skilled Immigration
on US Workers, submitted to the Senate Committee on the Judiciary, US Senate, February 25, 2016, https://www.judiciary.senate.gov/imo/media/doc/02-25-16%20Salzman
%20Testimony.pdf.

23. Revelio Labs, "Scientists Are Leaving Novartis," May 8, 2019, https://www.revelio
labs.com/news/business/scientists-are-leaving-novartis/.

24. See Teitelbaum, *Falling Behind?*, 75–83.

25. Stephanie Joyce, "Falling Oil Prices Leave Petroleum Engineering Students
Out in the Cold," Inside Energy, February 13, 2105, http://insideenergy.org/2015/02/13
/falling-oil-prices-leave-petroleum-engineering-students-out-in-the-cold/; Katherine
Dunn, "The Oil and Gas Industry Has Lost More Than 100,000 Jobs This Year," *Fortune*, October 4, 2020, https://fortune.com/2020/10/05/oil-gas-jobs-transition-climate
-coronavirus/.

26. Teitelbaum, *Falling Behind?*, 77–81.

27. Jesse Jenkins, Mark Muro, Ted Nordhaus, Michael Shellenberger, Letha Taw-
ney, and Alex Trembath, *Beyond Boom and Bust: Putting Clean Tech On a Path To Subsidy
Independence* (Washington, DC: Brookings Institution, 2012), https://www.brookings
.edu/research/beyond-boom-and-bust-putting-clean-tech-on-a-path-to-subsidy
-independence/; Juliet Eilperin, "Why the Clean Tech Boom Went Bust," *Wired*, January 20, 2012, https://www.wired.com/2012/01/ff_solyndra/.

28. Georges Vernez, Michael Dardia, Kevin F. McCarthy, Jesse D. Malkin, and Robert Nordyke, *California's Shrinking Defense Contractors: Effects on Small Suppliers* (Santa
Monica, CA: Rand Corporation, 1996).

29. See Teitelbaum, *Falling Behind?*, chapter 2; Neal, Smith, and McCormick, *Beyond
Sputnik*, 278. On petroleum engineering, see Lynn, Salzman, and Kuehn, "Dynamics
of Engineering Labor Markets," 243–62.

30. Joyce, "Engineering Students Out in the Cold."

31. Blind Staff Writer, "Nearly ⅓ of Professionals Are Worried About Layoffs In
2021," *Blind Blog—Workplace Insights*, Teamblind, February 2, 2021, https://www

.teamblind.com/blog/index.php/2021/02/02/nearly-%e2%85%93-of-professionals-are -worried-about-layoffs-in-2021/; Blind Staff Writer, "Worried About Layoffs? Tech Employees Weigh in About Layoff Anxiety," *Blind Blog—Workplace Insights*, Teamblind, February 11, 2019, https://www.teamblind.com/blog/index.php/2019/02/11/worried -about-layoffs-tech-employees-weigh-in-about-layoff-anxiety/. Methodologies are opaque here, as with most surveys done by businesses, but it almost certainly is the case that STEM workers commonly feel insecure at leading companies.

32. Kelly and Moen, *Overload*, 60–61.

33. Brent Orrell and Daniel A. Cox, *STEM Perspectives: Attitudes, Opportunities, and Barriers in America's STEM Workforce* (Washington, DC: American Enterprise Institute, July 2020), 10, https://www.aei.org/wp-content/uploads/2020/07/STEM-perspectives -Attitudes-opportunities-and-barriers-in-Americas-STEM-workforce.pdf.

34. Carrie M. Lane, *A Company of One: Insecurity, Independence, and the New World of White-Collar Unemployment* (Ithaca, NY: ILR Press, 2011), 5.

35. Lane, *Company of One*, 36.

36. Lane, *Company of One*, 46.

37. Lane, *Company of One*, 71.

38. Peter Cappelli found that during the mid-1990s, revenues for corporate recruiting firms tripled. Peter Cappelli, *The New Deal at Work: Managing the Market-Driven Workforce* (Boston: Harvard Business School Press, 1999), 215.

39. On job-hopping in California and in the computer sector, see Bruce Fallick, Charles A. Flieschman, and James B. Rebitzer, "Job-Hopping in Silicon Valley: Some Evidence Concerning the Microfoundations of a High-Technology Cluster," *Review of Economics and Statistics* 88 (2006): 472–81. It has also increased over time in all sectors of the economy for men, who had typically enjoyed the most job stability in those halcyon (for White men) decades in the middle of the twentieth century. See, for example, Raven Molloy, Christopher Smith, and Abigail K. Wozniak, "Changing Stability in US Employment Relationships: A Tale of Two Tails" (NBER Working Paper No. 26694, National Bureau of Economic Research, Cambridge, MA, January 2020), http:// www.nber.org/papers/w26694.

40. Stack Overflow, "Developer Survey Results 2019," accessed December 19, 2022, https://insights.stackoverflow.com/survey/2019.

41. Ferguson, Hitt, and Tambe, *Talent Equation*.

42. LiveCareer, *2018 Job Hopping Analysis: Trends by Generation & Education Level; A Study Conducted by LiveCareer in Conjunction with TIRO Communications* (Guyanabo, Puerto Rico: BOLD LLC, 2018), https://www.livecareer.com/wp-content/uploads/2018 /05/2018-Job-Hopping-Report.pdf.

43. Regarding nondegree credentials, tech companies such as Microsoft, Adobe, Cisco, VMware, and Oracle all provide certifications that will signal to any employer a level of proficiency (I discuss this more in chapter 5). On the rise of firm-provided certifications, see Clifford Adelman, *A Parallel Postsecondary Universe: The Certification System in Information Technology* (Washington, DC: Office of Educational Research and Development, 2000).

44. Jean Chatzky, "Job-Hopping Is on the Rise: Should You Consider Switching Roles to Make More Money?," NBC News, April 24, 2018, https://www.nbcnews.com

/better/business/job-hopping-rise-should-you-consider-switching-roles-make-more
-ncna868641; Jenny Darmody, "Why Do Employers Still See Job-Hopping as a Bad
Thing?," Silicon Republic, January 17, 2019, https://www.siliconrepublic.com/careers
/job-hopping-recruitment.

45. Gershon, *Down and Out*, 108.

46. Gershon, *Down and Out*, 115–16.

47. An insightful analysis of the rise of contracting and the meaning of employ-
ment, though focusing on less-skilled workers, is David Weil, *The Fissured Workplace:
Why Work Became So Bad for So Many and What Can Be Done to Improve It* (Cambridge,
MA: Harvard University Press, 2014).

48. See the analyses in Vicki Smith, *Crossing the Great Divide: Worker Risk and Op-
portunity in the New Economy* (Ithaca, NY: Cornell University Press, 2001); Jennifer JiHye
Chun, "Flexible Despotism: The Intensification of Insecurity and Uncertainty in the
Lives of Silicon Valley's High-Tech Assembly Workers," in *The Critical Study of Work:
Labor, Technology, and Global Production*, ed. Rick Baldoz, Charles Koeber, and Philip
Kraft (Philadelphia: Temple University Press, 2001), 127–54.

49. These accounts tend to group together all contractors, so that custodial staff,
shuttle drivers, and cafeteria workers are discussed right alongside top-level software
developers who may earn ten times as much. Mark Bergen and Josh Eidelson, "Inside
Google's Shadow Workforce," Bloomberg, July 25, 2018, https://www.bloomberg.com
/news/articles/2018-07-25/inside-google-s-shadow-workforce.

50. Ron Hira, "Bridge to Permanent Immigration or Temporary Labor? The H-1B
Visa Program Is a Source of Both," in Freeman and Salzman, *U.S. Engineering in a
Global Economy*, 263–83; Natalie M. Novick and John D. Skrentny, "The Innovation
Economy," in *Immigrant California: Understanding the Past, Present, and Future of US
Policy*, ed. David Scott FitzGerald and John D. Skrentny (Stanford, CA: Stanford Uni-
versity Press, 2021), 116–46.

51. Ellen Sheng, "Silicon Valley's Dirty Secret: Using a Shadow Workforce of Contract Employees to Drive Profits," CNBC, October 22, 2018, https://www.cnbc.com/2018
/10/22/silicon-valley-using-contract-employees-to-drive-profits.html; Daisuke Wakabayashi, "Google's Shadow Work Force: Temps Who Outnumber Full-Time Employees," *New York Times*, May 28, 2019, https://www.nytimes.com/2019/05/28/technology
/google-temp-workers.html; Joshua Brustein, "What It's Like to Work Inside Apple's
'Black Site,'" Bloomberg, February 11, 2019, https://www.bloomberg.com/news/features
/2019-02-11/apple-black-site-gives-contractors-few-perks-little-security.

52. Sam Harnett, "'Two-Tiered Caste System': The World of White-Collar Contracting in Silicon Valley," KQED, April 19, 2019, https://www.kqed.org/news/11741371/two
-tiered-caste-system-the-world-of-white-collar-contracting-in-silicon valley.

53. Wakabayashi, "Google's Shadow Work Force."

54. Brustein, "Inside Apple's 'Black Site.'"

55. Brustein, "Inside Apple's 'Black Site.'" On the YouTube shooting, see Wakabayashi, "Google's Shadow Work Force."

56. Sam Harnett, "Coronavirus Highlights Worker Privilege Disparities at Big Tech
Firms," KQED, March 14, 2020, https://www.kqed.org/news/11806387/coronavirus
-highlights-worker-privilege-disparities-at-big-tech-firms.

57. Debra Osnowitz, *Freelancing Expertise: Contract Professionals in the New Economy* (Ithaca, NY: Cornell University Press, 2010), esp. 152, 172, 174, and 181.

58. On organizing IT workers, see Immanuel Ness, "Globalization and Labor Resistance," and Danielle Van Jaarsveld, "Boom and Bust: Lessons from the Information Technology Workforce," in *Surviving the New Economy*, ed. John Amman, Tris Carpenter, and Gina Neff (Boulder, CO: Paradigm Publishers, 2007), 119–31; Chris Benner, "'Computers in the Wild': Guilds and Next Generation Unionism in the Information Revolution," *International Review of Social History* 48 (2003): 181–204; Danielle Van Jaarsveld, "Collective Representation among High-Tech Workers at Microsoft and Beyond: Lessons from WashTech/CWA," *Industrial Relations* 43 (2004): 364–85; Josh Eidelson and Hassan Kanu, "Microsoft Bug Testers Unionized, Then They Got Terminated," *Bloomberg Businessweek*, August 23, 2018, https://www.bloomberg.com/news/articles/2018-08-23/microsoft-bug-testers-unionized-then-they-were-dismissed; Osnowitz, *Freelancing Expertise*, 181.

59. On national growth of contracting (but saying little about STEM), see Lawrence F. Katz and Alan B. Krueger, "The Rise and Nature of Alternative Work Arrangements in the United States, 1995–2015," *ILR Review* 72 (2019): 382–416; and Vicki Smith and Esther B. Neuwirth, "Temporary Help Agencies and the Making of a New Employment Practice," *Academy of Management Perspectives* 23 (2009): 56–72. The large number of contractors in Silicon Valley (though including more than STEM workers) was identified in Alan Hyde, *Working in Silicon Valley: Economic and Legal Analysis of a High-Velocity Labor Market* (Armonk, NY: M. E. Sharpe, 2003).

60. A 2015 Government Accountability Office study of contingent labor showed the limits of the data but also some intriguing numbers. The contingent workforce in 2010 varied widely, from 5 percent of the total workforce to about 40 percent, depending on how it was counted, but it seemed to be mostly a phenomenon of the low-skilled sector. In 2012, about 6 percent of contingent workers were in "professional/technical services," and another 10 percent were in "administrative/support services," two categories where we might find STEM workers. This is helpful, but the percentage of STEM workers who are contractors is needed for a fuller analysis. US Government Accountability Office, *Contingent Workforce: Size, Characteristics, Earnings, and Benefits*, April 20, 2015, http://www.gao.gov/assets/670/669899.pdf.

61. Wakabayashi, "Google's Shadow Work Force."

62. Harnett, "'Two-Tiered Caste System'"; Wakabayashi, "Google's Shadow Work Force."

63. Stephen R. Barley and Gideon Kunda, *Gurus, Hired Guns, and Warm Bodies: Itinerant Experts in a Knowledge Economy* (Princeton, NJ: Princeton University Press, 2004), 40–45.

64. Another reason Google uses contractors is common to other companies: help in areas not central to the core business, such as food service, shuttle bus services, and customer support. Sheng, "Silicon Valley's Dirty Secret."

65. Katalin Szabó and Áron Négyesi, "The Spread of Contingent Work in the Knowledge-Based Economy," *Human Resource Development Review* 4 (2005): 63–85.

66. Barley and Kunda, *Gurus, Hired Guns, and Warm Bodies*, 45–47.

67. Lilly Irani, "Difference and Dependence among Digital Workers: The Case of Amazon Mechanical Turk," *South Atlantic Quarterly* 114 (2015): 225–34, at 231.

68. Bergen and Eidelson, "Inside Google's Shadow Workforce"; Robert H. Frank and Philip J. Cook, *The Winner-Take-All Society: Why the Few at the Top Get So Much More Than the Rest of Us* (New York: Penguin Books, 1996).

69. Barley and Kunda, *Gurus, Hired Guns, and Warm Bodies*, 47–49.

70. Sheng, "Silicon Valley's Dirty Secret."

71. Barley and Kunda, *Gurus, Hired Guns, and Warm Bodies*, 57–58.

72. Barley and Kunda, *Gurus, Hired Guns, and Warm Bodies*, 61–62.

73. Sheng, "Silicon Valley's Dirty Secret"; Harnett, "'Two-Tiered Caste System.'"

74. Davis, *Vanishing American Corporation*, 147.

CHAPTER 5

1. Some scholars believe these concerns are overblown. See Salzman and Benderly, "STEM Performance and Supply."

2. Joel Johnson, "The Unlikely Origins of USB, the Port That Changes Everything," *Fast Company*, May 29, 2019, https://www.fastcompany.com/3060705/an-oral-history-of-the-usb.

3. "New Apple CEO Tim Cook: 'I'm Thinking Printers,'" *Onion*, August 25, 2011, https://www.theonion.com/new-apple-ceo-tim-cook-im-thinking-printers-1819572893.

4. Gonzalo Valdés and Stephen R. Barley, "Be Careful What You Wish For: The Learning Imperative in Postindustrial Work," *Work and Occupations* 43 (2016): 466–501.

5. A final point: Here I emphasize training for STEM skills because those are the skills that employers and policymakers say are scarce in the US. I do not mean to imply that these are the most important skills a STEM worker can or should have. STEM workers need non-STEM skills, too, and employers very much value these foundational skills that allow organizations to function well, such as communication and teamwork skills.

6. Pew Research Center, *State of American Jobs*, 49, 52, 64, 68–69. See also Prudential, *Fifth American Workers Survey Fact Sheet*, December 2018, https://news.prudential.com/presskits/fifth-american-workers-survey.htm.

7. Pew Research Center, *State of American Jobs*, 67.

8. C. Jeffrey Waddoups, "Did Employers in the United States Back Away from Skills Training during the Early 2000s?," *ILR Review* 69 (2016): 405–34.

9. Waddoups, "Did Employers Back Away from Skills Training?"

10. See figure 3-27 in *Economic Report of the President Together with the Annual Report of the Council of Economic Advisers*, February 2015, 147. The report has been deleted from the White House website but is still available via the digital library FRASER, https://fraser.stlouisfed.org/title/economic-report-president-45/2015-492446/fulltext.

11. Brad Smith, "Microsoft Launches Initiative to Help 25 Million People," *Official Microsoft Blog*, June 30, 2020, https://blogs.microsoft.com/blog/2020/06/30/microsoft-launches-initiative-to-help-25-million-people-worldwide-acquire-the-digital-skills-needed-in-a-covid-19-economy/. This report relied on data from online surveys from

the Association for Talent Development, the American Management Association, and Microsoft-owned LinkedIn. In the 2020s, the tight job markets of the pandemic recovery may have helped boost training at least temporarily. A Harris Poll conducted between October 28 and November 1, 2021, found that only 39 percent of American workers thought their employer was helping them improve their skills. Harris Poll, *ASA Workforce Monitor: Training and Automation; American Staffing Association*, accessed December 21, 2022, https://d2m21dzi54s7kp.cloudfront.net/wp-content/uploads/2020 /05/ASA_Workforce_Monitor_Training_Automation.pdf.

12. The way NSF has asked its training question is, unfortunately, arguably out of date because it asks if workers have taken "any work-related training, such as workshops or seminars." This question would seem to discourage answers related to online, on-the-job, or any other informal training.

13. These analyses were conducted with Kevin Lewis. The STEM/non-STEM differences were statistically significant (at $p < .05$) in all survey years except 2013, though they are very small (ranging from 0.6 percent in 2013 to 3.1 percent in 2010). The NSCG asks respondents which reasons for training were *most important*. Looking only at respondents who said improving skills was the most important reason they trained, we see fewer saying they trained overall, but a higher percentage of STEM workers than non-STEM workers say they trained: 38.1 percent compared with 34.8 percent in 2003, 37.4 percent vs. 31.6 percent in 2010, 35.3 percent vs. 31.2 percent in 2013, and 34.7 percent vs. 30.4 percent in 2015. All these differences are statistically significant at $p < .001$. Skrentny and Lewis, "Beyond the 'STEM Pipeline.'"

14. Skrentny and Lewis, "Beyond the 'STEM Pipeline.'"

15. Cappelli, *New Deal at Work*, 209.

16. A thoughtful analysis of how there may be a skills gap even with a glut of educated workers is James Bessen, *Learning by Doing: The Real Connection between Innovation, Wages, and Wealth* (New Haven, CT: Yale University Press, 2015), esp. chap. 7.

17. Himanshu Sareen, "How Apps Overthrew Web Development and Changed the Internet," *Wired*, [June 2014], https://www.wired.com/insights/2014/06/apps-overthrew -web-development-changed-internet/.

18. Chris Benner, *Work in the New Economy: Flexible Labor Markets in Silicon Valley* (Malden, MA: Blackwell, 2002), 198–99.

19. A review of this debate, focusing on total overall employment, can be found in David Rotman, "How Technology Is Destroying Jobs," *MIT Technology Review*, June 12, 2013, https://www.technologyreview.com/2013/06/12/178008/how-technology -is-destroying-jobs/.

20. Jacob Mincer and Yoshio Higuchi, "Wage Structures and Labor Turnover in the United States and Japan," *Journal of the Japanese and International Economies* 2 (1988): 97–133.

21. Ann P. Bartel, "Technological Change and the Retirement Decisions of Older Workers," *Journal of Labor Economics* 11 (1993): 162–83.

22. Carol Ann Meares and John F. Sargent Jr., *The Digital Workforce: Building Infotech Skills at the Speed of Innovation* (Washington, DC: Office of Technology Policy, 1999), 86.

23. Congressional Commission on the Advancement of Women and Minorities in

Science, Engineering, and Technology Development, *Land of Plenty: Diversity as America's Competitive Edge in Science, Engineering, and Technology* (Arlington, VA: National Science Foundation, 2000), 10. A fascinating case study in how technology affected those working in media, creating something then called "new media," can be found in Rosemary Batt, Susan Christopherson, Ned Rightor, and Danielle Van Jaarsveld, "NET WORKING: Work Patterns and Workforce Policies for the New Media Industry" (CAHRS Working Paper Series, Cornell University Center for Advanced Human Resource Studies, Ithaca, NY, November 2000), https://hdl.handle.net/1813/77431.

24. National Research Council, *Building a Workforce for the Information Economy* (Washington, DC: National Academies Press, 2001), 254–55.

25. Robert N. Charette, "An Engineering Career: Only a Young Person's Game?," *IEEE Spectrum*, September 4, 2013, https://spectrum.ieee.org/an-engineering-career-only-a-young-persons-game.

26. National Academy of Engineering, *Understanding the Educational and Career Pathways of Engineers* (Washington, DC: National Academies Press, 2018), 7, 37, and chapter 2 generally.

27. Van Jaarsveld, "Collective Representation."

28. Siobhan O'Mahony, "Stretchwork: Managing the Career Progression Paradox in External Labor Markets," *Academy of Management Journal* 49 (2006): 918–41.

29. Sarah Overmyer, "What Do Tech Workers Really Want?," Indeed, August 22, 2019, https://www.indeed.com/lead/what-tech-workers-want.

30. Pew Research Center, *State of American Jobs*, 49, 52, 64, 68–69.

31. Skrentny and Lewis, "Beyond the 'STEM Pipeline,'" 12.

32. On non-STEM degree workers in STEM jobs, see Nirmala Kannankutty, "Multiple Pathways to Science and Engineering Employment: Characteristics of the U.S. S&E Workforce," 2007 Atlanta Conference on Science, Technology and Innovation Policy, https://ieeexplore.ieee.org/document/4472909?tp=&arnumber=4472909&queryText%3Dkannankutty=; National Science Board, *Revisiting the STEM Workforce: A Companion to Science and Engineering Indicators 2014* (Arlington, VA: National Science Foundation, 2015).

33. John D. Skrentny and Kevin Lewis, "Determinants of Training in STEM Careers" paper presented at the Annual Meeting of the American Sociological Association, San Francisco, August 2014.

34. John J. Horton and Prasanna Tambe, *The Death of a Technical Skill*, September 17, 2020, https://john-joseph-horton.com/papers/schumpeter.pdf.

35. Deming and Noray, "Earnings Dynamics."

36. Deming and Noray, "Earnings Dynamics." Also see Patrick McGovern, *HRM, Technical Workers and the Multinational Corporation* (New York: Routledge, 1998).

37. Deming and Noray, "Earnings Dynamics." Also see Johan Hombert and Adrien Matray, "Beware of Tech Bubbles: Long-Term Earnings of the Dot-Com Bubble Generation," *VoxEU*, Centre for Economic Policy Research, January 5, 2020, https://voxeu.org/article/long-term-earnings-dot-com-bubble-generation.

38. The Society for Human Resource Management provides an outline of what onboarding should look like. Roy Maurer, "New Employee Onboarding Guide," Society

for Human Resource Management, accessed December 21, 2022, https://www.shrm.org/resourcesandtools/hr-topics/talent-acquisition/pages/new-employee-onboarding-guide.aspx.

39. Suman Bhattacharyya, "You're New at a Company: How Can You Learn Its Technology?," *Wall Street Journal*, August 20, 2022, https://www.wsj.com/articles/onboarding-employees-company-technology-11660934964.

40. Brian X. Chen, "Simplifying the Bull: How Picasso Helps to Teach Apple's Style," *New York Times*, August 10, 2014, https://www.nytimes.com/2014/08/11/technology/-inside-apples-internal-training-program-.html.

41. Sam Colt, "Here's What It's Like to Attend Apple's Secret University," *Business Insider*, February 5, 2015, http://www.businessinsider.com/heres-what-its-like-to-attend-apples-secret-university-2015-2.

42. Cisco, "Cisco Learning Locator," accessed December 21, 2022, https://learninglocator.cloudapps.cisco.com/#/home.

43. Oracle, "Oracle University," accessed January 4, 2023, https://education.oracle.com/.

44. Microsoft, "AI Engineer," accessed December 21, 2022, https://docs.microsoft.com/en-us/learn/certifications/roles/ai-engineer.

45. Illumina, "Hands-on Training with Expert Instructors or Online Courses to Fit Your Schedule," accessed December 21, 2022, https://www.illumina.com/services/instrument-services-training/training.html.

46. See National Research Council, *Building a Workforce*, 251–53, for analysis of these certifications.

47. Google, "How We Care for Googlers," accessed January 20, 2022, https://careers.google.com/how-we-care-for-googlers/.

48. Pfizer, "Careers," accessed January 20, 2022, https://www.pfizer.com/about/careers.

49. ExxonMobil, "Careers: Engineering," accessed January 20, 2022, https://jobs.exxonmobil.com/go/Engineering/3845600/.

50. Adobe, "Careers: Why Adobe?," accessed January 20, 2022, http://www.adobe.com/careers/why-adobe.html.

51. Qualcomm Technologies, "Training and Development: Learn, Grow, Lead," accessed December 21, 2022, https://www.qualcomm.com/company/corporate-responsibility/our-people/training-development.

52. Heather Kelly, "Qualcomm Is Laying Off More Than 1,500 People," CNN Business, April 19, 2018, https://money.cnn.com/2018/04/19/technology/qualcomm-layoffs/index.html; Mike Freeman, "Qualcomm Laying off More Workers in San Diego, North Carolina to Cut Costs," *San Diego Union-Tribune*, December 7, 2018, https://www.sandiegouniontribune.com/business/technology/sd-fi-qualcomm-newlayoffs-20181207-story.html.

53. Mike Freeman, "Uncertain Local Job Market Awaits Qualcomm Workers: With Layoffs Pending at Tech Giant, Workers Could Need Retraining to Find Positions," August 17, 2015, *San Diego Union-Tribune*, https://www.sandiegouniontribune.com/business/technology/sdut-qualcomm-broadcom-nokia-layoffs-foreign-workers-2015aug17-htmlstory.html.

54. E. Kelly and Moen, *Overload*, 65.

55. Kiyoteru Tsutsui and Alwyn Lim, editors, *Corporate Social Responsibility in a Globalizing World* (New York: Cambridge University Press, 2016).

56. B. Smith, "Microsoft Launches Initiative."

57. Mary Jo Foley, "Microsoft Is Doing Its Usual Fiscal Year-End Layoffs, but Fewer than Usual," ZDNET, July 17, 2020, https://www.zdnet.com/article/microsoft-is-doing -its-usual-fiscal-year-end-layoffs-but-fewer-than-usual/; Geoff Baker, "Microsoft Jettisons Dozens of Full-Time MSN Jobs in Favor of Artificial Intelligence," *Seattle Times*, July 14, 2020, https://www.seattletimes.com/business/microsoft/microsoft-jettisons -dozens-of-full-time-msn-jobs-in-favor-of-artificial-intelligence/.

58. Jon Porter, "Google Donates Free Chromebooks and 100,000 Mobile Hotspots for Rural California Students," Verge, April 2, 2020, https://www.theverge.com/2020 /4/2/21204057/google-free-chromebooks-wi-fi-hotspots-california-schools-students -remote-learning-coronavirus.

59. See Google, "Our $1 Billion Commitment to Create More Opportunity for Everyone," accessed December 22, 2022, https://www.google.org/intl/en_us/billion -commitment-to-create-more-opportunity/; Google, "Helping Expand Learning for Everyone," accessed December 22, 2022, https://edu.google.com/why-google/our -commitment/.

60. Lindsay McKenzie, "Google's Growing IT Certificate," *Inside Higher Ed*, June 14, 2019, https://www.insidehighered.com/digital-learning/article/2019/06/14/google-it -certificate-program-expands-more-community-colleges. For Google's description of the effort, see Grow with Google, "Job-Ready Skills You Can Put to Work," accessed December 22, 2022, https://grow.google/certificates/.

61. Anna Kramer, "Laid-Off Google Cloud Workers Say They Found Out from Media Reports," *Protocol*, March 14, 2022, https://www.protocol.com/bulletins/google-cloud -layoffs-protest.

62. Sebastian Moss, "Google Cloud Workers Learned of Layoffs from Media Reports," DCD, March 15, 2022, https://www.datacenterdynamics.com/en/news/google -cloud-workers-learned-of-layoffs-from-media-reports/.

63. Jeff Horwitz, Salvador Rodriguez, and Miles Kruppa, "Meta Quietly Reduces Staff in Cost-Cutting Push," *Wall Street Journal*, September 21, 2022, https://www.wsj.com /articles/meta-and-google-are-cutting-staff-just-dont-mention-layoffs-11663778729.

64. John Mannes, "Airbnb Is Running Its Own Internal University to Teach Data Science," TechCrunch, May 24, 2017, https://techcrunch.com/2017/05/24/airbnb-is -running-its-own-internal-university-to-teach-data-science/.

65. Jack Kelly, "Airbnb Lays Off 25% of Its Employees: CEO Brian Chesky Gives a Master Class in Empathy and Compassion," *Forbes*, May 6, 2020, https://www.forbes .com/sites/jackkelly/2020/05/06/airbnb-lays-off-25-of-its-employees-ceo-brian-chesky -gives-a-master-class-in-empathy-and-compassion/#afde506ee307; for a more critical view of the layoff process, see Alex Torres, "Airbnb Employees Reportedly Say They Feel Betrayed as 1,900 Layoffs Rip Apart a Company Culture They Say Was Based on Trust and Loyalty," *Business Insider*, July 17, 2020, https://www.businessinsider.com/airbnb -under-scrutiny-for-laying-off-1900-employees-2020-7.

66. See, for example, W. Norton Grubb, *Learning to Work: The Case for Reintegrating*

Job Training and Education (New York: Russell Sage Foundation, 1996); Peter B. Berg, "Strategic Adjustments in Training: A Comparative Analysis of the US and German Automobile Industries," in *Training and the Private Sector: International Comparisons*, ed. Lisa M. Lynch (Chicago: University of Chicago Press, 1994), 77–108; Paul Osterman and Andrew Weaver, "Community Colleges and Employers: How Can We Understand Their Connection?," *Industrial Relations* 55 (2016): 523–45; Benner, *Work in the New Economy*, 188–90.

67. Mary Lindenstein Walshok, *Knowledge without Boundaries: What America's Research Universities Can Do for the Economy, the Workplace, and the Community* (San Francisco: Jossey-Bass, 1995).

68. Benner, *Work in the New Economy*, 191.

69. Mary Walshok and Joel West, "Serendipity and Symbiosis: UCSD and the Local Wireless Industry," in *Public Universities and Regional Growth: Insights from the University of California*, ed. Martin Kenney and David C. Mowery (Stanford, CA: Stanford Business Books, 2014), 127–52, at 143.

70. Extension or continuing education schools are not the only ways that research universities can play key roles in helping workers on the STEM-skills treadmill. For example, sociologist Mitchell Stevens has called for new visions of corporate–university partnerships, going beyond the extension model and taking advantage of new advances in technologies of learning. Mitchell L. Stevens, "Research Universities and the Future of Work," *Issues in Science and Technology* 35 (2018): 45–52.

71. Dan Primack, "Adecco Buys General Assembly for $413 Million," *Axios*, April 16, 2018, https://www.axios.com/general-assembly-1523667905-ce940016-11d9-4380-bdd3-d46ef18898f7.html.

72. I discussed the growing tendency of firms outside the tech sector to hire workers with computer expertise in chapter 2. Information from General Assembly was on the company website: General Assembly, "Corporate Digital Training: Why," accessed February 23, 2021, https://generalassemb.ly/corporate-digital-training#section-why; General Assembly, "Corporate Digital Training: Industries," accessed February 23, 2021, https://generalassemb.ly/corporate-digital-training#section-industries.

73. Quentin Hardy, "Gearing Up for the Cloud, AT&T Tells Its Workers: Adapt, or Else," *New York Times*, February 13, 2016, https://www.nytimes.com/2016/02/14/technology/gearing-up-for-the-cloud-att-tells-its-workers-adapt-or-else.html.

74. Hardy, "Gearing Up for the Cloud."

75. Markle Foundation Rework America Business Network, *Digital Blindspot: How Digital Literacy Can Create a More Resilient American Workforce* (New York: Markle Foundation, October 2019), 24.

76. Susan Caminiti, "Royal Dutch Shell Reskills Workers in Artificial Intelligence as Part of Huge Energy Transition," CNBC.com, April 3, 2020, https://www.cnbc.com/2020/04/03/royal-dutch-shell-reskills-workers-in-ai-part-of-energy-transition.html; Alex McFarland, "Shell Begins to Reskill Workers in Artificial Intelligence," Unite.AI, updated December 9, 2022, https://www.unite.ai/shell-begins-to-reskill-workers-in-artificial-intelligence/.

77. For example, Amazon created "Amazon Technical Academy" to move non-STEM

workers into software careers. As Amazon explained, "Combining instructor-led, project-based learning with real-world application, graduates of the program master the most widely used software engineering practices and tools required to thrive into a career at Amazon. This tuition-free program was created by Amazon software engineers for Amazon employees who want to move into the field." Amazon, "Amazon Pledges to Upskill 100,000 US Employees for In-Demand Jobs by 2025," press release, July 11, 2019, https://press.aboutamazon.com/news-releases/news-release-details/amazon-pledges-upskill-100000-us-employees-demand-jobs-2025.

78. Amazon eventually opened up Machine Learning University to anyone, following the market-share training strategy, as it centered on AWS, or Amazon Web Services, a cloud-computing platform. Other programs included Amazon Apprenticeship, which offered paid classroom work and on-the-job training, and free access to AWS training and certification for skills in working with the cloud to provide "opportunities both within Amazon and in organizations around the world as demand for cloud talent continues to grow." Amazon, "Amazon Pledges to Upskill." The apprenticeship program was certified by the US Department of Labor.

79. Doug Lederman, "Amazon Snags a Higher Ed Superstar," *Inside Higher Ed*, January 29, 2018, https://www.insidehighered.com/digital-learning/article/2018/01/29/amazons-high-profile-hire-higher-education-candace-thille.

80. Paul Fain, "Employers as Educators," *Inside Higher Ed*, July 17, 2019, https://www.insidehighered.com/digital-learning/article/2019/07/17/amazon-google-and-other-tech-companies-expand-their.

81. Gary Becker, *Human Capital* (New York: Columbia University Press, 1964). Mindful of this, some firms have offered general skills training, but only with contracts that state that workers need to pay back training costs if they leave within a specified number of years. A problem here, however, is the possible effect on employee morale. (Who wants to keep an unhappy employee, resentful of a kind of indentured servitude status?) Cappelli, *New Deal at Work*, 200–201.

82. Rothwell, *Still Searching*; Bersin, *Rethinking the Build vs. Buy Approach*.

83. Michael J. Feuer, Henry Glick, and Anand Desai, "Firm Financed Education and Specific Human Capital: A Test of the Insurance Hypothesis," in *Market Failure in Training? New Economic Analysis and Evidence on Training in Employed Adults*, ed. D. Stern and J. M. M. Ritzen (Berlin: Springer-Verlag, 1991), 41–60. See also the review in Berg, "Strategic Adjustments in Training," 78.

84. Jason Wingard, *Learning to Succeed* (New York: AMACOM, 2015), 99–126.

85. Bersin, *Rethinking the Build vs. Buy Approach*.

86. William Lazonick, *Sustainable Prosperity in the New Economy? Business Organization and High-Tech Employment in the United States* (Kalamazoo, MI: W. E. Upjohn Institute for Employment Research, 2009), 270.

87. National Research Council, *Building a Workforce*, 255.

88. In Rothwell's study of the length of time that STEM jobs remain open when compared with non-STEM jobs, he describes without comment the overwhelming focus on buying skills outside the incumbent workforce, at the expense of training: "In order for businesses to succeed, they need to match the right employee to the right

position. Accordingly, businesses invest heavily in searching for the right employees, through methods such as advertising their vacancies and thoroughly evaluating candidates." Rothwell, *Still Searching*.

89. Cappelli, *New Deal at Work*, 198–99.

90. Pablo Illanes, Susan Lund, Mona Mourshed, Scott Rutherford, and Magnus Tyreman, "Retraining and Reskilling Workers in the Age of Automation," McKinsey Global Institute, January 22, 2018, https://www.mckinsey.com/featured-insights/future -of-work/retraining-and-reskilling-workers-in-the-age-of-automation.

91. Lauren Weber, "Why Companies Are Failing at Reskilling," *Wall Street Journal*, April 19, 2019, https://www.wsj.com/articles/the-answer-to-your-companys-hiring -problem-might-be-right-under-your-nose-11555689542.

92. Dariusz Jemielniak, *The New Knowledge Workers* (Northampton, MA: Edward Elgar, 2012), 123–24.

93. Abigail Marks and Cliff Lockyer, "Producing Knowledge: The Use of the Project Team as a Vehicle for Knowledge and Skill Acquisition for Software Employees," *Economic and Industrial Democracy* 25 (2004): 219–45.

94. Horton and Tambe, *Death of a Technical Skill*.

95. ErichTheRed, "Hard Truth: Be a lifelong learner or get out of IT," comment on Slashdot, "What Are Some Hard Truths That IT Must Learn to Accept?," October 16, 2017, 7:51 p.m., https://ask.slashdot.org/comments.pl?sid=11242913&cid=55380605. Emphasis and ellipses in the original.

96. For an excellent overview of the IEP, see Gail Belsky, "What Is an IEP?," Understood, accessed December 22, 2022, https://www.understood.org/en/school-learning /special-services/ieps/what-is-an-iep.

CHAPTER 6

1. Josh Harkinson, "Jesse Jackson Is Taking on Silicon Valley's Epic Diversity Problem," *Mother Jones*, June 30, 2015, https://www.motherjones.com/politics/2015/06/tech -industry-diversity-jesse-jackson/. Harkinson also noted that the problem extended to the top of these firms—their boards of directors. Clayton S. Rose and William T. Bielby showed that resistance to integration of boards of directors is common and tends toward only token representation of African Americans as a way to appease those applying social pressure. Clayton S. Rose and William T. Bielby, "Race at the Top: How Companies Shape the Inclusion of African Americans on Their Boards in Response to Institutional Pressures," *Social Science Research* 40 (2011): 841–59.

2. Josh Harkinson, "The Combined Black Workforces of Google, Facebook, and Twitter Could Fit on a Single Jumbo Jet," *Mother Jones*, July 2, 2015, https://www .motherjones.com/politics/2015/07/black-workers-google-facebook-twitter-silicon -valley-diversity/.

3. Peter Arcidiacono, V. Joseph Hotz, and Songman Kang, "Modeling College Major Choices Using Elicited Measures of Expectations and Counterfactuals" (NBER Working Paper No. 15729, National Bureau of Economic Research, Cambridge, MA, revised December 2011), http://www.nber.org/papers/w15729; Maya A. Beasley, *Opting*

Out: Losing the Potential of America's Young Black Elite (Chicago: University of Chicago Press, 2011).

4. Sull, Sull, and Zweig, "Toxic Culture Driving Resignation"; Sull et al., "Why Every Leader Needs to Worry about Toxic Culture."

5. Margaret O'Mara, "Why Can't Tech Fix Its Gender Problem?," *MIT Technology Review*, August 11, 2022, https://www.technologyreview.com/2022/08/11/1056917/tech -fix-gender-problem/.

6. Donald Tomaskovic-Devey and Joo-Hee Han, *Is Silicon Valley Tech Diversity Possible Now?*, Center for Employment Equity, University of Massachusetts Amherst, January 2018, https://www.umass.edu/employmentequity/silicon-valley-tech-diversity -possible-now.

7. Jessica Guynn and Marco della Cava, "Uber Looks Like the Rest of Tech: White, Asian and Male," updated March 29, 2017, *USA Today*, https://www.usatoday.com /story/tech/news/2017/03/28/uber-diversity-reports-shows-familiar-tech-deficiencies /99726318/.

8. Guynn and della Cava, "Uber Looks Like the Rest of Tech."

9. Allison Scott, Freada Kapor Klein, Frieda McAlear, Alexis Martin, and Sonia Koshy, *The Leaky Tech Pipeline: A Comprehensive Framework for Understanding and Addressing the Lack of Diversity across the Tech Ecosystem* (Oakland: Kapor Center for Social Impact, February 28, 2018), 5, https://mk0kaporcenter5ld71a.kinstacdn.com/wp -content/uploads/2018/02/KC18001_report_v6-1.pdf.

10. Jessica Guynn, "Facebook Diversity Report: Efforts Still Failing Black and Hispanic Employees, Especially Women," *USA Today*, July 15, 2020, https://www.usatoday .com/story/tech/2020/07/15/facebook-diversity-african-american-black-hispanic-latino -employees/5430124002/.

11. Josh Trapani and Katherine Hale, "Demographic Attributes of S&E Recipients: S&E Degrees by Sex," in *Higher Education in Science and Engineering* (Alexandria, VA: National Center for Science and Engineering Statistics, September 4, 2019), https:// ncses.nsf.gov/pubs/nsb20197/demographic-attributes-of-s-e-degree-recipients#s-e -degrees-by-sex.

12. See, for example, Sarah Klevan, Sharon L. Weinberg, and Joel A. Middleton, "Why the Boys Are Missing: Using Social Capital to Explain Gender Differences in College Enrollment for Public High School Students," *Research in Higher Education* 57 (2016): 223–57.

13. National Science Foundation / National Center for Science and Engineering Statistics, "Field of Degree: Women," accessed December 22, 2022, https://ncses.nsf .gov/pubs/nsf19304/digest/field-of-degree-women#computer-sciences.

14. Allison Scott et al., *Leaky Tech Pipeline*, 19; Elizabeth Weise and Jessica Guynn, "Black and Hispanic Computer Scientists Have Degrees from Top Universities, but Don't Get Hired in Tech," *USA Today*, updated July 20, 2020, https://www.usatoday.com /story/tech/2014/10/12/silicon-valley-diversity-tech-hiring-computer-science-graduates -african-american-hispanic/14684211/; also see June Park John and Martin Carnoy, "The Case of Computer Science Education, Employment, Gender, and Race/Ethnicity in Silicon Valley, 1980–2015," *Journal of Education and Work* 32 (2019): 421–35.

15. Trapani and Hale, "Demographic Attributes of S&E Recipients."

16. Center for Talent Innovation (CTI) and Biotechnology Innovation Organization (BIO), *Measuring Diversity in the Biotech Industry: Building an Inclusive Workforce*, January 2020, 12, http://go.bio.org/rs/490-EHZ-999/images/Measuring_Diversity_in_the _Biotech_Industry_Building_an_Inclusive_Workforce.pdf.

17. CTI and BIO, *Measuring Diversity in the Biotech Industry*, 13.

18. Ulrike Von Lonski, Andrea Ostby, Shelly Trench, Paul Goydan, Pierce Riemer, Tor Fjaeran, Pedro Miras Salamanca, Whitney Merchant, and Claire Gauthier-Watson, "Untapped Reserves 2.0: Driving Gender Balance in Oil and Gas," World Petroleum Council and Boston Consulting Group, December 7, 2021, https://www.bcg.com /publications/2021/gender-diversity-in-oil-gas-industry.

19. Kassia Yanosek, Sana Ahmad, and Dionne Abramson, "How Women Can Help Fill the Oil and Gas Industry's Talent Gap," October 16, 2019, McKinsey & Company, https://www.mckinsey.com/industries/oil-and-gas/our-insights/how-women-can-help -fill-the-oil-and-gas-industrys-talent-gap.

20. Yanosek, Ahmad, and Abramson, "Oil and Gas Industry's Talent Gap."

21. These numbers were calculated by Karina Shklyan (2017) and by Kevin Lewis for our previously cited article, Skrentny and Lewis, "Beyond the 'STEM Pipeline.'"

22. Joyce Tang, *The Career Attainment of Caucasian, Black, and Asian-American Engineers* (Lanham, MD: Rowman and Littlefield, 2000); Roli Varma, "High-Tech Coolies: Asian Immigrants in the US Science and Engineering Workforce," *Science as Culture* 11 (2002): 337–61; Johanna Shih, "Circumventing Discrimination: Gender and Ethnic Strategies in Silicon Valley," *Gender & Society* 20 (2006): 177–206.

23. National Science Foundation / National Science Board, "Women in the S&E Workforce," in *Science and Engineering Labor Force* (Alexandria, VA: National Center for Science and Engineering Statistics, September 2019), https://ncses.nsf.gov/pubs /nsb20198/demographic-trends-of-the-s-e-workforce#women-in-the-s-e-workforce.

24. Alison T. Wynn found that tech firm executives tend to assign responsibility for gender inequality to women and to the wider society, while the human resource leaders at firms typically believe that firms are contributing to inequality but doubt that changes will succeed. The result is that nothing gets done. See Alison T. Wynn, "Pathways toward Change: Ideologies and Gender Equality in a Silicon Valley Technology Company," *Gender and Society* 34 (2020): 106–30.

25. Jessica Guynn, "Facebook's Sheryl Sandberg on Tech's Diversity Gap," *USA Today*, updated August 15, 2014, https://www.usatoday.com/story/tech/2014/08/12/face book-sheryl-sandberg-diversity-gap/13787731/.

26. Sheryl Sandberg, "Supporting Black and Diverse Communities," Meta, June 18, 2020, https://about.fb.com/news/2020/06/supporting-black-and-diverse-communities/; Matt Weinberger, "Facebook Says It Wants to 'Double Our Number of Women Globally and Black and Hispanic Employees in the US' as It Reports Its Annual Workforce Diversity Stats," *Business Insider*, July 9, 2019, https://www.businessinsider.com/facebook -diversity-report-women-workforce-2019-7.

27. Scott et al., *Leaky Tech Pipeline*, 19; Elizabeth Weise and Jessica Guynn, "Black and Hispanic Computer Scientists Don't Get Hired"; also see John and Carnoy, "Case of Computer Science."

28. National Academy of Sciences, National Academy of Engineering, and Institute of Medicine, *Rising Above the Gathering Storm: Energizing and Employing America for a Brighter Economic Future* (Washington, DC: National Academies Press, 2007). For a similar focus on STEM education to improve STEM worker diversity, see also National Academy of Sciences, National Academy of Engineering, and Institute of Medicine, *Expanding Underrepresented Minority Participation: America's Science and Technology Talent at the Crossroads* (Washington, DC: National Academies Press, 2011), 177, 246.

29. Anne Kim, *STEM Voices: The Experiences of Women and Minorities in Science, Technology, Engineering, and Math Occupations* (Washington, DC: American Enterprise Institute, 2022), 8.

30. Erin Cech, Brian Rubineau, Susan Silbey, and Caroll Seron, "Professional Role Confidence and Gendered Persistence in Engineering," *American Sociological Review* 76 (2011): 641–66; see the review in Mary Ayre, Julie Mills, and Judith Gill, "'Yes, I Do Belong': The Women Who Stay in Engineering," *Engineering Studies* 5 (2013): 216–32.

31. Shelly J. Correll, "Constraints into Preferences: Gender, Status, and Emerging Career Aspirations," *American Sociological Review* 69 (2004): 93–113; Wendy Faulkner, "The Power and the Pleasure? A Research Agenda for 'Making Gender Stick' to Engineers," *Science, Technology, & Human Values* 25 (2000): 87–119.

32. Erin A. Cech and Mary Blair-Loy, "Perceiving Glass Ceilings? Meritocratic versus Structural Inequality among Women in Science and Technology," *Social Problems* 57 (2010): 371–97.

33. I explored firms leveraging the perceived "racial abilities" of minority employees in Skrentny, *After Civil Rights*, chap. 3.

34. Mark S. Luckie, "Facebook is failing its black employees and its black users," Facebook, November 8, 2018, https://www.facebook.com/notes/mark-s-luckie/facebook-is-failing-its-black-employees-and-its-black-users/1931075116975013/; Sam Levin, "Facebook Removed Post by Ex-Manager Who Said Site 'Failed' Black People," *Guardian*, December 4, 2018, https://www.theguardian.com/technology/2018/dec/04/facebook-mark-s-luckie-african-american-workers-users; Jessica Guynn, "Facebook Has a Problem with Black People, Former Employee Charges," *USA Today*, updated July 9, 2020, https://www.usatoday.com/story/news/2018/11/27/facebook-has-problem-black-people-former-employee-says/2126056002/.

35. FB Blind, "Facebook Empowers Racism Against Its Employees of Color," Medium, November 7, 2019, https://medium.com/@blindfb2020/facebook-empowers-racism-against-its-employees-of-color-fbbfaf55ab76; Guynn, "Facebook Diversity Report."

36. Elizabeth Dwoskin, "Complaint Alleges that Facebook Is Biased against Black Workers," *Washington Post,* July 2, 2020, https://www.washingtonpost.com/technology/2020/07/02/facebook-racial-bias-suit/.

37. Antonio García Martínez, "About Antonio García Martínez," accessed December 23, 2022, https://antoniogarciamartinez.com/about-antonio-garcia-martinez/.

38. Martínez, *Chaos Monkeys*, 220.

39. Lauren A. Rivera, *Pedigree: How Elite Students Get Elite Jobs* (Princeton, NJ: Princeton University Press, 2015).

40. Elizabeth Dwoskin and Nitasha Tiku, "A Recruiter Joined Facebook to Help It

Meet Its Diversity Targets: He Says Its Hiring Practices Hurt People of Color," *Washington Post*, April 6, 2021, https://www.washingtonpost.com/technology/2021/04/06/facebook-discrimination-hiring-bias/.

41. Dwoskin and Tiku, "Practices Hurt People of Color."

42. This is a common organizational pattern, explored in detail decades ago by management scholar Rosabeth Moss Kanter, when women found their entry into the upper echelons of corporate America blocked. Rosabeth Moss Kanter, *Men and Women of the Corporation* (New York: Basic Books, 1977).

43. Jason Del Rey, "Bias, Disrespect, and Demotions: Black Employees Say Amazon Has a Race Problem," Recode (*Vox*), February 26, 2021, https://www.vox.com/recode/2021/2/26/22297554/amazon-race-black-diversity-inclusion.

44. Della Cava, "Uber Engineer Killed Himself"; Said, "Suicide of an Uber Engineer."

45. Law Firm Newswire, "Widow Blames Suicide of Uber Engineer on Work Stress, Discrimination," August 11, 2017, https://www.lawfirmnewswire.com/2017/08/widow-blames-suicide-of-uber-engineer-on-work-stress-discrimination/.

46. Kantor and Streitfeld, "Inside Amazon."

47. Donovan and Anand, "Uber's Hard-Charging Corporate Culture."

48. Susan Fowler, "Reflecting on One Very, Very Strange Year at Uber," *Susan Fowler* (blog), February 19, 2017, https://www.susanjfowler.com/blog/2017/2/19/reflecting-on-one-very-strange-year-at-uber. The impact of the Fowler blog post is discussed in both the BuzzFeed and *New York Times* exposés: Donovan and Anand, "Uber's Hard-Charging Corporate Culture"; Isaac, "Uber's Unrestrained Workplace."

49. Emily Chang, *Brotopia: Breaking Up the Boys' Club of Silicon Valley* (New York: Portfolio, 2018); Sean Illing, "Uber and the Problem of Silicon Valley's Bro Culture," *Vox*, February 28, 2017, https://www.vox.com/conversations/2017/2/28/14726004/uber-susan-fowler-travis-kalanick-sexism-silicon-valley.

50. Emi Nietfeld, "After Working at Google, I'll Never Let Myself Love a Job Again," *New York Times*, April 7, 2021, https://www.nytimes.com/2021/04/07/opinion/google-job-harassment.html.

51. Quoted in Koul and Shaw, "We Built Google." For more, see Daisuke Wakabayashi, Erin Griffith, Amie Tsang, and Kate Conger, "Google Walkout: Employees Stage Protest Over Handling of Sexual Harassment," *New York Times*, November 1, 2018, https://www.nytimes.com/2018/11/01/technology/google-walkout-sexual-harassment.html; Ben Tarnoff and Moira Weigel, "Silicon Valley's White-Collar Workers Aren't Done Yet," *New York Times*, January 26, 2021, https://www.nytimes.com/2021/01/26/opinion/silicon-valley-tech-workers.html; Kate Conger, "Hundreds of Google Employees Unionize, Culminating Years of Activism," *New York Times*, January 4, 2021, https://www.nytimes.com/2021/01/04/technology/google-employees-union.html. For union complaints targeting discriminatory workplaces at video game developers, see D'Anastasio, "Big Union Wants to Make Videogame Workers' Lives More Sane."

52. Pew Research Center, *Women and Men in STEM Often at Odds Over Workplace Equity*, January 2018, https://www.pewsocialtrends.org/wp-content/uploads/sites/3/2018/01/PS_2018.01.09_STEM_FINAL.pdf.

53. Jennifer Hunt, "Why Do Women Leave Science and Engineering?," *ILR Review*

69 (2016): 199–226. Hunt also found that women's departure rates from engineering looked similar to rates from other fields dominated by men, suggesting nothing distinctive about engineering. However, once again, it is important to stress that it is STEM fields where employers complain loudly and often about worker shortages, so their lack of support for women is especially problematic in these cases.

54. Nadya A. Fouad and Romila Singh, "Stemming the Tide: Why Women Engineers Stay in, or Leave, the Engineering Profession," Appendix D in National Research Council and National Academy of Engineering, *Career Choices of Female Engineers: A Summary of a Workshop* (Washington, DC: National Academies Press, 2014), 32.

55. Fouad and Singh, "Stemming the Tide," 33.

56. Erin A. Cech and Mary Blair-Loy, "The Changing Career Trajectories of New Parents in STEM," *Proceedings of the National Academy of Sciences* 16 (2019): 4182–87; Mary Blair-Loy and Erin A. Cech, "Demands and Devotion: Cultural Meanings of Work and Overload among Women Researchers and Professionals in Science and Technology Industries," *Sociological Forum* 32 (2016): 5–27.

57. Sull, Sull, and Zweig, "Toxic Culture Driving Resignation"; Sull et al., "Why Every Leader Needs to Worry about Toxic Culture."

58. Alison T. Wynn and Shelley J. Correll, "Puncturing the Pipeline: Do Technology Companies Alienate Women in Recruiting Sessions?," *Social Studies of Science* 48 (2018): 149–64.

59. National Research Council and National Academy of Engineering, *Career Choices of Female Engineers*, 8–9. This section of the report summarized the research of Fouad and Singh.

60. Behroozi et al., "Does Stress Impact Technical Interview Performance?"

61. Orosz explained on Twitter how this worked. Gergely Orosz, "When at Uber, I remember this change," Twitter, May 4, 2022, 5:42 p.m., https://twitter.com/GergelyOrosz/status/1521983607925055489.

62. Jennifer L. Glass, Sharon Sassler, Yael Levitte, and Katherine M. Michelmore, "What's So Special about STEM? A Comparison of Women's Retention in STEM and Professional Occupations," *Social Forces* 92 (2013): 723–56, at 744–45.

63. Fouad and Singh, "Stemming the Tide."

64. Wendy Faulkner, "Doing Gender in Engineering Workplace Cultures I: Observations from the Field," *Engineering Studies* 1 (2009): 3–18.

65. Christine L. Williams, Chandra Muller, and Kristine Kilanski, "Gendered Organizations in the New Economy," *Gender & Society* 26 (2012): 549–73.

66. Abigail Powell, Barbara Baghilhole, and Andrew Dainty, "How Women Engineers Do and Undo Gender: Consequences for Gender Equality," *Gender, Work and Organization* 16 (2009): 411–28; Wendy Faulkner, "Doing Gender in Engineering Workplace Cultures II: Gender In/Authenticity and the In/Visibility Paradox," *Engineering Studies* 1 (2009): 169–89.

67. Lauren Alfrey and France Winddance Twine, "Gender-Fluid Geek Girls: Negotiating Inequality Regimes in the Tech Industry," *Gender & Society* 31 (2017): 28–50.

68. Kim, *STEM Voices*, 30.

69. Sharla Alegria, "Escalator or Step Stool? Gendered Labor and Token Processes in Tech Work," *Gender & Society* 33 (2019): 722–45.

70. Rebecca C. Franklin, "Black Workers in Silicon Valley: Macro and Micro Boundaries," *Ethnic and Racial Studies* 45 (2022): 69–89, at 80–81.

71. Franklin, "Black Workers in Silicon Valley," 86.

72. Kim, *STEM Voices*, 32.

73. Kim, *STEM Voices*, 23.

74. Payscale, "By the Numbers: Comparing Tech Employee Salary, Age, Stress and More," accessed December 23, 2022, https://www.payscale.com/data-packages/top -tech-companies-compared/tech-salaries.

75. See, for example, Michelle Castillo, "35 Isn't Too Old to Work in Tech—But You May Feel Over the Hill, Say Software Engineers," CNBC, September 18, 2017, https:// www.cnbc.com/2017/09/18/even-35-year-olds-may-feel-ageism-in-tech-google-amazon -engineers.html; Jon Swartz, "Ageism Is Forcing Many to Look Outside Silicon Valley, but Tech Hubs Offer Little Respite," *USA Today*, updated September 13, 2017, https:// www.usatoday.com/story/tech/columnist/2017/08/04/ageism-forcing-many-look -outside-silicon-valley-but-tech-hubs-offer-little-respite/479468001/; Stephanie Czeka-linski and National Journal, "Does Your STEM Degree Have a Shelf Life?," *Atlantic*, March 12, 2014, https://www.theatlantic.com/business/archive/2014/03/does-your-stem -degree-have-a-shelf-life/425295/.

76. Mark Coker, "Startup Advice for Entrepreneurs from Y Combinator," VentureBeat, March 26, 2007, https://venturebeat.com/2007/03/26/start-up-advice-for -entrepreneurs-from-y-combinator-startup-school/.

77. Vivek Wadha, "The Case for Old Entrepreneurs," *Washington Post*, December 2, 2011, https://www.washingtonpost.com/national/on-innovations/the-case-for-old -entrepreneurs/2011/12/02/gIQAulJ3KO_story.html.

78. Kantor and Streitfeld, "Inside Amazon."

79. Noam Scheiber, "The Brutal Ageism of Tech," *New Republic*, March 23, 2014, https://newrepublic.com/article/117088/silicons-valleys-brutal-ageism.

80. Karen Wickre, "Surviving as an Old in the Tech World," *Wired*, August 2, 2017, https://www.wired.com/story/surviving-as-an-old-in-the-tech-world/.

81. Swartz, "Ageism Is Forcing Many to Look Outside."

82. Raj Mukherjee, "Ageism in the Tech Industry," Indeed, October 19, 2017, https:// www.indeed.com/lead/tech-ageism-report.

83. Allison+Partners Research + Insights, *Modis 2017 STEM Workplace Trends Survey Results*, September 2017, https://www.modis.com/en-us/-/media/US/modis-stem -insights-survey-2017.pdf.

84. Dice, *Dice Diversity and Inclusion Report 2018* (New York: DHI Group, 2018), https://marketing.dice.com/pdf/2018-06_DiceDiversity_InclusionReport_FINAL.pdf. Not surprisingly, older IT workers in the US are more likely to feel pressure to continually train for new skills. Tracey L. Adams and Erin I. Demaiter, "Knowledge Workers in the New Economy: Skill, Flexibility, and Credentials," in *Aging and Working the New Economy: Changing Career Structures in Small IT Firms*, ed. Julie Ann McMullin and Victor W. Marshall (Northampton, MA: Edward Elgar, 2010), 119–42, at 133.

85. Jon Swartz, "90 Age-Discrimination Suits Reflect Growing Issue for Tech," *USA Today*, updated December 2, 2016, https://www.usatoday.com/story/tech/news/2016/11 /22/90-age-discrimination-suits-reflect-growing-issue-tech/93110594/.

86. Swartz, "90 Age-Discrimination Suits."

87. Betsey Guzior, "EEOC Investigates Intel Over Age Discrimination Claims," *Bizwomen*, May 29, 2018, https://www.bizjournals.com/bizwomen/news/latest-news /2018/05/eeoc-investigates-intel-over-age-discrimination.html?page=all; Mike Rogoway, "Age Discrimination: Intel Investigation Drags on for Years, Worker Protections Lag," *Oregonian*, December 8, 2019, https://www.oregonlive.com/silicon-forest /2019/12/age-discrimination-intel-investigation-drags-on-for-years-highlighting-legal -pitfalls.html.

88. Peter Gosselin and Ariana Tobin, "Cutting 'Old Heads' at IBM," *Propublica*, March 22, 2018, https://features.propublica.org/ibm/ibm-age-discrimination-american -workers/.

89. Lazonick, *Sustainable Prosperity in the New Economy?*, 264.

90. Stuart D. Galup, Ronald Dattero, and Jim J. Quan, "The Effect of Age on Computer Programmer Wages," *Journal of Computer and Information Systems* 45 (2004): 57–68; Norman S. Matloff, "The Adverse Impact of Work Visa Programs on Older US Engineers and Programmers," *California Labor & Employment Law Review* 4 (2006): 5–6, 24.

91. Laura Langbein, *An Analysis of Unemployment Trends Among IEEE U.S. Members* (Washington, DC: Institute of Electrical and Electronics Engineers, 1998), https://silo.tips/download/an-analysis-of-unemployment-trends-among-ieee-us -members-laura-langbein-phd.

92. Tammy Duerden Comeau and Candace L. Kemp, "Intersections of Age and Masculinities in the Information Technology Industry," *Ageing and Society* 27 (2007): 215–32.

93. Matloff, "Adverse Impact of Work Visa Programs on Older US Engineers and Programmers."

94. CBS News Los Angeles, "Not Happy With Work? Wait Until You're 50 Or Older," CBS News, October 27, 2013, https://www.cbsnews.com/losangeles/news/not-happy -with-work-wait-until-youre-50-or-older/. For an academic view, see Roman Raab, "Workplace Perception and Job Satisfaction of Older Workers," *Journal of Happiness Studies* 21 (2020): 943–63.

95. Data from the 2017 National Survey of College Graduates. Analysis performed by Karina Shklyan.

96. Peter Gosselin, "If You're Over 50, Chances Are the Decision to Leave a Job Won't be Yours," *ProPublica*, December 28, 2018, https://www.propublica.org/article /older-workers-united-states-pushed-out-of-work-forced-retirement.

97. Philip Oreopoulos, "Why Do Skilled Immigrants Struggle in the Labor Market? A Field Experiment with Thirteen Thousand Resumes," *American Economic Journal: Economic Policy* 3 (November 2011): 148–71, at 166.

98. Hira, *Outsourcing America*; Xiang Biao, *Global "Body Shopping": An Indian Labor System in the Information Technology Industry* (Princeton, NJ: Princeton University Press, 2007); Ron Hira, "Top 10 H-1B Employers Are All IT Offshore Outsourcing Firms, Costing US Workers Tens of Thousands of Jobs," *Working Economics Blog*, Economic Policy Institute, August 22, 2016, https://www.epi.org/blog/top-10-h-1b-employers-are -all-it-offshore-outsourcing-firms-costing-u-s-workers-tens-of-thousands-jobs/; Ron Hira, "New Data Show How Firms Like Infosys and Tata Abuse the H-1B Program," *Working Economics Blog*, Economic Policy Institute, February 19, 2015, https://www

.epi.org/blog/new-data-infosys-tata-abuse-h-1b-program/; Martin, "High-Skilled Migrants."

99. Michael Roach and John D. Skrentny, "Why Foreign STEM PhDs Are Unlikely to Work for US Technology Startups," *Proceedings of the National Academy of Sciences* 116 (2019): 16805–10; Michael Roach and John D. Skrentny, "Rethinking Immigration Policies for STEM Doctorates," *Science* 371 (2021): 350–52; Novick and Skrentny, "Innovation Economy."

100. Lauren Kaori Gurley, "'Do Not Discuss the Incident,' Facebook Told Employee Fired After Speaking about Worker Suicide," *Vice*, October 21, 2019, https://www.vice.com/en/article/qvgn9q/do-not-discuss-the-incident-facebook-told-employee-fired-after-speaking-about-worker-suicide.

101. E. Kelly and Moen, *Overload*, 64–65.

102. Schuyler Velasco, "Americans Are Losing Jobs to a Visa Program: Can It Be Fixed?," *Christian Science Monitor*, February 3, 2016, https://www.csmonitor.com/Business/2016/0203/Americans-are-losing-jobs-to-a-visa-program.-Can-it-be-fixed.

103. Patrick Thibodeau, "Southern California Edison IT Workers 'Beyond Furious' Over H-1B Replacements," *Computerworld*, February 4, 2015, https://www.computerworld.com/article/2879083/southern-california-edison-it-workers-beyond-furious-over-h-1b-replacements.html.

104. Michael Hiltzik, "How the University of California Exploited a Visa Loophole to Move Tech Jobs to India," *Los Angeles Times*, January 6, 2017, https://www.latimes.com/business/hiltzik/la-fi-hiltzik-uc-visas-20170108-story.html. See Complaint of Employment Discrimination before the State of California Department of Fair Employment and Housing, DFEH No. 610653-262315, filed November 14, 2016, https://assets.documentcloud.org/documents/3254052/Ho-DFEH-Complaint-Copy.pdf. Matloff has argued that the H-1B impacts older workers most. Matloff, "Adverse Impact of Work Visa Programs on Older US Engineers and Programmers."

105. Ron Hira, "Outsourcing STEM Jobs: What STEM Educators Should Know," *Journal of Science Education and Technology* 28 (2019): 41–51.

106. Julie Bykowicz, "Tech Industry Warns That More Remote-Work Jobs Are Headed Out of US," *Wall Street Journal*, May 10, 2022, https://www.wsj.com/articles/tech-industry-warns-that-more-remote-work-jobs-are-headed-out-of-u-s-11652175000?mod=hp_lead_pos10.

107. Kai Ryssdal and Daisy Palacios, "A Workforce Crisis Hurting Women, Especially Mothers," *Marketplace*, January 22, 2021, https://www.marketplace.org/2021/01/22/a-workforce-crisis-hurting-women-especially-mothers/.

108. Beasley, *Opting Out*.

109. Kim, *STEM Voices*, 19.

110. I explored the practice of using minority employees for signaling openness to minorities in Skrentny, *After Civil Rights*. Another reason African Americans avoided STEM majors and jobs included the value African Americans placed on meaningful work that contributed to improving outcomes in their community, which steered them toward jobs in teaching, legal work for defendants, social work, and nonprofits. See Beasley, *Opting Out*, esp. chapters 5–7.

111. Fouad and Singh, "Stemming the Tide," 32.

112. National Research Council and National Academy of Engineering, *Career Choices of Female Engineers*, 10.

113. Frank Dobbin and Alexandra Kalev, "Why Firms Need Diversity Managers and Task Forces," in *How Global Migration Changes the Workforce Diversity Equation*, ed. Massimo Pilati et al. (Newcastle, UK: Cambridge Scholars Publishing, 2014), 170–98; Alexandra Kalev, Frank Dobbin, and Erin Kelly, "Best Practices or Best Guesses? Assessing the Efficacy of Corporate Affirmative Action and Diversity Policies," *American Sociological Review* 71 (2006): 589–617; Frank Dobbin and Alexandra Kalev, *Getting to Diversity: What Works and What Doesn't* (Cambridge, MA: Belknap Press of Harvard University Press, 2022). Dobbin related this and other advice at a National Academies of Sciences, Engineering, and Medicine conference on diversity in STEMM (the extra *M* was for *medicine*). National Academies of Sciences, Engineering, and Medicine, *Addressing Diversity, Equity, Inclusion, and Anti-Racism in 21st Century STEMM Organizations: Proceedings of a Workshop in Brief* (Washington, DC: National Academies Press, 2021).

114. Isabelle Solal and Kaisa Snellman, "Women Don't Mean Business? Gender Penalty in Board Composition," *Organization Science* 30 (2019): 1270–88.

115. Mark R. DesJardine, Emilio Marti, and Rodolphe Durand, "Why Activist Hedge Funds Target Socially Responsible Firms: The Reaction Costs of Signaling Corporate Social Responsibility," *Academy of Management Journal* 64 (2021): 851–72.

116. O'Mara, "Why Can't Tech Fix Its Gender Problem?"

CHAPTER 7

1. Moretti, *New Geography of Jobs*, 55.

2. The classic text on how Americans find meaning in their lives is Robert N. Bellah, Richard Madsen, William M. Sullivan, Ann Swidler, and Steven M. Tipton, *Habits of the Heart: Individualism and Commitment in American Life* (Berkeley: University of California Press, 1985).

3. For a review, see Brent D. Rosso, Kathryn H. Dekas, and Amy Wrzesniewski, "On the Meaning of Work: A Theoretical Integration and Review," *Research in Organizational Behavior* 30 (2010): 91–127.

4. Rosso, Dekas, and Wrzesniewski, "On the Meaning of Work."

5. Kristen Bell DeTienne, Bradley R. Agle, James C. Phillips, and Marc-Charles Ingerson, "The Impact of Moral Stress Compared to Other Stressors on Employee Fatigue, Job Satisfaction, and Turnover: An Empirical Investigation," *Journal of Business Ethics* 110 (2012): 377–91; Ron Carucci and Ludmila N. Praslova, "What to Do if Your Job Compromises Your Morals," *Harvard Business Review*, April 29, 2022, https://hbr.org/2022/04/what-to-do-if-your-job-compromises-your-morals.

6. Sull et al., "Why Every Leader Needs to Worry about Toxic Culture."

7. Sull et al., "Why Every Leader Needs to Worry about Toxic Culture."

8. Naomi Oreskes and Erik M. Conway, *Merchants of Doubt: How a Handful of Scientists Obscured the Truth on Issues from Tobacco Smoke to Global Warming* (New York: Bloomsbury, 2010).

9. Mei Li, Gregory Trencher, and Jusen Asuka, "The Clean Energy Claims of BP,

Chevron, ExxonMobil and Shell: A Mismatch Between Discourse, Actions and Investments," *PLoS ONE* 17 (2022): e0263596.

10. A. Gordon Smith, "Price Gouging and the Dangerous New Breed of Pharma Companies," *Harvard Business Review*, July 6, 2016, https://hbr.org/2016/07/price-gouging-and-the-dangerous-new-breed-of-pharma-companies; Wayne Drash, "Anatomy of a 97,000% Drug Price Hike: One Family's Fight to Save Their Son," CNN, June 29, 2018, https://www.cnn.com/2018/06/29/health/acthar-mallinckrodt-questcor-price-hike-trevor-foltz/index.html.

11. Jan Hoffman, "Purdue Pharma Is Dissolved and Sacklers Pay $4.5 Billion to Settle Opioid Claims," *New York Times*, September 1, 2021, https://www.nytimes.com/2021/09/01/health/purdue-sacklers-opioids-settlement.html.

12. Rachel Aviv, "A Valuable Reputation: After Tyrone Hayes Said That a Chemical Was Harmful, Its Maker Pursued Him," *New Yorker*, February 2, 2014, https://www.newyorker.com/magazine/2014/02/10/a-valuable-reputation.

13. Patricia Cohen, "Roundup Maker to Pay $10 Billion to Settle Cancer Suits," *New York Times*, June 24, 2020, https://www.nytimes.com/2020/06/24/business/roundup-settlement-lawsuits.html.

14. Ashlee Vance, "This Tech Bubble Is Different," *Bloomberg Businessweek*, April 14, 2011, https://www.bloomberg.com/news/articles/2011-04-14/this-tech-bubble-is-different.

15. On the early spread of the Hammerbacher quotation, see Quote Investigator, "The Best Minds of My Generation Are Thinking about How to Make People Click Ads: Jeff Hammerbacher? Anonymous?," June 12, 2017, https://quoteinvestigator.com/2017/06/12/click/.

16. Amazon, which nearly everyone knows has an e-commerce near monopoly with massive warehouses and thousands of employees in the US, actually makes most of its profit from cloud computing (Amazon Web Services) and ads that it sells on its platform. Motley Fool Staff, "How Amazon Actually Makes Money," Motley Fool, April 10, 2019, https://www.fool.com/investing/2019/02/19/how-amazon-actually-makes-money.aspx; Jason Goldberg, "Amazon Reveals Its Most Profitable Business," *Forbes*, February 4, 2022, https://www.forbes.com/sites/jasongoldberg/2022/02/04/amazon-reveals-its-most-profitable-business/?sh=56a19b88679f.

17. Shoshana Zuboff, *The Age of Surveillance Capitalism: The Fight for a Human Future at the New Frontier of Power* (New York: PublicAffairs, 2019).

18. Lauren Smiley, "Stitch Fix's Radical Data-Driven Way to Sell Clothes—$1.2 Billion Last Year—Is Reinventing Retail," Fast Company, February 19, 2019, https://www.fastcompany.com/90298900/stitch-fix-most-innovative-companies-2019.

19. As a writer for CNBC stated, "Profitable end uses for Generative AI are currently rare. A lot of today's excitement revolves around free or low-cost experimentation." Kif Leswing, "Why Silicon Valley Is So Excited About Awkward Drawings Done by Artificial Intelligence," CNBC, October 8, 2022, https://www.cnbc.com/2022/10/08/generative-ai-silicon-valleys-next-trillion-dollar-companies.html.

20. Steve Kovach, "Here's How Zuckerberg Thinks Facebook Will Profit by Building a 'Metaverse,'" CNBC, July 29, 2021, https://www.cnbc.com/2021/07/29/facebook

-metaverse-plans-to-make-money.html; Sarah E. Needleman and Meghan Bobrowsky, "The Metaverse Lures Brands Like Nike and Gap with New Ways to Market and Make Money," *Wall Street Journal*, June 20, 2022, https://www.wsj.com/articles/metaverse -marketing-companies-11655493807.

21. Insight, "Insight Fellows Programs," accessed December 26, 2022, https:// insightfellows.com/. Also see Thomas H. Davenport and D. J. Patil, "Data Scientist: The Sexiest Job of the 21st Century," *Harvard Business Review*, October 2012, https:// hbr.org/2012/10/data-scientist-the-sexiest-job-of-the-21st-century.

22. Marcel Haas, "I Regret Quitting Astrophysics," *Marcel Haas—Data, Science, & More* (blog), December 16, 2020, http://www.marcelhaas.com/index.php/2020/12/16/i -regret-quitting-astrophysics/. Steve Herrin, December 16, 2020, comment on Haas, "I Regret Quitting Astrophysics."

23. Wendy Liu, *Abolish Silicon Valley: How to Liberate Technology from Capitalism* (London: Repeater Books, 2020).

24. Kate Conger, "Google Removes 'Don't Be Evil' Clause From Its Code of Con- duct," Gizmodo, May 18, 2018, https://gizmodo.com/google-removes-nearly-all -mentions-of-dont-be-evil-from-1826153393.

25. Koul and Shaw, "We Built Google."

26. Levi Sumagaysay, "Life After Google: Ex-Employees Keep Speaking Out as They Move On," *Protocol*, February 7, 2020, https://www.protocol.com/employees-life-after -google-activism.

27. Megan Farokhmanesh, "Google's LGBTQ Employees Are Furious about You- Tube's Policy Disasters," Verge, June 7, 2019, https://www.theverge.com/2019/6/7/1865 6540/googles-youtube-lgbtq-employees-harassment-policies-pride-month.

28. Amanda Bartlett, "San Francisco Pride Members Pass Resolution to Ban Google, YouTube from Future Parades," SFGATE, January 16, 2020, https://www.sfgate.com /pride/article/San-Francisco-Pride-Google-YouTube-Alphabet-ban-14981446.php#.

29. This approach was critiqued with an insider's expertise in Jaron Lanier, *Who Owns the Future?* (New York: Simon and Schuster, 2013).

30. Karen Hao, "How Facebook Got Addicted to Spreading Misinformation," *MIT Technology Review*, March 11, 2021, https://www.technologyreview.com/2021/03/11/10 20600/facebook-responsible-ai-misinformation/.

31. Petter Törnberg, "How Digital Media Drive Affective Polarization through Parti- san Sorting," *Proceedings of the National Academy of Sciences* 119, no. 42 (October 2022): e2207159119, https://doi.org/10.1073/pnas.2207159119.

32. Joseph B. Bak-Coleman et al., "Stewardship of Global Collective Behavior," *Pro- ceedings of the National Academy of Sciences* 118, no. 27 (July 2021): e2025764118, https:// doi.org/10.1073/pnas.2025764118.

33. Shannon Bond, "Facebook's Most Viewed Article in Early 2021 Raised Doubt about COVID Vaccine," NPR, August 21, 2021, https://www.npr.org/2021/08/21/103003 8616/facebooks-most-viewed-article-in-early-2021-raised-doubt-about-covid-vaccine.

34. Hao, "Facebook Addicted to Misinformation."

35. Ryan Mac and Craig Silverman, "After the US Election Key People Are Leav- ing Facebook and Torching the Company in Departure Notes," BuzzFeed News,

December 11, 2020, https://www.buzzfeednews.com/article/ryanmac/facebook-rules
-hate-speech-employees-leaving. Emphasis in the original.

36. Ryan Mac and Craig Silverman, "'Hurting People at Scale': Facebook's Employees Reckon with the Social Network They've Built," BuzzFeed News, July 23, 2020, https://www.buzzfeednews.com/article/ryanmac/facebook-employee-leaks-show-they
-feel-betrayed.

37. Mac and Silverman, "'Hurting People at Scale.'"

38. Craig Silverman and Ryan Mac, "Facebook Fired an Employee Who Collected Evidence of Right-Wing Pages Getting Preferential Treatment," BuzzFeed News, August 6, 2020, https://www.buzzfeednews.com/article/craigsilverman/facebook
-zuckerberg-what-if-trump-disputes-election-results.

39. David Mack, Ryan Mac, and Ken Bensinger, "'If They Won't Hear Us, They Will Fear Us': How the Capitol Assault Was Planned on Facebook," BuzzFeed News, January 19, 2021, https://www.buzzfeednews.com/article/davidmack/how-us-capitol
-insurrection-organized-facebook.

40. Craig Silverman, Ryan Mac, Pranav Dixit, "'I Have Blood on My Hands': A Whistleblower Says Facebook Ignored Global Political Manipulation," BuzzFeed News, September 14, 2020, https://www.buzzfeednews.com/article/craigsilverman/facebook
-ignore-political-manipulation-whistleblower-memo.

41. April Glaser, "Kickstarter's Year of Turmoil," Slate, September 12, 2019, https://
slate.com/technology/2019/09/kickstarter-turmoil-union-drive-historic-tech-industry
.html.

42. See Cecilie Schou Andreassen, Joel Billieux, Mark D. Griffiths, Daria Kuss, Zsolt Demetrovics, Elvis Mazzoni, and Ståle Pallesen, "The Relationship between Addictive Use of Social Media and Video Games and Symptoms of Psychiatric Disorders: A Large-Scale Cross-Sectional Study," Psychology of Addictive Behaviors 30 (2016): 252–62; Cecilie Schou Andreassen, Ståle Pallesen, and Mark D. Griffiths, "The Relationship between Addictive Use of Social Media Narcissism, and Self-Esteem: Findings from a Large National Survey," Addictive Behaviors 64 (2017): 287–93.

43. Samuel Axon, "Apple Had Made Nearly $100 Billion So Far This Year," Ars Technica, April 28, 2022, https://arstechnica.com/gadgets/2022/04/apple-has-made-nearly
-100-billion-so-far-this-year/.

44. See, for example, a book by Senator Amy Klobuchar (D-MN): Amy Klobuchar, Antitrust: Taking on Monopoly from the Gilded Age to the Digital Age (New York: Knopf, 2021).

45. Brian Kateman, "Investors Are Looking Toward Plant-Based Food—But What Are They Seeing?," Forbes, January 19, 2021, https://www.forbes.com/sites/brian
kateman/2021/01/19/investors-are-looking-towards-plant-based-food--but-what-are
-they-seeing/?sh=132c47f54895.

46. See Margaret Pugh O'Mara, Cities of Knowledge: Cold War Science and the Search for the Next Silicon Valley (Princeton, NJ: Princeton University Press, 2005); Fred Block and Matthew R. Keller, eds., State of Innovation: The US Government's Role in Technology Development (New York: Taylor & Francis, 2011); Steven C. Currall, Ed Frauenheim, Sara Jansen Perry, and Emily Hunter, Organized Innovation: A Blueprint for Renewing

America's Prosperity (New York: Oxford University Press, 2014); and Jerald Hage, *Restoring the Innovative Edge: Driving the Evolution of Science and Technology* (Stanford, CA: Stanford Business Books, 2011).

47. David Hart, "On the Origins of Google," National Science Foundation, August 17, 2004, https://www.nsf.gov/discoveries/disc_summ.jsp?cntn_id=100660.

48. Greg Perkins and Johann Peter Murmann, "What Does the Success of Tesla Mean for the Future Dynamics in the Global Automobile Sector?," *Management and Organization Review* 14 (2018): 471–80.

49. Charley Grant, "Tesla's Stock Is the Original Gamestop," *Wall Street Journal*, January 27, 2021, https://www.wsj.com/articles/tesla-stock-is-the-original-gamestop -11611798484; Keris Lahiff, "Tesla Could Be the Most Dangerous Stock on Wall Street, Investment Researcher Says," CNBC, updated September 7, 2020, https://www.cnbc .com/2020/09/06/tesla-could-be-the-most-dangerous-stock-on-wall-street-investment -researcher-says.html.

50. Josh Lerner and Ramana Nanda, "Venture Capital's Role in Financing Innovation: What We Know and How Much We Still Need to Learn," *Journal of Economic Perspectives* 34 (2020): 237–61, at 245.

51. Jonathan Gruber and Simon Johnson, *Jump-Starting America: How Breakthrough Science Can Revive Economic Growth and the American Dream* (New York: Public Affairs, 2019), 99–100.

52. Joan Farre-Mensa, Deepak Hegde, and Alexander Ljungqvist, "What Is a Patent Worth? Evidence from the US Patent 'Lottery,'" *Journal of Finance* 75 (2020): 639–82, at 676.

53. Gruber and Johnson, *Jump-Starting America*, 99.

54. Gruber and Johnson, *Jump-Starting America*, 86–90.

55. Lerner and Nanda, "Venture Capital's Role," 254.

56. Lerner and Nanda, "Venture Capital's Role," 246.

57. Gruber and Johnson, *Jump-Starting America*, 101. Emphasis in the original.

58. Gruber and Johnson, *Jump-Starting America*, 102.

59. Devashree Saha and Mark Muro, "Cleantech Venture Capital: Continued Declines and Narrow Geography Limit Prospects," Brookings, May 16, 2017, https://www .brookings.edu/research/cleantech-venture-capital-continued-declines-and-narrow -geography-limit-prospects/.

60. PwC/CB Insights MoneyTree Report Q4 2020, slide 76, accessed January 7, 2022, https://www.pwc.com/us/en/moneytree-report/assets/pwc-moneytree-2020-q4.pdf.

61. Lerner and Nanda, "Venture Capital's Role," 246.

62. Lerner and Nanda, "Venture Capital's Role," 253.

63. Jason Owen Smith, Massimo Riccaboni, Fabio Pammolli, Walter W. Powell, "A Comparison of U.S. and European University-Industry Relations in the Life Sciences," *Management Science* 48 (2002): 24–43.

64. Gruber and Johnson, *Jump-Starting America*, 104.

65. Stephen Buranyi, "Big Pharma Is Fooling Us," *New York Times*, December 17, 2020, https://www.nytimes.com/2020/12/17/opinion/covid-vaccine-big-pharma.html.

66. Lerner and Nanda, "Venture Capital's Role," 246.

67. Gruber and Johnson, *Jump-Starting America*, 105.

68. Pisano, *Science Business*.

69. William Lazonick, Philip Moss, Hal Salzman, and Öner Tulum, "Skill Development and Sustainable Prosperity: Cumulative and Collective Careers versus Skill-Biased Technical Change" (AIR Working Paper #14-13/01, Academic-Industry Research Network, December 8, 2014), 53–54.

70. National Science Foundation / National Science Board, Figure 4-11: "Federal Obligations for Research, by Agency and Major S&E Field; FY 2017," in *Research and Development: US Trends and International Comparisons* (Alexandria, VA: National Center for Science and Engineering Statistics, January 2020), https://ncses.nsf.gov/pubs /nsb20203/recent-trends-in-federal-support-for-u-s-r-d#distribution-of-federal-funding -for-research-by-s-e-fields. For an insightful discussion, see Stephan, *How Economics Shapes Science*, 111–50.

71. Buranyi, "Big Pharma Is Fooling Us"; Arthur Allen, "For Billion-Dollar COVID Vaccines, Basic Government-Funded Science Laid the Groundwork," *Scientific American*, November 18, 2020, https://www.scientificamerican.com/article/for-billion-dollar -covid-vaccines-basic-government-funded-science-laid-the-groundwork/.

72. Anna Goldstein, Claudia Doblinger, Erin Baker, and Laura Díaz Anadón, "Patenting and Business Outcomes for Cleantech Startups Funded by the Advanced Research Projects Agency-Energy," *Nature Energy* 5 (2020): 803–10. One analysis of the emergence of new industries concluded that wind turbines, solar panels, and battery technology will all continue to require government direct funding or tax credits to spur new innovation. Jeffrey L. Funk, *Technology Change and the Rise of New Industries* (Stanford, CA: Stanford University Press, 2013), 158–76.

73. See White House, "President Biden Takes Bold Executive Action to Spur Domestic Clean Energy Manufacturing," Fact Sheet, June 6, 2022, https://www.whitehouse .gov/briefing-room/statements-releases/2022/06/06/fact-sheet-president-biden-takes -bold-executive-action-to-spur-domestic-clean-energy-manufacturing/; White House, "Biden-Harris Administration Driving US Battery Manufacturing and Good-Paying Jobs," Fact Sheet, October 19, 2022, https://www.whitehouse.gov/briefing-room /statements-releases/2022/10/19/fact-sheet-biden-harris-administration-driving-u-s -battery-manufacturing-and-good-paying-jobs/. Organizations working toward clean energy saw benefits from these actions. Lachlan Carey and Jun Ukita Shepard, "Congress's Climate Triple Whammy: Innovation, Investment, and Industrial Policy," RMI, August 22, 2022, https://rmi.org/climate-innovation-investment-and-industrial-policy/.

74. See, for example, Eric Lipton, "With Federal Aid on the Table, Utilities Shift to Embrace Climate Goals," *New York Times*, November 29, 2022, https://www.nytimes .com/2022/11/29/us/politics/electric-utilities-biden-climate-bill.html.

75. Gina Melchner von Dydiowa, Sander van Deventer, and Daniela S. Couto, "How Large Pharma Impacts Biotechnology Startup Success," *Nature Biotechnology* 39 (2021): 266–69.

76. Eric Wesoff, "Where Can Cleantech Startups Find Funding in 2019?," *Greentech Media*, January 24, 2019, https://www.greentechmedia.com/articles/read/how-do-clean tech-startups-get-funded-in-2019.

77. Bill Gates, *How to Avoid a Climate Disaster: The Solutions We Have and the Breakthroughs We Need* (New York: Knopf, 2021).

78. Breakthrough Energy, "Our Approach: Letting Science Lead the Way," accessed January 8, 2023, https://www.breakthroughenergy.org/our-story/our-story.

79. Business Wire, "Impossible Foods Confirms Approximately $500 Million in New Funding," March 16, 2020, https://www.businesswire.com/news/home/20200316005301 /en/Impossible-Foods-Confirms-Approximately-500-Million-in-New-Funding.

80. Eric J. Savitz, "Amazon Unveils Plan for $2 Billion Green Tech Venture-Capital Fund," *Barron's*, June 23, 2020, https://www.barrons.com/articles/amazon-unveils-plan -for-2-billion-green-tech-venture-capital-fund-51592938279.

81. David Roberts, "YouTube Has a Big Climate Misinformation Problem It Can't Solve," *Vox*, January 27, 2020, https://www.vox.com/energy-and-environment/2020/1/26 /21068473/youtube-climate-change-misinformation-epistemic-crisis.

82. John Doerr, *Speed and Scale: An Action Plan for Solving Our Climate Crisis Now* (New York: Portfolio, 2021).

83. Mark Bergen, "Investor John Doerr: Silicon Valley Should 'Triple Down' on Clean Tech," *Bloomberg News*, May 23, 2022, https://www.bloomberg.com/news/articles /2022-05-23/investor-john-doerr-silicon-valley-should-triple-down-on-clean-tech.

84. Responding to shareholders means doing what shareholders want, which can change over time. Gourevitch and Shinn, *Political Power and Corporate Control*; Peter Gourevitch and James Shinn, "The Perplexing Roles of Institutional Investors in a World of Multiple Investing Entities," in *The Emergence of Corporate Governance*, ed. Knut Sogner and Andrea Colli (New York: Routledge, 2021), 187–205.

85. Benji Jones, "Why Investors Suddenly Care about Saving the Environment," *Vox*, June 15, 2022, https://www.vox.com/down-to-earth/2022/6/15/23161482/esg-investing -environment-biodiversity-risk-tnfd. Emphasis in the original.

86. Dieter Holger, "Costco Shareholder Vote Signals Focus on Supply-Chain Emissions," *Wall Street Journal*, January 26, 2022, https://www.wsj.com/articles/costco-share holder-vote-signals-focus-on-supply-chain-emissions-11643194803.

87. Cara Lombardo, "Relentless Wall Street Billionaire Has a Secret Cause," *Wall Street Journal*, February 8, 2022, https://www.wsj.com/articles/carl-icahn-mcdonalds -pigs-gestation-crates-11644335198.

88. Timothy Puko, "GOP Lawmakers Lobby Oil Industry to Denounce Tax-and-Climate Bill," *Wall Street Journal*, August 6, 2022, https://www.wsj.com/articles/gop-law makers-lobby-oil-industry-to-denounce-tax-and-climate-bill-11659778202.

89. J. Adam Cobb, "How Firms Shape Income Inequality: Stakeholder Power, Executive Decision Making, and the Structuring of Employment Relationships," *Academy of Management Review* 41 (2016): 324–48, at 325; Derek C. Jones, Takao Kato, and Adam Weinberg, "Managerial Discretion, Business Strategy, and the Quality of Jobs: Evidence from Medium-Sized Manufacturing Establishments in Central New York," in *Low-Wage America: How Employers Are Reshaping Opportunity in the Workplace*, ed. Eileen Appelbaum, Annette Bernhardt, and Richard J. Murnane (New York: Russell Sage Foundation, 2003), 479–525.

90. Ton, *Good Jobs Strategy*, viii.

91. Thomas Kochan, *Shaping the Future of Work: What Future Worker, Business, Government, and Education Leaders Need to Do for All to Prosper* (New York: Business Expert Press, 2016), 78.

92. Matt Stoller, Sarah Miller, and Zephyr Teachout, "Addressing Facebook and Google's Harms Through a Regulated Competition Approach" (Working Paper Series on Corporate Power #2, American Economic Liberties Project, April 2020), 7–9, https://www.economicliberties.us/wp-content/uploads/2020/04/Working-Paper-Series -on-Corporate-Power_2.pdf.

93. Gilad Edelman, "Why Don't We Just Ban Targeted Advertising?," *Wired*, March 22, 2020, https://www.wired.com/story/why-dont-we-just-ban-targeted-advertising/; Jeff Gary and Ashkan Soltani, "First Things First: Online Advertising Practices and Their Effects on Platform Speech," Knight First Amendment Institute at Columbia University, August 21, 2019, https://knightcolumbia.org/content/first-things-first-online -advertising-practices-and-their-effects-on-platform-speech; K. Sabeel Rahman and Zephyr Teachout, "From Private Bads to Public Goods: Adapting Public Utility Regulation for Informational Infrastructure," Knight First Amendment Institute at Columbia University, February 4, 2020, https://knightcolumbia.org/content/from-private-bads -to-public-goods-adapting-public-utility-regulation-for-informational-infrastructure.

94. Edelman, "Why Don't We Just Ban Targeted Advertising?"; David Dayen, "Ban Targeted Advertising," *New Republic*, April 10, 2018, https://newrepublic.com/article/14 7887/ban-targeted-advertising-facebook-google.

95. Dipayan Ghosh and Nick Couldry, "Digital Realignment: Rebalancing Platform Economies from Corporation to Consumer" (M-RCBG Associate Working Paper No. 155, Mossavar-Rahmani Center for Business and Government, Harvard Kennedy School, 2020), 2, https://www.hks.harvard.edu/centers/mrcbg/publications/awp/aw p155.

96. Neal, Tobin, and McCormick, *Beyond Sputnik*, 287. Also see Peter Whalley and Stephen R. Barley, "Technical Work in the Division of Labor: Stalking the Wily Anomaly," in *Between Craft and Science: Technical Work in US Settings*, ed. Stephen R. Barley and Julian E. Orr (Ithaca, NY: ILR Press, 1997), 23–52, at 30.

INDEX

Abolish Silicon Valley (Liu), 161

Accel Partners, 9

Accenture, 61, 116

Accreditation Board for Engineering and Technology, 99

Activision Blizzard, 44

Actuarial Foundation, 7

Adecco, 111

Adobe, 36, 61, 105, 111, 204n43; Flash software, 101, 117–18

Advanced Research Projects Agency–Energy (ARPA-E), 173

aerospace, 78

Aetna, 26, 111

African Americans: at Amazon, 133; at biotech companies, 123–25, 148; at Facebook, 130–31; and feelings of exclusion, 140; fitting in, 140; and relational labor, 140; in Silicon Valley, 140; STEM majors, avoidance of, 222n110; as STEM workers, 121–27, 130, 135, 139–40, 148–49, 153–55, 166, 168, 170, 172–73, 175–77, 179; at Uber, 133

age discrimination, 141–44, 150; and layoffs, 143

Age Discrimination in Employment Act, 82

ageism, 142

agency, 20, 176

Airbnb, 9, 110, 123; Data University, 109

Alfred P. Sloan Foundation, 14, 195n57

Alphabet, 9, 161–62, 166. *See also* Google

Alphabet Workers Union, 109

alternative work arrangements, growth of, 86

Always Punch Nazis (comic book), 165

Amazon, 57, 99, 111, 132, 159–60, 163, 166; absolutist language at, 62; African Americans at, 133; Amazon Technical Academy, 212n77; "Amhole," as derisive nickname, 63, 69; as "bruising workplace," 63; buying and building passion, 61–62; Climate Pledge, 174; cloud computing, 224n16; culture fit, 133; "Customer Obsession" principle, 62; "Deliver Results" principle, 62; diversity officers, 149; forced ranking, use of, 62, 65; "Frugality" principle, 62; *Hunger Games* atmosphere of, 63; "Insist on the Highest Standards" principle, 62; Leadership Principles, 62; "Learn and Be Curious" principle, 62; Machine Learning University, 113; older workers at, 142; "Organizational Level Review" at, 63; overwork at, 62; "Ownership" principle, 62; "passion" at, 63–64; purposeful Darwinism at, 63; sense of limitlessness, 62; stress, of workers, 63; as toxic workplace, 61; training, of workers, 113; women at, 133

America COMPETES Act, 6, 12–14, 22, 173